Praise for *Mindstuck*

"With its deft mix of research, humor, and practical advice, *Mindstuck* offers a timely—and much-needed—guide for restoring the lost art of civil discourse. If you want to learn how to change minds, Michael McQueen opens the door."

Daniel H. Pink, #1 *New York Times* bestselling author of *To Sell is Human, Drive,* and *The Power of Regret*

"Michael McQueen shows readers how to master the art of healthy persuasion. He shares a range of proven techniques that are invaluable and easy to implement. *Mindstuck* is a must-read if you want to make a greater impact!"

Mel Robbins, *New York Times* bestselling author and host of The Mel Robbins Podcast

"In *Mindstuck*, Michael McQueen dispels many common myths about what it really takes to move others. This book is a must-read guide for anyone looking for practical insights into how to persuade even the most stubborn and strong-willed individuals."

Jonah Berger, PhD, Wharton professor and bestselling author of *Contagious, Magic Words,* and *The Catalyst*

"*Mindstuck* shows readers how to gain and wield the superpower of persuasion using clear examples and the latest science. You, too, can be a persuasion pro when you read this book."

Paul J. Zak, PhD, professor of neuroeconomics and author of *Immersion: The Science of the Extraordinary and the Source of Happiness*

"Saturated with science yet practical and funny! *Mindstuck* grabbed my attention from the very first page. This book will help you win hearts even when minds are on the defensive."

Zoe Chance, PhD, senior lecturer, Yale School of Management, and author of *Influence is Your Superpower*

"Prepare to have your mind blown as Michael McQueen dives into the inner workings of human cognition. *Mindstuck* is like a rollercoaster ride for your brain with unexpected twists and turns that will have you laughing out loud and re-evaluating everything you thought you knew about thinking."

Jay Van Bavel, professor of psychology, New York University

"In an age where it's harder than ever to inspire change in people who are fixed in their ways or thinking, this book is incredibly timely. *Mindstuck* is a refreshingly practical look at what it takes to meaningfully persuade others."

Josh Linkner, *New York Times* bestselling author, serial tech entrepreneur, venture capital investor

"*Mindstuck* serves up a firehose of facts and insights about how to help yourself to become more open-minded and how to help others take on new perspectives. In a time of heated intransigence based on ideology more than evidence, this book reviews a formidable amount of research about what drives opinion and how to deploy that research to make the truth more likely to prevail."

Steven Sloman, PhD, professor of cognitive, linguistic, and psychological sciences, Brown University

"Michael McQueen has done it again! This intriguing book confronts and examines how people form perspectives and how those can be challenged or changed. As the leader of an international non-profit organization, I can say *Mindstuck* has powerfully shaped my thinking too."

Stephanie Urchick, Rotary International global president, 2024-2025

"This lively read pulls back the curtain on the hidden forces that lead people to embrace change. Essential insights for anyone in the business of bringing new ideas into the world."

Loran Nordgren, PhD, Kellogg professor of management and bestselling author of *The Human Element*

"This thoroughly engaging book provides a highly accessible summary of the latest research in psychology and neuroscience. Readers wanting to gain a better understanding of attitude change will not find a more clearly written, comprehensive, and thought-provoking summary. Better yet, Michael McQueen provides many concrete and practical recommendations based on empirical research."

Frank Keil, PhD, psychology professor and director of the Cognition and Development Lab, Yale University

"Michael McQueen's book is a contemporary masterpiece. The extensive use of literature, academic resources, and quotes to underpin the ideas is impressive. The real-world applications of tools and tips are a unique and invaluable resource. I found myself constantly engaged and challenged by the information presented, unable to put it down."

Professor Mark Hutchinson, PhD, president of Science & Technology Australia and director of the Australian Research Council Centre of Excellence for Nanoscale BioPhotonics

"The challenges in our societies require all of us to change the way we think, act, and see the world. Many of us want change but few want to be changed. This book leads to the roots of wisdom and provides evidence for how change can be realistically achieved."

Olli-Pekka Heinonen, director general of the International Baccalaureate and former Finnish Minister of Education

"In an era of half-truths and increasing polarization, *Mindstuck* shows readers how to harness the power of persuasion to bring people closer together. With engaging stories and insightful research, Michael McQueen reveals how even the most stubborn of minds can become 'unstuck.'"

Dr. Sander van der Linden, Cambridge University professor of social psychology and author of *Foolproof: Why We Fall for Misinformation and How to Build Immunity*

"*Mindstuck* is an incredibly timely book for leaders trying to navigate a changed world. Michael offers a toolkit for making better decisions ourselves and influencing others to do the same."

Neil J. Solomon, vice president, Asia Pacific/Latin America, UKG

"This book is an incredibly enlightening, timely, and essential read. In this polarized age, Michael McQueen lays out a compelling roadmap for how we all can approach dialogue and persuasion more productively."
Jun Sochi, former APAC COO, Cushman & Wakefield

"*Mindstuck* is essential reading in a world where our attention and opinions are constantly under bombardment. With a skillful blend of philosophy and science, Michael provides readers with real and usable tools to improve their critical thinking."
Foad Safari, e-Commerce Leader, Optus

"If you are trying to drive organizational change in the face of resistance, *Mindstuck* is the book for you. I am not in 'two minds' about the value of this book and its learnings—it is well researched and packed with practical tools."
Kylie Bromley, PhD, vice president and managing director, Biogen United Kingdom & Ireland

"Michael McQueen has done a masterful job of conveying a wealth of evidence-based knowledge about the ways our minds deceive us as we struggle to make rational decisions in today's complex, deceptive, and dangerous world."
Dr. Paul Slovic, professor of psychology, University of Oregon

"Insightful and delightful. *Mindstuck* is a fabulous and practical evidence-based guide to understanding why we think the way we do and how to shift perceptions for the better."
Dr. Justin Coulson, four-time bestselling author, television host, and parenting expert

"*Mindstuck* is a wonderful blend of straight talk and neuroscience. This is one of those rare books that is both enjoyable and enlightening. It is simple enough to understand and technical enough to trust. Highly recommended."
Thomas R. Verny MD, DHL (Hon), clinical psychiatrist and author of *The Embodied Mind*

"If you ever wonder why it's so hard for people to calmly and rationally discuss their differing viewpoints, then *Mindstuck* is for you. Michael McQueen engagingly explains how the process of changing people's minds relies less on rationality than we realize—and how to use this knowledge to become more effective persuaders."

David B. Strohmetz, PhD, professor of psychology, University of West Florida

"*Mindstuck* is an engaging take on the complicated and often counterintuitive world of influence. Michael McQueen smartly reminds us that we can't fully understand persuasion without understanding why people resist it."

Josh Compton, professor of speech, Dartmouth College

"Michael has a unique ability to translate complex psychological insights into practical tools. Engaging, entertaining, and inspiring, *Mindstuck* is a masterclass in human judgment and decision making."

Phil Slade, psychologist and author of *Behavioural Economics for Business*

"Michael McQueen has really nailed it again with *Mindstuck*. Whether you are transacting an idea, pitching an argument, or making a sale, this is one book everyone needs to read and put into practice."

David Mulham, global chief sales officer, Usana Health Sciences

an imprint of Amplify Publishing Group

www.amplifypublishinggroup.com

Mindstuck: Mastering the Art of Changing Minds

For more information, please contact:
Amplify Publishing, an imprint of Amplify Publishing Group
620 Herndon Parkway, Suite 220
Herndon, VA 20170
info@amplifypublishing.com

Library of Congress Control Number: 2023913263

CPSIA Code: PRV0823A

ISBN-13: 978-1-63755-739-6

Printed in the United States

MASTERING THE ART OF
CHANGING MINDS

MICHAEL McQUEEN

an imprint of Amplify Publishing Group

To receive weekly tips for thinking well—and helping others do the same—scan the QR code below or visit **www.MondayMindhack.com.**

ABOUT THE AUTHOR

Michael McQueen has spent the past two decades helping organizations and leaders win the battle for relevance. From Fortune 500 brands to government agencies and not-for-profits, Michael specializes in helping clients navigate uncertainty and stay one step ahead of change.

He is a bestselling author of nine books and a familiar face on the international conference circuit, having shared the stage with the likes of Bill Gates, Dr. John C. Maxwell, and Apple co-founder Steve Wozniak. Michael has spoken to hundreds of thousands of people across five continents since 2004 and is known for his high-impact, research-rich, and entertaining conference presentations.

Having formerly been named Australia's Keynote Speaker of the Year, Michael has been inducted into the Professional Speakers Hall of Fame.

He and his family live in Sydney, Australia.

WWW.MICHAELMCQUEEN.NET

CONTENTS

INTRODUCTION
THERE'S SOMETHING IN THE WATER

"**M**y colleagues call me the poo lady," Danielle said with a wry smile. This was not quite the response I expected when I asked one of the parents at my son's day care what they did for work.

I vaguely knew that Danielle worked for one of Australia's major water utilities but had no idea what this had to do with effluent. I soon found out.

Danielle explained that she had spent the last few years working with a team trying to get funding approval for a wastewater recycling program in Sydney. When she explained the science behind purified recycled water and how safe it was, I couldn't help but agree it was a fantastic idea. In theory, that is.

"Would you like to try some?" she asked. Having just come from a presentation to a community group to raise awareness, Danielle had a few leftover sample bottles of recycled water in her car.

With a mixture of curiosity and caution, I put on a brave face. "Sure, why not?"

When Danielle returned a few minutes later, I knew I had a choice to make. The idea of drinking recycled effluent made logical sense to me, but as I cracked the screw cap on a bottle of the stuff, being willing to take a gulp was a different matter entirely.

As you might expect, there was nothing remarkable about the water at all. In texture, color, and taste, it was identical to the water you'd normally pay a few dollars a bottle for. "In fact, it's even cleaner than bottled spring water," Danielle informed me. "But it's no easy task to get people on board with the idea. The resistance has been enormous."

I learned that the concept of recycling wastewater for human consumption actually dates back decades with one of the early projects being trialed during the late 1960s in Namibia's arid capital city, Windhoek. One of the key proponents for Namibia's project, Dr. Lucas van Vuuren, had argued that "Water should not be judged by its history, but by its quality." Eventually, van Vuuren won over the local regulators and a few years later had successfully proved to the world that recycled wastewater was both a safe and incredibly sensible idea.

However, the road to acceptance in other parts of the world has been far tougher and remains an uphill battle.

In Los Angeles, for instance, plans to begin recycling drinking water in the early 1990s were met with fierce opposition. The media and several local politicians dismissed the idea with the pithy but ultimately misleading term "Toilet to Tap." Even the National Academy of Sciences flinched at the idea, deeming recycled wastewater as the "option of last resort" for shoring up water supply.

It was much the same experience in the Australian city of Toowoomba when the prospect of wastewater recycling was suggested in 2006. Despite a record-breaking drought making the pressing need clearly evident, community opposition was fierce and effective. Various false claims were made by those opposing the idea including that it would shrink men's penises, cause fish to change gender, and that the city would become known as "Poowoomba." The scare campaign worked so well that the proposal was decisively defeated in a referendum.

Fear trumps facts

Reflecting on the implications of this experience, Australia's former Prime Minister Malcolm Turnbull lamented, "You don't need to have facts on your side to mount a vigorous political campaign. Science denial and scare campaigns" are more than enough to halt the march of progress.[1]

To Turnbull's point, both the science and common sense of recycled wastewater is irrefutable. After all, anyone who understands even basic hydrology knows that *all* drinking water is essentially recycled wastewater. Yet most of us operate as if this were not the case. We tend to think of water use as a linear process where water is received, used, and then disposed of when dirty.

Even outside of the natural water cycle, the reality is that the reuse of wastewater has been common practice for many decades. It's just that most of us have never connected the dots. For instance, anyone living on inland river systems already consumes water that has been used and then treated by communities upstream. The technical term for this is "unacknowledged reuse," and it gives rise to the commonly used industry adage that water goes through "seven sets of kidneys" between falling as rain and being evaporated again.[2]

This dynamic was certainly the case in the U.S. city of San Diego. Owing to its dry climate and lack of groundwater supplies, 85 percent of San Diego's water has been piped from the Colorado River for decades. Given the fact that this river system has 400 intakes upstream of San Diego's supply, much of the city's drinking water was already recycled wastewater—and had been for years.

With costs for importing water having increased threefold in a decade and the supply pipes themselves dangerously crossing numerous active seismic fault lines, San Diego's governing officials realized the need in the early 2000s to become water self-sufficient by way of wastewater recycling. The key challenge was to get the public on board with the idea.

When independent polls were conducted in 2004, just 26 percent of people were open to the possibility. Indicative of the public sentiment, a 2006 headline in *The San Diego Union-Tribune* read "Yuck! San Diego should flush 'toilet to tap' plan." The article itself began with the words, "Your golden retriever may drink out of the toilet but that doesn't mean humans should do the same."

On top of this general sense of repulsion, a rumor gained traction that sensationally claimed that the effluent of San Diego's wealthy suburbs would be treated and piped to the poorer areas of the city for consumption. While this was not remotely true, it added to a feeling of disgust at the whole plan.

Stigma sticks

Industry expert Linda Macpherson suggests that part of the challenge is that the descriptions and imagery associated with recycled wastewater have traditionally had a "poisoning" effect for the general community. As Macpherson describes it, they have led to "gut-based reactions and stigma" that make reasoned, evidence-based judgments near impossible. She added, "We're all fearful of things we don't fully understand. It's become really clear that without education, stigmatized reactions will continue to kill otherwise sound and sustainable (wastewater) projects."[3]

In an effort to turn the tide of public opinion, authorities in San Diego realized that a multifaceted approach would be necessary. The first step was to change the language of reused water. In addition to avoiding industry jargon such as "indirect potable reuse" and "microconstituents," they recognized that using terms such as "wastewater" and even the word "recycled" were part of the issue. Their focus on calling the initiative Pure Water was a step in the right direction as was the decision to focus on talking about "reused" and "purified" drinking water.

Proactive educational initiatives also played a key role in addressing misconceptions and fear. Chief amongst these was the Pure Water visitors center, which gave people the chance to understand the process of treating reused water and also the opportunity to try some. A series of online educational videos and resources were also created which reduced stigma and heavily used images and language of cleanliness and purity to counteract the imagined notions of disgust. Researchers and educators quickly discovered that information for the public needed to be "Simple enough to understand and technical enough to trust."

In an ingenious move, the team in San Diego also joined forces with an initiative in the U.S. state of Oregon to use reclaimed drinking water to produce special craft-brew beer. Not only did this reframe recycled drinking water in a completely new way, it also increased familiarity and led to ample opportunities for light-hearted community engagement.

The impact of these combined efforts was extraordinary. Polls revealed that by late 2019, public acceptance of purified recycled drinking water stood at 79 percent and the very newspaper editors that so actively ridiculed the idea in 2006 had certainly changed their tune.

A *San Diego Union-Tribune* headline in 2017 proclaimed "San Diego Will Drink Water Recycled from Sewage. Cheers." The article began with something of a confession: "The San Diego Union-Tribune Editorial Board used to be among the skeptics who maligned 'toilet to tap'. Then six years ago we changed our minds."[4]

This about-face is as incredible as it is instructive.

If San Diegans could be persuaded to change their minds and eagerly drink water that had repulsed them for no logical reason just a few years earlier, there are powerful lessons for us all when it comes to shifting even the most stubborn views.

This is a theme that has grown to fascinate me in recent years. Having spent two decades researching the trends and technology that will rewrite the future, my work has centered on helping organizations and individuals stay at the cutting edge.

As I have worked with clients over those years, there's one question that I've come back to time and time again: what stops people from changing—even when they want to change and know they should?

Recent years have provided plenty of cautionary tales of what happens when organizations and leaders don't keep pace with the rate of disruption around them. But while it may be convenient to assume that the likes of Kodak, Blackberry, or Sears failed as a result of ineptitude or incompetence, this is simply not the case. In these and many other instances, those at the helm of formerly successful organizations were well-read, well-informed, and had incredibly sharp minds.

Instead, I'd suggest it is mental inflexibility—or being "mindstuck"—rather than a lack of intelligence or insight that most often trips us up. Something about the process of making up our minds gets in the way of us making good decisions. Failing to account for this in ourselves and others is dangerous indeed.

While stubbornness is nothing new, we live in an era when it is more prevalent than ever. You could almost describe obstinance as one of the hallmarks of our age.

Of course, it's not you or I that are stubborn. *Our* views are completely reasonable and sensible, and we pride ourselves on the fact that we're always open to different opinions or perspectives. We'd like to assume that we willingly embrace the best thinking, the smartest ideas, and the soundest reasoning. The problem is that *everyone else* is so stubborn, pig-headed, and close-minded.

The reality is that stubbornness is much like arrogance—we can spot it in other people from a mile away but can find it near-impossible to detect in ourselves.

In fairness, it's not that people today are inherently less rational or reasonable than previous generations. Rather, our modern epidemic of stubbornness is largely due to the fact that we tend to have very little real understanding of how humans actually think, reason, and arrive at points of judgment. And it's far from the linear and logical process we'd like to imagine is the case.

On top of this is the fact that we've never had to make up our minds about so many things, so quickly, and with access to so much information. Overwhelm and obstinance go hand in hand.

Please make up your mind

At any given moment, modern society demands we form and defend a view about pretty much everything. From the ethics of where we buy our clothes to whether we should get vaccinated, wear a mask, drink fluoridated water, or buy an electric car, it's mandatory that we pick a side, form an opinion, and make up our minds.

According to Timothy Wilson, professor of psychology at the University of Virginia, the sheer volume of ideas and input we are exposed to in modern times has a huge influence on this process.

Wilson cites data showing our brains are exposed to roughly 11 million pieces of information at any moment.[5] Given that we can only consciously process forty of those inputs, we are left with little choice but to go with our gut or defer to tribal instincts. Our minds become made up depending on whether an idea feels intuitively right, or based on a vague sense of what people like us think about things like this.[6]

But what matters more than the way we make our minds up is what happens next. Once we've formed a view or an opinion, we immediately start fortifying it.

Mark Stephens in his book, *The End of Thinking,* describes this very dynamic. "Our initial responses are pretty automatic, what we might call a gut-level reaction. And then our reasoning follows our gut, playing the role of an 'inner lawyer' who defends our intuition." As a result, when we are confronted with an idea that challenges our opinions, our reaction isn't "think and then respond. It's respond and then defend."[7]

It's this defensive reflex that we've honed into a fine art in recent years. And it's something that has enormous implications for anyone in the business of persuasion—which is, of course, every single one of us.

Impact at the speed of influence

Whether we realize it or not, our success and effectiveness in most areas of life is determined by how good we are at changing the perspective of others. The level of our impact will be determined by our ability to exert influence.

It is estimated that the "soft skill" of persuasion is responsible for generating a quarter of economic output in today's "knowledge economy."[8] In fact, 40 percent of our professional time is spent trying to influence and convince others to make certain decisions or adopt new perspectives. As Dan Pink observes in his brilliant book *To Sell is Human*, roughly twenty-four minutes of every hour of the workday is dedicated to "moving people."[9]

To this point, the only diploma that Warren Buffett displays on the wall of his office is one from a Dale Carnegie course that he credits for teaching him how to influence others. Buffett routinely advises young professionals to improve their persuasion skills—something he suggests will immediately boost their professional value by 50 percent.[10]

Beyond the professional arena, mastering the art of changing minds is an indispensable skill in everyday life. Perhaps you are a father attempting to persuade your teenager to stop playing video games long enough to get his homework done. Or perhaps you are the adolescent trying to get your parents on board with the idea of you getting a nose ring. Maybe you're an adult child trying to convince your elderly parents to take their medication or consider going into care. You might be trying to get your husband to fix the light on the back porch or put the toilet seat down.

Then there are those delicate situations when you want your neighbor to cut back the tree that's overhanging your fence. Or maybe you're an apartment-dweller wanting the people living upstairs to stop playing music at 2 o'clock on a Sunday morning.

Regardless of the context, our ability to persuade stubborn people can make all the difference. And that is the focus of this book.

In examining the latest research and thinking in disciplines ranging from neuroscience to behavioral economics, I'd suggest what we need is a total upgrade in our understanding of what it takes to shift the thinking of other people (and ourselves).

Many of the persuasion strategies we have been taught are fundamentally flawed in that they are based on a notion of what we'd like human nature to be—not what it is. We are still using nineteenth- and twentieth-century techniques for trying to persuade twenty-first-century minds and are wondering why it's not working.

In the chapters ahead, we'll look at the surprising truth about how we actually make up our minds. We will explore the psychology of stubbornness and look at the factors that *really* shape our opinions, beliefs, and judgments—often in ways we don't understand or are not aware of.

But while we may be more stubborn than ever, this need not be the end of the story. Even the most mindstuck people can be persuaded to change their minds.

As we will see, the art of persuasion dates back to ancient Athens and the original masters Aristotle and Plato. In describing the art of influence and its importance, Plato once suggested that the entirety of world history is the story of "the victory of persuasion over force."[11]

And yet recent times have seen us forget and, in many instances, flip this axiom on its head. Today when we encounter those who disagree with or resist our efforts, we tend to resort to force in an attempt to bend others to our will. We shout, we get offended, we get upset, or we play power games.

Then there are those who try motivating others to change through the dangling of carrots or the waving of sticks. And although coaxing and coercing others can seem to get results, the change tends to only last as long as the threats or incentives that motivated it do.

Making this sort of change stick is both costly and exhausting. It requires constant monitoring and intervention. What's more, even if someone conforms to our wishes out of grudging compliance or incentivized self-interest, it's highly unlikely their mind has changed in the slightest. As Dale Carnegie famously observed in his iconic bestseller *How to Win Friends and Influence People*, "A person convinced against their will is of the same opinion still."[12]

Those with a more intellectual bent tend to try and get the upper hand in persuasion by resorting to logic. Part of the reason we make this mistake can be traced back to the eighteenth-century Enlightenment which was dubbed by Immanuel Kant as the "Age of Reason."[13] This was a period when presenting your argument or views in the most rational possible way became highly important.[14]

As inheritors of this philosophical paradigm, we too easily fall into the trap of assuming that someone who holds an unenlightened to uninformed view must lack the information they need to "see reason." We therefore imagine that if we can present someone with better evidence or watertight logic, they'll come to their senses and change their minds.

In their bestselling book *Switch: How to Change Things When Change Is Hard*, Chip and Dan Heath pick up on this theme. They suggest that many of us operate under the assumption that if we present an "impeccably rational case for change," the other person will have no choice but to see reason and joyfully exclaim 'You're right... how could I have not seen this before!'[15]

If only the human mind worked this way.

As the legendary American comedian and talk show host Dick Cavett once observed, "It's a rare person who wants to hear what he doesn't want to hear."[16]

As we will see in the coming pages, even the most flawless logic tends to be of little value and can even be counterproductive. In the words of Irish essayist Jonathan Swift, "It is useless to attempt to reason a person out of what they were never reasoned into."[17]

However, this is not a book about what doesn't work in persuading others but rather what does. We will explore a host of practical and proven techniques for shifting even the most mindstuck people. And be forewarned that you are likely to have many of your own preconceptions about persuasion challenged along the way.

The old proverb tells us you can lead a horse to water, but you cannot make it drink. But what if this is not true?

The good news is that persuading others need not be an onerous or over-whelming task. Just as horse whisperers know how to win over even the most rebellious or obstinate bronco, so master persuaders know how to shift even the most stubborn mind.

Let's explore how.

PART I
WHAT MAKES
UP A MIND

Behavioral scientist Kurt Lewin once noted, "If you want to truly understand something, try to change it." But the reverse is also true. Before we can try changing anything, it helps to understand how it works.[1]

Given that this book is about changing minds and shifting stubborn opinions, we'd do well to start by looking at the very nature of thinking itself.

When it comes to any one of a million subjects, if I were to ask you *what* you think, the answer would be fairly straightforward. Whether it's the most reliable carmaker on the market, the best smartphone brand, or the perfect wine to serve with steak, you'd be able to come up with a fairly certain answer in the blink of an eye.

This answer will seem infinitely sensible to you and it might even seem to you like the only answer that a reasonable person would give. And that would be an entirely human thing to do. It's worth remembering that everything a person thinks or believes makes perfect sense to them. No matter how crazy, irrational, or strange another person's ideas may seem to us, for them it is an entirely sensible way to view the world.

But before we explore *why* you and I might hold the opinions, views, and beliefs that we do, it's helpful to first examine the all-important question of *how* thinking happens.

When people say they have "made up their mind" about a certain idea or issue, this is more than simply stating that they have accumulated sufficient information or activated enough neurons to trigger a point of judgment or decision. The process by which our minds get made up is nowhere near this neat.

The truth is that much of what shapes our conclusions and choices has less to do with our rational faculties than most of us would assume. The influence of subliminal instincts sees us arrive at points of stubborn certainty that often have little to do with the rational parts of our brain. Further still, we're coming to realize that the human mind itself is multifaceted and prone to drawing conclusions that *feel* right but can be wildly inaccurate. As we will see, you and I would do well to not believe everything we think.

Returning to the words of Kurt Lewin, understanding what makes up our minds—both figuratively and literally—is the essential first step in discovering how minds can be changed. So, let's start there.

CHAPTER 1
A TALE OF TWO MINDS

When my wife and I were doing the research to purchase a new car recently, the decision ended up coming down to two models. One was a reliable and fairly boring option, while the other was a sexier car with mixed reviews online. As we tried to make a choice, I remarked, "I'm of two minds about the whole decision..."

As soon as this familiar phrase came out of my mouth, I was struck by the profound truth it contains.

The reality is that in so much of life, we *do* operate in two minds—and not just in an indecisive sense. Plato described the difference between our two minds as the distinction between the "rational charioteer" who had to rein in the "unruly horse of emotion." Freud described the two-mind reality as the difference between our selfish and conscientious egos.[1] Numerous Eastern philosophies speak of the "monkey mind" that must be trained through discipline and focus,[2] while Christian theology distinguishes between the mind of the Spirit and the mind of the Flesh.[3]

In recent decades, an important new distinction has been drawn between the two minds we operate in as humans—a distinction that has profoundly shifted our understanding of what drives our judgments and how they can be influenced. Nowhere has this revision of thought been more significant than in the relatively young discipline of behavioral economics. This field of study emerged out of a recognition that traditional economic theories failed to account for the reasons people make the decisions they do.

For centuries, the world of economics had operated under the assumption that when confronted with a choice, humans would always make the most rational and reasonable one. In the field of economics, this became known as Expected Utility Theory.

However, you don't have to look far to see evidence that we often make decisions that go against common sense or even self-interest. In fact, we frequently make decisions that are highly irrational, to our own detriment, and just plain absurd. Behavioral economists set out to understand why this is the case.[4]

Two of the founding fathers of behavioral economics, Daniel Kahneman and Amos Tversky, were the first to methodically challenge centuries of economic assumptions and propose a new way of understanding human thinking.[5] For his part, Kahneman's most important contribution to the field was the concept that humans have two distinct ways of thinking. These two minds, so to speak, shape the way we process information and therefore make decisions.[6]

Building on Kahneman's ideas and the work of psychologists Keith Stanovich and Richard West, much of this book is going to revolve around the notion that the two minds you and I operate in every day could be referred to as our Inquiring Mind and our Instinctive Mind.

The reason the distinction between these two minds matters is that the vast majority of our most stubborn opinions, judgments, and beliefs are informed by our Instinctive Mind. Yale academic Zoe Chance suggests in her book *Influence is Your Superpower* that the Instinctive Mind is responsible for up to 95 percent of our decisions and behavior.[7] Harvard marketing professor Gerald Zaltman agrees, suggesting that over 90 percent of our thoughts, emotions, and learning occur without our conscious awareness.[8]

While these numbers may be hard to prove, they are also hard to ignore. What's clear is that our Instinctive Mind plays such an outsized role in how we respond to the world and to each other. For instance, it was San Diegans' Instinctive Minds that initially reacted with disgust to the idea of recycled wastewater despite logical evidence that there was nothing to fear. Then there are the numerous studies over the years which have revealed that voters tend to primarily use their Instinctive Mind when making decisions at the ballot box. As a result, many of us cast our vote based on, for instance, whether or not we like the look of a candidate or whether we get a good vibe about them.[9]

Whether it's who we choose to vote for or any number of the other 35,000 decisions we make each day on average, our Instinctive Minds shape more of who we are and what we do than most of us realize.[10]

So, what are these two minds and how do they work?

The Inquiring Mind[11]

Our Inquiring Mind is typically the one we associate with "thinking" in the classic sense. It is characterized as being:

1. **Meticulous** – Detail and precision matter when processing information.
2. **Effortful** – The process of inquiry is taxing and time-consuming.
3. **Self-aware** – Making sense of thought processes is easy because they are linear and sequential.
4. **Reasoned** – Processing information is about employing logic and rationality.
5. **Deliberate** – Engaging the Inquiring Mind requires an active choice.
6. **Cerebral** – Gut reactions are discounted and viewed with suspicion.
7. **Nuanced** – Complexity and uncertainty are embraced as a key component of quality thought.

The Instinctive Mind[12]

Unlike our methodical and critical Inquiring Mind, the Instinctive Mind tends to be:

1. **Quick** – Highly efficient at processing information.
2. **Effortless** – Isn't mentally taxing.
3. **Opaque** – We are generally unaware of its processes.
4. **Emotion-driven** – How an idea feels matters in how we evaluate it.
5. **Automatic** – We don't need to decide to use our Instinctive Mind.
6. **Relies on gut reaction** – Impressions and inclinations are core.
7. **Simplistic** – Ambiguity and nuance are ignored or dismissed.

While thinking and making decisions with our Instinctive Minds has its limitations, there are scores of good reasons we do so. For a start, using our Instinctive Mind requires much less effort and concentration than engaging our Inquiring Mind. As Daniel Kahneman points out, our brains are not just busy, they're lazy.[13] Or, as Carl Jung is often credited as saying, "Thinking is difficult, that's why most people judge."

This shouldn't necessarily be considered an indictment of our thinking habits. In fact, Wharton School professor Katy Milkman goes as far as suggesting that our mental preference for the path of least resistance can work in our favor. "Instead of seeing our inherent laziness as a bug, I regard it as a feature with many upsides."[14] Psychology professors Erin Devers and Jason Runyan agree, pointing to the fact that using our Instinctive Mind frees us up to think slowly and deliberately about certain matters. "Deliberate thinking is a limited resource that needs to be used wisely," they suggest.[15]

The two minds in action

In their bestselling book *Nudge*, celebrated behavioral economists Richard Thaler and Cass Sunstein examine how our two minds function in practice.

They point to the fact that it's the Instinctive Mind at work when you duck because a ball is thrown at you unexpectedly or smile when you see a cute puppy. Spontaneous and creative ideas like the ones we tend to have in the shower or just as we drift off to sleep are also our Instinctive Mind at work.

In comparison, if you were asked to multiply 17 times 34, figure out how to navigate from point A to B in an unfamiliar city, or to speak a language that is not your native tongue, it'll be your Inquiring Mind that swings into action.[16]

While the Instinctive Mind has a genius of its own, it also has numerous shortcomings we'd do well not to ignore.

As an illustration of this, try reading the text below and pay attention to anything that stands out as you do:

A BIRD IN THE
THE HAND IS WORTH
TWO IN THE BUSH

Did you notice anything unusual?

Perhaps try reading the three lines again but this time look out for the duplicate of the word "the" at the beginning of the second line. Now that you're engaging your Inquiring Mind, it becomes obvious, doesn't it?

In his bestselling book *The Black Swan*, Nassim Nicholas Taleb points out that we fail to see the error in this above example because our Instinctive Mind so easily operates without conscious awareness.[17] As this exercise shows, we tend to read with our Instinctive Minds—seeing what we expect to see and believing it unquestioningly when we see it. Beyond making proofreading our own work perilously difficult, it also makes us vulnerable to drawing inaccurate conclusions.[18]

Speak to the Instinctive Mind first

The sequence in which our two minds process information has a significant impact on the judgments we make. If the Inquiring Mind is activated first, it can actually *prevent* our Instinctive Mind from having too much influence on our decisions and thinking.

In comparison, something powerful happens when our Instinctive Mind forms an impression, inclination, or sense of certainty, which is then logically reinforced by our Inquiring Mind.[19] This process of reverse-engineering reason is a surefire path to stubbornness.

According to critical thinking researcher Peter Ellerton, the key in persuading or influencing others is to follow this same pattern. We must start by creating, modifying, or reinforcing a narrative in the other person's Instinctive Mind and then give them logical Inquiring Mind reasons why their judgments are accurate.[20]

Research by behavioral psychologist Susan Weinschenk shows just how important this sequence is when it comes to influencing others. Weinschenk suggests that appealing to the wrong "mind" or in the wrong order could see persuasive attempts backfire entirely.[21]

Salespeople know this well. For instance, if someone is looking to sell you a car, they will appeal first to the features that stimulate your emotions and ego. They'll have you imagine how you'll look in the car, the heads that will turn as you drive down the street, or the roar of the car accelerating from a standing start.

Only then will they turn your attention to the logical elements of the decision such as fuel economy and safety ratings. In comparison, the same salesperson knows that if we start the buying consideration process in analytical mode, it's very hard to engage the gut-level emotions as a secondary motivator.[22]

None of this is to say that our Instinctive Minds are somehow inferior when it comes to thinking and decision-making. On the contrary, there are times when our Instinctive Mind will help us make the best decision and arrive at the most sensible conclusion.

This was the central theme in Malcolm Gladwell's bestselling book *Blink: The Power of Thinking Without Thinking*. According to Gladwell, there are times when instinctive decisions are in fact best. "There are moments, particularly in times of stress, when haste does not make waste, when our snap judgments and first impressions can offer a much better means of making sense of the world."[23]

That said, there are many instances when our Instinctive Minds do not serve us well and can even work against our best interests.

When our Instinctive Minds don't serve us well

When asked in a 2014 interview what the greatest challenge facing the modern world was, famed science educator Dr. Bill Nye wasted no time in singling out the accelerating rate of climate change. "The problem is the speed at which things are changing," said Nye, lamenting the apathy toward taking action. "We are inducing a sixth mass extinction event."[24]

While it's hard to argue with Nye's point, you might be surprised to learn that there's growing research that shows that the biggest challenge in garnering commitment to taking action on climate change is that it is actually happening too *slowly*.

According to Harvard psychology professor Daniel Gilbert, the issue is that our Instinctive Minds are ill-equipped to process information that is abstract, complex, and slow. "We can duck a baseball in milliseconds and while we have come to dominate the planet because of such traits, threats that develop over decades rather than seconds circumvent the brain's alarm system." Gilbert concludes that "Many environmentalists say climate change is happening too fast. No, it's happening too slowly. It's not happening nearly quickly enough to get our attention."[25] That is, the attention of our Instinctive Minds.

Speaking to this same theme, Greg Harman wrote in an article for *The Guardian* that our Instinctive Mind isn't "wired to respond easily to large, slow-moving threats." Nor is it very good at assessing probability when risks are extreme—either very high or very low. As science and technology journalist Liam Mannix observes, "It's hard to imagine what 0.00009 percent means, so our (Instinctive Minds) think 'very low risk,' when the risk is actually much lower than that."[26]

Added to this is the fact that our Instinctive Minds are also prone to confuse probability with plausibility. Put simply, just because something is plausible (i.e. it could happen), doesn't necessarily mean it is probable (i.e. likely to happen).

This helps explain why few of us think twice about driving a car while roughly 40 percent of people get nervous when boarding a plane. This is despite the statistical fact that we have a 1 in 84 chance of dying in a car accident in our lifetime, as opposed to a 1 in 5,000 chance of meeting the same fate in a plane crash. Similarly, we are more likely to die from falling down the stairs than at the hands of a terrorist, but that doesn't correlate with our real fears.[27]

The work of Richard Thaler and Cass Sunstein is helpful in understanding why our Instinctive Minds tend to get probability mixed up with plausibility. In their book *Nudge,* Thaler and Sunstein presented research participants with the following two scenarios and asked them to forecast the probability or likelihood of each:

- A massive flood somewhere in North America next year, in which more than 1,000 people drown.
- An earthquake in California sometime next year, causing a flood in which more than 1,000 people drown.

While the notion of an earthquake in California may seem more plausible given that it straddles the San Andreas Fault, the first option is statistically more probable. And yet, significantly more people believed that the probability was higher for option 2.

This research illustrates one of the key limitations of our Instinctive Mind and its judgments. By including additional qualifying details to a scenario, our perceptions of plausibility increase despite the fact that this causes the scenario's actual probability to decrease. In practical terms, this means additional details don't necessarily bring clarity or context when making decisions—rather they can deceive us by creating a narrative that *seems* more likely.[28]

The anatomy of thought

Beyond outlining the attributes of our two minds, it's worth taking a few moments to examine their physical anatomy too.

Our Inquiring Mind, for instance, tends to be dominated by our brain's frontal lobe, which biologists will tell you is the part of the brain that developed most recently from an evolutionary standpoint. The frontal lobe is associated with things such as rational consideration, concentration, and planning. Because these activities require focus, self-control, and energy, our frontal lobe tends to be the last port of call when thinking and making decisions unless it is engaged deliberately.

In contrast, our Instinctive Mind is driven and defined by some of the more "ancient" parts of our brain. Chief among these is our limbic system, which is the part of our brain responsible for many of our primal impulses. First conceptualized by American neuroscientist Paul MacLean in 1952, our limbic system consists of brain regions including the amygdala, hippocampus, and basal ganglia.[29] Buried close to the back of the brain and underneath the cerebral cortex, the limbic system plays a big role in emotion processing, tribal instincts, and our fight/flight reflexes.[30]

Our Instinctive Minds keep us safe

In functional terms, one of the things our Instinctive Mind does best is protect us. After all, it is our limbic system—and our amygdala in particular—that swings into action at the first hint of a threat.

One of the complicating factors, however, is that our Instinctive Minds react in much the same way whether a threat is physical or psychological. If confronted with information or ideas that are perceived as threatening, our neurological instinct is to batten down the hatches and retreat to stubbornness. When this happens, even the best evidence and logic will struggle to get a fair hearing. As leadership author and pastor Andy Stanley suggests, our actions may speak louder than our words, but our reactions speak louder than both.

In an effort to observe the mechanics of this very process, Emory University psychologist Drew Westen monitored which parts of people's brains lit up when they were exposed to negative information about a political party or candidate they supported. Weston expected the brain's frontal lobe (the Inquiring Mind) to swing into action as individuals processed the information and considered how they could refute or dismiss it.

But this isn't what happened at all.

Instead, the frontal lobe stayed dormant while the limbic system (Instinctive Mind) roared to life. Weston's conclusion was that we don't really engage objectively or intellectually when confronted with disconfirming or inconvenient evidence. Instead, we instinctively defer to bias and emotion.[31] This is something commonly referred to as an "amygdala hijack."

Even if you are unfamiliar with the term, you probably know what an amygdala hijack feels like. We've all had the experience of jumping to the defensive or going on the attack when our opinions or beliefs are challenged—even when part of us knows that we are overreacting. But once an amygdala hijack gets under way, it can be hard to back down. Our pulse races, our hands get clammy, our face reddens. We are angry, incensed, and ready for a fight.

When we are in this state, our focus narrows, our memory becomes compromised, and, as award-winning mediator Diane Musho Hamilton observes, "We find ourselves trapped in the one perspective that makes us feel the most safe: 'I'm right and you're wrong.'"[32]

Although this dynamic is an entirely natural response and nothing new, there is little doubt that the digital age and social media in particular has heightened the "fight" instincts of our limbic system as we will see in Chapter 2.

Naturally, we are not powerless victims of our Instinctive Mind and its response reflexes. In an ideal world, our brain's frontal lobe ought to evaluate our instinctive responses and apply a good dose of reason, consideration, and judgment. However, recent research by University of California Professor Matthew Lieberman has shown just how powerful a role the amygdala plays in helping sustain and safeguard our deeply held beliefs—and how increasingly hard it is to fight this.

Interestingly, neuroscientist Bridget Queenan of UCSB's Brain Initiative points to evidence that the reflex to resist ideological threats is largely absent in young children and only kicks in and strengthens as we age. "Kids do not appear to be emotionally or cognitively shattered by new or contradictory information. (Children) are perfectly capable of updating their belief systems and behaviors based on evidence. In fact, they find new and contradictory things really appealing."

"So why do we stop?" Queenan ponders. "Why do we suddenly say: That's it, I'm done, I don't want to learn anymore. The world continues to be fascinating and unpredictable and open for exploration. So why do we as adults decide that we don't care anymore?"[33]

These are important questions and ones we will explore in the coming pages.

The impact of isolation

While it might be a natural, adult instinct to reject ideas that threaten our beliefs and opinions, there are certain factors that can cause our Instinctive Minds to be more sensitive to threat than is otherwise reasonable. The first of these is isolation.

Numerous studies in recent years have pointed to the power and importance of social connectedness. Not only has loneliness been shown to negatively impact our immune systems, cardiovascular health, and general well-being, new research indicates the degree to which it impacts the functioning of our Instinctive Minds too.

For instance, a study conducted by the University of Chicago in the early stages of the COVID pandemic sought to examine how lockdowns and social distancing were impacting our brains. The results confirmed that the size of an individual's amygdala grew or shrank in proportion to how socially connected that individual was.[34]

The reason this matters is that a smaller amygdala appears to be correlated with a more acute fight/flight response. Given this, is it any wonder that the pandemic years of social isolation were marked by a sense of trigger-happy outrage?

The important principle here is that lonely brains lash out. Isolation has a physical and psychological impact that makes our Instinctive Minds more stubborn and reactive. Significantly, the sort of connections that nurture healthy minds tend to be in-person ones. Video conference calls and digital interactions might make us feel connected to others but they just don't cut it when it comes to having balanced and healthy brains.

How fatigue makes us foolish

While loneliness can prevent our Instinctive Minds from thinking clearly, fatigue can cause just as many problems.

In an indication of just how consequential this can be, consider a study reported in Proceedings of the National Academy of Sciences looking at how fatigue affects legal judgments. In the study, the decision-making processes of eight parole judges were monitored. These judges have the unenviable task of reviewing an enormous quantity of parole applications on any given day. On average, each application is considered for six minutes by each judge, and only 35 percent are approved on an average day.

On this particular day, researchers measured the parole evaluations and judgments across the course of the day taking into account three food breaks—a morning break, a lunch break, and an afternoon break. An interesting pattern emerged. It turns out that approvals for parole spiked significantly straight after each meal break. In fact, it turned out that 65 percent of all approvals are granted shortly following a break.

This finding, while confronting ethically, is a clear indication that even the most rational and logical among us can fall into the trap of deferring to our Instinctive Mind when fatigue comes into play.[35]

It's worth noting that although taking regular breaks may cause us to feel fresher and think more clearly, what we consume while on a break can have a big impact on our reasoning skills too.

The trouble with trimethylxanthine

You might be surprised to learn that there is a legal and widely available drug called 1,3,7-trimethylxanthine that makes you more gullible if you take it— and makes you more persuasive if you give it to others. This drug is routinely dispensed through what are essentially "trimeth labs" that you'll find in almost every neighborhood.

While you've probably never heard of 1,3,7-trimethylxanthine, you've definitely heard this drug called by another name: caffeine.

The impact of caffeine on our evaluations and judgments was first examined back in 2005 by Pearl Martin at the University of Queensland in Australia. In Martin's research, attempts were made to convince participants to change their opinions about the controversial topic of voluntary euthanasia.

Participants for the study were already of the view that voluntary euthanasia ought to be legalized and Martin was curious as to what it would take to change this opinion. Before the persuasion attempt began, the participants were asked to consume an orange beverage that resembled juice. What they didn't know is that half of the group's drinks contained a moderate dose of caffeine (the equivalent to two espresso shots) and the other half were given a placebo. Each group was then exposed to six moving stories that made the case for not allowing euthanasia.

After reading each of the stories, the attitudes of the group were surveyed and those who had consumed the caffeine were found to be 35 percent more favorably disposed toward the arguments they'd read than those who'd consumed the placebo.[36]

In explaining the results, Pearl Martin suggests that caffeine increases arousal leading our Instinctive Minds to be more open to new ideas and information. Numerous studies have since confirmed this finding.[37]

■ ■ ■

While an awareness of the nature and limitations of our two minds is powerful in itself, this is only the beginning.

As we have explored, the vast majority of our deeply held opinions and views are formed by our Instinctive Minds. But how exactly does the Instinctive Mind get made up? What's the process by which we arrive at points of stubborn certainty and conviction?

This is where we will turn our attention next.

In the coming pages, we'll examine the mechanisms by which we become mindstuck. And as we will discover, not only does the Instinctive Mind extend well beyond our physical brains, it tends to operate at a powerfully subliminal level too.

CHAPTER 2
HOW CAN YOU BE SO SURE?

We all have things about which we are certain.

Two plus two is four.

What goes up must come down.

The sun always rises in the East and sets in the West.

While it's one thing to be certain about issues of science, it's another thing to hold fixed and firm ideas about matters that are entirely subjective. And yet there are countless things about ourselves, others, and the world around us about which we feel absolutely certain—even though there may be no objective reason for our conviction. We simply know that we know.

Building on what we explored in the previous chapter about the Instinctive Mind and how it influences our judgments, this chapter will examine the fundamental aspects of certainty. How do we arrive at points of stubborn assurance? And what does this mean for the process of trying to persuade others to reconsider the things they already think they know?

Many of us assume that knowledge is the cumulative outcome of considered thought and evaluated experience. As we have meandered our way through life, we have read, seen, and heard things that have informed our idea of what's true about the world. Our opinions and views, we presume, are the sum of our experiences and everything they have taught us.

In his superb book *On Being Certain*, neurologist Robert Burton questions this very assumption. According to Burton, the familiar sense we all have that we "just know" something to be true or accurate is actually more of a sensation than a reasoned conclusion.[1] This is something Burton refers to as the "feeling of knowing."

In drawing together the latest findings in disciplines as diverse as neuroscience, philosophy, and psychology, it's clear there are three distinct factors involved in our sense of certainty. When our Instinctive Minds arrive at a point of "knowing," most if not all of these three factors are involved:

1. Identity
2. Ideology
3. Intuition

Like any good triad, these elements tend to be most powerful when they work in unison. Just as the symmetry of three harmonizing notes makes up a musical chord, so too we often equate the feeling of knowing as being like something that "strikes a chord" or "resonates" with us. When our Instinctive Minds arrive at a point of knowing, the resultant feeling of certainty just *feels* right—even if we can't explain why.

More importantly, these three factors determine the sorts of ideas and information our Instinctive Minds are willing—or even able—to consider. As such, they can either act as a pathway or a roadblock when it comes to persuading others.

1. Identity

In October 2020, the father of a good friend of mine was admitted to a hospital in southern Florida for emergency surgery. Given that the COVID-19 pandemic was in full flight with escalating cases daily, a general sense of nervousness about being admitted to a hospital was understandable. However, it was not COVID that worried my friend's father the most. As a passionate Republican, he said his deepest hope was that he wouldn't receive a blood transfusion from a Democrat. "If I come back home liking Trump a bit less, you'll know why," he'd wryly told the family in a text message.

And he was only half joking.

The sheer enmity my friend's father felt toward those on the "other side" of the political divide was perhaps best characterized less than a month later with the victory of Republican David Andahl in his bid for the North Dakota state legislature. What was most unusual about Andahl's win was the fact he had died a month earlier. That's right—people opted to vote for a man who had died in order to prevent a living candidate from the opposing party getting into power.[2]

It's only funny if...

In an effort to understand what underpins this dynamic, researchers at La Trobe University asked a group of students to listen to a series of audio recordings and make judgments about what they heard. The researchers standing on the other side of a two-way mirror, however, were only interested in one particular reaction—laughter.

As the students donned the headphones and settled in, what they heard was a recording of a stand-up comedian. For some listeners, the audio simply featured the voice of the comedian. Others had canned laughter tracks dubbed over the comedian's act at deliberate points. What became immediately apparent was that the students laughed significantly more when they heard the sound of others laughing too.

This may not seem like an enormously significant discovery, and it's not. The power of canned laughter has been well understood for decades.

Where things got interesting was when the researchers assigned personas to the laughter tracks. One group of listeners were told that those laughing were similar to them (i.e. other students who they'd identify with and probably enjoy spending time with). Importantly, though, a different group of research participants were informed that those laughing at the comedian's jokes in the recording supported a political party that the students were likely to strongly disagree with.

The results were extraordinary. When the students heard laughter that had been ascribed to people "just like them," they laughed nearly four times as long. In contrast, when the students were told that the audience in the recording were people they wouldn't identify or agree with, they laughed about as much as if there had been no laughter track at all.[3]

Birds of a feather think together

While most of us would like to think we'd never be so partisan, there is growing evidence that this tendency is both universal and instinctual.

According to psychologist Daniel Haun, the human compulsion toward tribalism is a foundational element of our existence. As an indication of this, brain scans reveal that when we choose to fit in with "our herd," it's our Instinctive Mind and its desire for self-protection at work. In contrast, when we hold on to an opinion that is at odds with the rest of our group, our brains produce an error signal that warns us that we are probably wrong.[4]

The degree to which our Instinctive Mind gravitates toward tribal thinking can pose a number of problems. Firstly, it leaves us prone to thinking and believing things simply because everyone else in our tribe does—whether we genuinely hold the view or not. Beyond creating significant internal angst and confusion, this also means we outsource moral and mental assessments of what's right to others rather than thinking for ourselves.

Secondly, tribalism can cause us to defer to group consensus rather than considering what is best for all concerned. Something dangerous happens when popularity becomes a proxy for veracity. Just because a lot of people believe a certain thing doesn't mean it is correct—the majority can indeed be wrong.[5]

As Canadian bioethicist George Dvorsky describes it, "When our individualized brains start to shut down and enter into a kind of 'groupthink', (this) often causes behaviors, social norms, and memes to propagate among groups of individuals — regardless of the evidence or motives in support."[6]

Further still, Dvorsky points to the role of the social bonding hormone oxytocin in helping us forge close bonds with our tribe while making us suspicious, fearful, and even disdainful of people who we don't identify with.[7] Significantly, oxytocin is produced—largely, but not exclusively—by one of the brain structures that makes up our limbic system, the hypothalamus.

The practical implications of tribalism emerged strongly in the 2023 Edelman Trust Index data, which revealed that more than three-quarters of us would refuse to help someone in need if the other individual strongly disagreed with our views.[8]

Similar research conducted by the University of Calgary found that the average person would rather talk to a stranger who shares their political views than a friend who doesn't.[9] Consider that for a moment!

This is more than merely a case of enjoying a sense of commonality with those we agree with. Instead, it speaks to the compulsion we have to evaluate others and their ideas through the lens of identity.

What would people like me think about something like this?

Our sense of collective identity has a powerful impact on how we think and make judgments. In fact, a recent meta-analysis of fifty studies by the psychologist Peter Ditto confirms that "identity-motivated reasoning" is the single biggest factor in determining whether we accept or reject information.[10]

The reason for this is that when exposed to unfamiliar information or ideas, we tend to be unconsciously guided by the question, *What would people like me think about an idea like this?* Identity tends to trump inquiry.

One study that illustrates the power of identity in shaping perceptions and judgments involved showing a group of research participants a photo featuring an assembly of protesters standing in front of a building. When the researchers specified that it was a protest outside a health clinic against abortion, conservatives described it as a peaceful protest, whereas liberals saw it as an aggressive mob trying to intimidate innocent people.

It was a very different story when the same image was shown to another group of participants and was described as a protest against the exclusion of homosexuals outside a military recruitment center. According to the researchers, when conservatives were asked to characterize the scene, they saw "pitchforks and torches" while the liberals saw "Mahatma Gandhi." Remember, in both these instances, the image hadn't changed at all.[11]

Cognitive scientists Steven Sloman and Philip Fernbach explore the dynamics of identity-based reasoning in their book *The Knowledge Illusion: Why We Never Think Alone.* They argue that the vast majority of our strong views and opinions "do not emerge from deep understanding" but rather, are shaped by the sense that others we perceive to be like us hold a certain view.[12]

Beyond shaping perceptions, our sense of shared identity also has a huge influence on how we react when we encounter inconvenient truths. Upon being confronted with evidence or information that threatens or challenges our identity, we don't merely jump on the defensive but we invariably double down. Commonly referred to as "reactance," this response tends to be especially strong when values, morals, and politics are at the center of an argument. When our deeply held views are threatened, we dig our heels in and try to convince ourselves that our viewpoint is truer than even we suspect it is.[13]

When the best logic backfires

Dartmouth's Brendan Nyhan and Jason Reifler of the University of Exeter termed this tendency the "Backfire Effect."[14] In their famed 2006 study examining this quirk of our Instinctive Minds, Nyhan and Reifler presented research participants with fabricated news articles that reported weapons of mass destruction had indeed been discovered in Iraq following the U.S. invasion. Participants that were politically liberal dismissed the "facts" almost immediately while individuals who self-identified as conservatives were very open to accepting the news reports without question.

Where things got interesting was when Nyhan and Reifler subsequently presented the conservative participants with factual evidence that no weapons had indeed been discovered. This revelation saw their belief in the original mock article's claims grow stronger—despite having been informed that it was a complete fabrication.[15]

It was a similar story when researchers informed a group of volunteers that tax cuts had been demonstrated to actually increase government revenue. Despite the researchers later retracting the claim and apologizing for their mistake, right-leaning voters who were taking part in the study reported still believing the statement to be true. Even when the researchers admitted that the lie had been a deliberate part of the research, the conservative individuals simply chose to still believe it was true because it gelled with their existing assumptions.[16]

It is this dynamic that powerfully informs the conclusions our Instinctive Minds draw when evaluating information. We are always on the lookout for cues as to whether someone is on "our side" or not. Regardless of whether an idea is reasonable, rational, or logical, one of our primary processing filters is whether we can identify with the person presenting it. Only then do we decide whether we can identify with the other person's idea.

In an interesting experiment to explore how this dynamic plays out online, sociologist Chris Bail set out to see if exposure to the views of ideological opponents would change an individual's mind or shift their viewpoint—even slightly. His approach was to recruit 1,500 Twitter users and have them follow accounts that exposed them to opposing points of view. For a month they saw messages that directly contradicted their worldview—and the view of those they identified with as "their people." Liberals saw content from the likes of Fox News, while conservatives saw content posted from Planned Parenthood and key Democrats.

At the conclusion of the month, Bail and his team measured the attitudes of the participants in the hope that this broadening of exposure to different ideas may have also broadened people's thinking. Sadly, it was exactly the opposite. Something about the process of being exposed to the "other side" of key issues had caused each individual to become *more* entrenched in their prevailing views.[17]

Whether in the digital or analogue world, we can all too easily feel that a challenge to our ideas is an assault on our identity.

Left behind by liberalism

The challenge of course is that recent years have seen more and more issues become framed as ones of identity. Added to this, the sheer pace of social and moral change has seen many people feel that their values and identity no longer have a place.

In her book, *Cultural Backlash,* Harvard political scientist Pippa Norris suggests that this goes a long way to explaining the rise of right-wing conservative parties and leaders from the early 2010s onwards. According to Norris, the advancement of social liberalism has caused many people to feel left behind. These individuals tend to feel a collective sense of disorientation as they no longer recognize the modern world—and the modern world seems increasingly unwilling to recognize them.

Those who find themselves in this position tend to hold views relating to morality and national pride, for instance, that were considered mainstream or even virtuous until a few short years ago. But now those same values and opinions are considered outdated or bigoted and can lead you to be canceled if you dare voice them. It's hard to underestimate how threatening this is for people who suddenly feel that their opinion is no longer permissible and that their identity no longer has a place.

Of course, when a political leader or party promises a return to the values and norms of the past, this can seem irresistibly appealing. Once this nostalgic vision is coupled with a vow to defy the enemy (i.e. elites, the liberal media, and the political establishment) the battle lines for an identity-fueled clash quickly emerge. It is this very dynamic we have seen play out in scores of countries around the globe in recent years.

Our penchant for outrage

Whether in the context of populist politics or the culture wars more broadly, identity-motivated reasoning tends to be characterized by a sense of outrage and offense.

A case in point was the online reaction to climate change rallies in Sydney in late 2019. In an effort to discredit the many thousands of young people who had gathered in protest of government inaction regarding climate change, members of the Australian Youth Coal Committee shared an image on social media falsely claiming to be of rubbish that protesters had left behind in Sydney's Hyde Park. The idea was that climate protesters were hypocritical and should therefore be ignored.

However, anyone even vaguely familiar with the location would have immediately picked up on the fact that the photo wasn't at Sydney's Hyde Park, but rather Hyde Park in London. Further still, investigations revealed that the image was of rubbish left behind in the aftermath of a marijuana legalization rally in April 2019.

This fact scarcely mattered to those who were outraged by "evidence" of what they had already concluded to be true. Despite the accuracy of the image being quickly debunked, it went on to be shared almost 40,000 times in the following days.[18] Our Instinctive Minds love preventing the facts from getting in the way of a good story.

Blinded by belonging

Herein lies an important point: the very factors that drive tribalism have a unique ability to blind us. As Jonathan Haidt and Greg Lukianoff observed in their book *The Coddling of the American Mind*, "In tribal mode, we seem to go blind to arguments and information that challenge our team's narrative."[19]

In reflecting on the role that this dynamic plays in our willingness to deny facts or evidence, Adrian Bardon suggests that denial is "notoriously resistant to facts because it isn't about facts in the first place. (It) is an expression of identity."[20]

As a case in point, consider how the identity-fueled resistance to mask wearing during the COVID-19 pandemic was reminiscent of the reaction to seatbelt use in cars being mandated during the 1980s.

"Compelling the use of seat belts," declared a prominent conservative thinker at the time, was "one of the purest examples of paternalism." Emblematic of this view was a judge in Michigan who refused to fine drivers ticketed for not wearing seat belts despite the law compelling him to do so. Some conservative members of the federal judiciary publicly questioned whether seat belt laws were unconstitutional. Why? Simply because seatbelt use was perceived as an idea being pushed by the "other side."

While it's one thing to stubbornly cling to a bad idea merely because our identity is wrapped up in it, it's another entirely to dismiss a good idea for the simple reason that an "outsider" suggested it.

Even when our identity-fueled opinions could harm or disadvantage us, our zeal in defending them is extraordinary indeed—even to the point of hypocrisy.

Consider how this has played out over recent years in the political arena. For instance, shortly after Barack Obama was sworn in as president in 2009, numerous Republicans set about stymying the legislative agenda, even voting against bills they themselves had created before the election. Why? For no other reason than that the "other side" were the ones now supporting and promoting these issues.[21]

Of course, this is a game that both sides of the ideological divide play all too readily. In July 2021, Joe Biden's Press Secretary Jen Psaki cautioned of the dangers of misinformation, lamenting "the number of people dying around the country because they're getting misinformation that is leading them to not take a (COVID-19) vaccine." However, it's worth remembering that only 12 months earlier it had been leading Democrats who had been the ones stirring up misinformation and warning Americans against getting the "Trump vaccine."

At the time, Joe Biden suggested that it was likely the Trump administration would rush approvals and cut corners, while Kamala Harris made her feelings even more clear: "If Donald Trump tells us that we should take it, I'm not taking it." Then there was the Democratic Governor of New York, Andrew Cuomo, who stoked concerns saying, "I think it's going to be a very skeptical American public about taking the vaccine, and they should be.... You're going to need someone other than this FDA and this CDC saying it's safe."

It's hard to make a case for these perspectives being based in scientific thinking. Instead, these were essentially statements of identity. In other words, if the "other side" were suggesting something, it was probably an idea to be dismissed or ridiculed regardless of its possible merit. As Tim Urban suggests in his book *What's Our Problem?,* "Their point was more about Trump than the vaccine."[22]

Unified by enmity

When it comes to identity-motivated reasoning, knowing who is not on our side matters just as much as knowing who is—and perhaps more.

Speaking to this point, Duke University professor Chris Bail argues that the human impulse toward tribalism is as much about belonging as it is about "drawing boundaries between ourselves and others we deem to be less capable, honest, or moral." Bail suggests that "The sense of superiority that we derive from categorizing people into groups of 'us' and 'them' fulfills our intrinsic need for status."[23]

A story I heard recounted by the pastor of a small rural church in the aftermath of the COVID pandemic underscored just how destructive this propensity is. One day the pastor in question was approached by a representative group of parishioners who demanded to know which of their fellow churchgoers had chosen to be vaccinated. Those making the request had conscientiously refused the COVID vaccine and felt it was important they knew who, in their minds, ought to be ostracized or at least shamed for having succumbed to worldly and government pressure. Despite sharing the same faith and being part of the same tight-knit community, the choice to be vaccinated was cause enough for these individuals to be seen as the enemy.

This dynamic is a powerful tactic used in the world of brand marketing. Sometimes the most effective thing for a brand to have is a clearly defined adversary. In the words of David Foster Wallace, "Nothing brings you together like a common enemy."[24]

Consider how Pepsi people don't define themselves merely as drinkers of Pepsi, but as non-drinkers of Coke. In the same way, American truck drivers tend to be Ford or Chevy people, while iPhone and Android users relish in the fact that they are one and not the other.

In fact, there are few brands that have elicited as strong a tribal instinct as Apple. When researchers placed Apple devotees into an fMRI machine and mentioned the brand, the very same regions of their brains activated as those associated with religious belief.[25]

The lure of labels

When it comes to categorizing people as insiders or outsiders, one of ways we often do this is by resorting to labels. Our Instinctive Minds love labels because they help us make sense of people and ideas quickly. The trouble of course is that when we're too quick to apply simplistic labels to people and ideas that are inherently complex, we start drawing dangerously inaccurate conclusions. As Mark Twain once said, "If you label me, you negate me."

Labels are invariably the vehicles of prejudice. For instance, calling someone a "temporary migrant worker" as opposed to an "expat" carries a very different connotation. Both are essentially the same thing, but the connotations of the words are entirely different.

The key point here is not the label itself but how the process of applying it shuts down consideration. Once an individual or idea gets boxed and labeled, views and perspectives are seen through the narrow prism of what your label is commonly accepted to mean.[26]

This tendency is alive and well in political discourse. For instance, if you dare criticize any element of democracy, you'll be dismissed as a "fascist." Question whether capitalism would benefit from a few checks and balances on its characteristic excesses, and you'll be labeled a "Marxist." Or go to bat for the underprivileged and marginalized and you'll be seen as a "bleeding-heart liberal."

The trouble is that once a philosophical view becomes an identity we assign others or assume ourselves, things start getting tricky. It's no longer about the battle between the ideas of "conservatism" or "progressivism," for instance, but becomes a battle between "conservatives" and "progressives" whose primary goal is asserting their correctness and the folly (or evil) of their opponents.[27] Life, ideas but most importantly people quickly become two-dimensional.

The 2-D Trap

As human history attests, the moment we begin to see people as two-dimensional, dangerous things begin to happen. For a start, we tend to readily defer to our Instinctive Mind at the expense of reasoned consideration. When this happens, we invariably make the mistake of *demonizing* or *deifying* others— something I call the 2-D Trap.

Time and time again we have seen how simplistic narratives that demonize others can cause people to draw conclusions and take actions they would otherwise find unconscionable. As Tim Urban observes, "It's hard for people to truly hate a real human. It's hard to pillage a settlement where real humans live. It's hard to commit heinous violence against a real human. But is it hard to do awful things to filthy vermin and vile cockroaches and revolting scum of the Earth and agents of the underworld? Not really."[28]

It's important to note that demonizing the "other" in order to gain power is far from something that only the despots and dictators of our history books have engaged in. At some level, all conflict is based on an unwillingness to appreciate the multifaceted nuances of a person or circumstance. Whether it's quarreling spouses, bickering coworkers, menacing schoolyard bullies or warring nations, our Instinctive Mind's reluctance to see another individual as complex, nuanced, and truly human lies at the heart of all enmity.

Social commentator Dr. Natasha Moore suggests that the best warning sign for when we are falling into this trap is the language we use. "Every time we find ourselves starting a sentence with the immortal and deeply satisfying phrase 'I just don't understand how *anyone* could...' alarm bells should be ringing," Moore cautions.[29]

While it's easy to see the inherent danger in demonizing those who are not "on our side," the opposite dynamic is equally problematic. The process of dehumanization is not just about seeing outsiders as less than human—it is also about elevating people on our side to being superhuman. To *deify* them.

Either extreme feeds into the binary narratives that we've been taught since birth. We are conditioned to believe the notion that our heroes are perfect and blameless, while our enemies are evil and irredeemable. This two-dimensional view of reality, the 2-D trap, feeds right into the tribal nature of our Instinctive Minds and prevents us from thinking clearly.

Over the years, one of the personal rules of thumb I have come back to often is simply this: "No one is as good as they seem, and no one is as bad as they might otherwise appear to be."

This is always a timely reminder when I am tempted to write someone off without pausing to consider whether there is more to the story (and their story) than I realize. By the same token, I've learned the hard way that no one is perfect and placing my complete trust in another human being simply because we may be "on the same team" is dangerous and delusional. Doing so gets in the way of exercising my critical thinking.

The limitations of self-labels

While it is unhelpful to see other people or groups as two-dimensional, the labels we place on ourselves can be just as problematic.

Speaking to this dynamic, YCombinator founder Paul Graham suggests, "The more labels you have for yourself, the dumber they make you." By attaching our viewpoints to our identities, Graham warns that we lose an ability to engage with someone else's point of view. Aiming to be open-minded is always a good start, but Graham dares people to go one step further. "There is a step beyond thinking of yourself as x but tolerating y: not even to consider yourself an x."[30]

In a similar vein, Tim Urban in his book *What's Our Problem?*, writes "Think about your identity. The truth is, you're not a progressive or a conservative or a moderate or radical or some other political noun. Those are words for ideas, not people. Attaching a political category to your identity is a heavy piece of baggage to carry around, and putting it down makes learning and exploring much easier and less stressful."[31]

Wharton School psychologist Adam Grant suggests that no meaningful persuasion can occur unless we can help someone detach their opinions from their identity. According to Grant, this is the single biggest factor that prevents people from recognizing when they may not have a complete view of reality.[32]

As much as we'd like to think we're immune to the psychological impacts of tribalism, the reality is that many of our deeply held views and opinions are a statement of identity rather than fact. This has a powerful influence on how open our Instinctive Minds are to new perspectives or unfamiliar ideas and is something we must always factor in when it comes to changing other people's minds (and our own).

Political economist John Stuart Mill powerfully summed up the danger of shielding ourselves from people and ideas that we don't identify with. "It is hardly possible to overrate the value of placing human beings in contact with persons dissimilar to themselves, and with modes of thought and action unlike those with which they are familiar. Such communication has always been one of the primary sources of progress."[33]

But identity is just the first element that contributes to our sense of stubborn certainty. Something powerful happens when identity joins forces with the second factor that shapes the judgments of our Instinctive Minds: ideology.

2. Ideology

The old adage tells us that seeing is believing. We'd like to imagine that if we see clear evidence that something is true, we will adjust our beliefs accordingly. And yet, this is far from the case. As humans, our Instinctive Minds have a uniquely powerful ability to only see what we already believe to be true.

We tend to see and agree with ideas that fit our preconceptions and to ignore or dismiss information that conflicts with them. In the words of eighteenth-century German physicist Georg Christoph Lichtenberg, "Unbelief in one thing tends to spring from blind belief in another."

The fabled story of Christopher Columbus's voyages to the new world in the 1490s are a powerful demonstration of this principle. As we all learned in school, Columbus was so convinced that he was heading to Asia that he could not accept any alternate explanation for the lands he encountered. After all, Asia was what he hoped and expected to encounter as he headed west.

Having been heavily influenced by the accounts of Marco Polo's travels to Mongolia and China, Columbus mistook the Caribbean Island of Hispaniola for Japan, and assumed Cuba was mainland China. In a subsequent voyage, he concluded that the southward direction of Cuba's coastline could only mean that the landmass he was seeing was the Malay peninsula.

Due to his entrenched assumptions, Columbus instructed his crew to selectively collect botanical samples to take back to Spain that would support his thesis. He even mandated that officers and crew sign a deposition stating that the coastline they had seen was indeed part of the Asian continent. The punishment for refusing to sign was to have your tongue cut out. Despite mounting skepticism in the late 1490s that Columbus had encountered the Asian continent, the explorer couldn't accept the possibility that he had discovered a fourth continent and died with this conviction.

As hard as it can be to admit, Columbus' mistake is one any of us could have made. We all have deeply ingrained assumptions that warp the perceptions and judgments our Instinctive Minds make. The challenge comes when we live our lives as if this were not the case.

One of the complicating features of our beliefs is that they prevent us from testing our basic assumptions. In a way, this is a necessary process—otherwise we could never make sense of all the countless and varied experiences in life.[34] We simply can't evaluate every thought, interaction, or piece of information from first principles—it'd be exhausting and impractical.

Speaking to this theme, Andrew O'Keeffe in his book *Hardwired Humans* suggests that our Instinctive Minds have always relied on established assumptions to help categorize things as good or bad—and this served our ancestors well on the plains of Africa. "It meant the difference between life and death," observes O'Keeffe.[35] But this same trait can work to our detriment in a modern age when ideas that challenge our existing beliefs, experiences, and assumptions become seen as a threat.[36]

The Prism of Precedence

According to Aristotle, all new knowledge is learned through the lens of our experiences — what I refer to as the Prism of Precedence. What we have discovered or decided on in the past powerfully shapes the meaning we attach to all new ideas. More significantly, precedence doesn't only shape the way we perceive new information, it sometimes prevents us from even considering new ideas at all. Old knowledge can indeed prevent new knowledge.[37]

This was the key insight of Thomas Kuhn in 1962. Until we experience what Kuhn described as a paradigm shift, taking on new knowledge is incredibly difficult. It's been argued that science would have progressed much faster if we were not so constrained by ideology.

Scientists, like all humans, easily get mindstuck when their existing beliefs and assumptions get in the way of untethered thinking and learning.[38] To this point, Wharton School psychologist Adam Grant cautions that high levels of intelligence can make it difficult to achieve a high level of mental flexibility. "The brighter you are, the harder it can be to see your own limitations. Being good at thinking can make you worse at rethinking." As Grant describes it, ideological flexibility "means being actively open-minded. It requires searching for reasons why we might be wrong—not for reasons why we must be right—and revising our views based on what we learn."[39]

And yet, this is advice most of us find very difficult to put into practice. In examining why this is the case, Bertrand Russell observed that it is human nature to scrutinize and instinctively reject ideas that challenge our established assumptions. In comparison, if new information affirms our ideology, our Instinctive Minds will "accept it even on the slightest evidence."[40]

David McRaney describes this dynamic in his book *You Are Not So Smart*: "When you watch your preferred news program or read your favorite newspaper or blog, you tend to believe you are an independent thinker. You may disagree with people on the issues, but you see yourself as having an open mind, as a person who looks at the facts and reaches conclusions after rational objective analysis."[41]

In other words, if we agree with what we're reading, we're more likely to engage with it thoughtfully. However, if something challenges our existing views, our Instinctive Mind is inclined to dismiss it more readily and reactively.[42] As an indication of this, an Ohio State University study showed people spend 36 percent more time reading an essay or piece of information if it aligns with their existing opinions.[43] The father of modern psychology William James put it best when he said, "A great many people think they are thinking when they are merely rearranging their prejudices."

In a stark example of this principle at play, consider the explosive evidence uncovered in March 2023 as part of Dominion Voting Systems' defamation case against Fox News. Dominion's primary complaint was that high profile Fox programs and news anchors deliberately aired false information about the voting machine company's technology in the tumultuous weeks following the 2020 election. Viewers were deceived into thinking that Dominion Voting Systems had allowed anti-Trump forces to secretly alter voting tallies and that the company itself was the brainchild of deceased Venezuelan dictator, Hugo Chavez.

Of course, there was no evidence of any of these claims, and those propagating them at Fox News knew this full well. Private correspondence tabled for the court case revealed that Fox employees joked with each other about how "crazy" and "insane" the claims were and that the guests touting them on their broadcasts were "lying."

However, former NPR assistant managing editor Bill Wyman suggests that the most significant element of this story was not the ethical and editorial choices made by Fox News. Rather, it was how Fox viewers reacted when the channel did start accurately reporting the news. When TV hosts eventually acknowledged that Trump had indeed lost the election and that there had been no fraud, this was information that scores of Fox viewers simply would not or could not hear. So they simply chose not to listen and changed the channel en masse.[44]

Exploring this quirk of human nature in an article for *The New York Times*, psychologist Daniel Gilbert said: "When our bathroom scale delivers bad news, we hop off and then on again, just to make sure we didn't misread the display or put too much pressure on one foot. When our scale delivers good news, we smile and head for the shower. By uncritically accepting evidence when it pleases us, and insisting on more evidence when it doesn't, we subtly tip the scales in our favor."[45]

Why logic and facts have little impact

While the human reflex to resist ideas that challenge our beliefs is something we have all experienced firsthand, the process by which this actually happens has been largely a mystery until recently. In a landmark study a few years ago, researchers at UCLA monitored the brain activity of politically liberal individuals while they were being exposed to arguments that challenged or contradicted their views.

The brain scans revealed that participants' strength of belief was significantly lower for non-political statements than for more ideology-based, political ones. Unsurprisingly, people were far more willing to concede that taking multivitamins was not essential, for instance, than they were open to reconsidering their views on abortion. The data showed that participants were up to five times more likely to re-evaluate non-ideological beliefs than ideological ones.

Paradoxically, the UCLA researchers found that the response time for reconsidering views was much faster for deeply held beliefs—indicating that little real consideration was given to counterevidence. This was the Instinctive Mind doing what it does best: reacting.

These findings correlate with the natural sequence we are all familiar with feeling. If we are exposed to something that challenges an idea or assumption that doesn't really matter to us, we are curious or even excited to explore and learn. However, when our core beliefs are questioned, we tend to shut down or double down rather than open up.[46]

Psychologist Dr. Joe Pierre has witnessed this human propensity for resisting ideological counterarguments many times in his interactions with Flat Earth Society members. Reflecting on these experiences, Pierre remarked, "I would love to see a Flat Earther purchase a SpaceX ticket to 'see for themselves' what the Earth looks like from above 35,000 feet and beyond." However, he suggests that even this firsthand experience may make little difference: "Some die-hard Flat Earthers would even reject that personal experience. Indeed, if you look online, you'll see some people suggesting that the Earth's atmosphere acts as a spherical lens that gives the illusion of curvature."[47]

In examining the similar role that ideology plays in shaping anti-vaccination sentiment, Dartmouth's Brendan Nyhan and his colleagues exposed research participants to an article actively refuting the claims of anti-vaxxers. Despite clearly showing evidence that disproved any linkage between vaccines and autism, for instance, anti-vaccination attitudes actually *increased*.[48]

Similarly, when people who were hesitant to take the flu vaccine were shown irrefutable evidence that the immunization does not give you the flu, their degree of willingness to get vaccinated dropped by half.[49]

In other words, vaccine skeptics were so entrenched in their belief that immunizations are bad, that even if one reason for this belief was allayed, other assumptions immediately swung into action to reinforce the originally held ideology.[50]

The unraveling effect

Far from something that is particular to anti-vaxxers and flat earthers, the trap of defending our ideology at any cost is something we're all prone to. One of the key reasons for this is what's often described as the unraveling effect. When our beliefs are challenged with counterevidence, the process of re-evaluation can be a confronting one. There can be a sense that "if this one thing is not true or accurate, what else have I believed to be true that is not?" This can be extraordinarily unsettling.

Added to this is the fact that our deeply held ideology is often inherited and linked to our identity. We are each given core narratives and belief systems from our families, communities, and cultures that help us answer the major questions of life. To have these undermined means not just abandoning an ideology but, in some cases, can feel like forsaking our heritage and community.[51]

Professor Richard Tedlow from Harvard Business School has spent years examining how this dynamic affects our judgment. "Sometimes we divert information from our awareness because it is too painful or stressful," according to Tedlow. "More commonly we do so because the offending information contradicts assumptions with which we are comfortable, and it is easier to reject the information than to change our assumptions."[52]

Wharton School psychologist Adam Grant suggests that this tendency is near-universal, saying "We favor the comfort of conviction over the discomfort of doubt. We laugh at people who still use Windows 95, yet we still cling to opinions that we formed in 1995."[53]

One of the reasons for this is that reconsidering our ideology can be confronting indeed. Being "in-between beliefs"—where we are no longer sure of what we previously assumed but unconvinced about an alternative—can feel unstable and unsettling. This psychological discomfort tends to be all the motivation our Instinctive Minds need to look for a resolution that will restore the safety of certainty—even if that means ignoring evidence and returning to old beliefs despite a nagging sense that something's not right.[54]

The implications of this for persuasion are significant. After all, when we ask someone to consider a new idea or we are challenged to do so ourselves, this is no small ask. It means not just adopting a new viewpoint but discarding or re-evaluating an old one.

Feeling right feels good

Beyond the psychological aspects of ideology-driven thinking, there is a physiological process involved too. In their book *Denying to the Grave: Why We Ignore the Facts That Will Save Us*, Jack and Sara Gorman cite fascinating research that shows that we experience a genuine sense of pleasure in the form of a dopamine rush when exposed to information that reinforces our existing beliefs. "It feels good to 'stick to our guns' even if we are wrong," according to the Gormans.[55]

Because feeling right feels so good, we are rarely judging the world as it is—but rather the way we expect to see it. And if there's one thing the Instinctive Mind is brilliant at, it's finding evidence to support what it already thinks is true.

Neuroscientist Robert Burton suggests that this is because one of our Instinctive Mind's primary tendencies is to seek out the familiar. "The closer the fit between previously learned patterns and the new incoming pattern, the greater the feeling of correctness will be." This process of pattern recognition results in our Instinctive Minds automatically deeming something to have a high probability of correctness even before our Inquiring Minds get involved. If an idea "seems right," we tend to only see evidence that will convince us that we are right.[56]

This leads to one of the most blinding aspects of our beliefs—and that is their ability to delude us.

Clinging to untruth

According to the *Diagnostic and Statistical Manual of Mental Disorders*, delusions are "fixed and strongly held beliefs that are not amenable to change in light of conflicting evidence."[57]

Put simply, while we all create belief systems that influence our perceptions and judgments, delusion sets in when our Instinctive Minds hold onto ideology so strongly that we lack the will or ability to reconsider it.

Importantly, delusion isn't the same as confusion about what is or isn't true. Rather it is a complete confidence and belief in things that are demonstrably *untrue*. The question of who decides what's true or not and how they determine this is where things get messy of course—especially in a post-modern age when truth is seen as relative. As *Seinfeld's* George Costanza put it, "It's not a lie if you believe it."[58] A motto for delusional thought if ever there was one!

To overcome this inherent subjectivity, psychiatrists tend to diagnose delusionality based on the degree to which a belief differs from popular opinion. It follows then that we tend to label as "deluded" those who hold deep convictions about things that are considered implausible and ridiculous to the average person.[59]

In a practical sense, this has always meant that holding wildly contentious beliefs that deviated from those in your immediate surroundings was dangerous. After all, it could see you dismissed as delusional or downright insane.

This self-referential nature of delusion can quickly become complicated. David Streitfeld of the *New York Times* points to the fact that prior to the introduction of social media, a deluded individual may have struggled to find someone in their village, suburb, or city that held the ideology and convictions they did.[60] In modern times, however, anyone can seek out and find people who agree with even the most obscure ideology, and then band together online.

Intelligence offers little immunity

It's important to clarify that delusion is not a function of ignorance—the undiscerning are not necessarily unintelligent. In fact, high levels of intelligence or education make little difference in our susceptibility to ideology-driven thinking. To this point, a 2017 study found that highly educated or knowledgeable individuals are *more* likely to defend ideological viewpoints even when confronted with reliable counterevidence.[61]

In looking at how this contributes to intelligent people falling prey to conspiracy belief, Dr. Steven Novella suggests that highly educated and intelligent people are just as prone to conspiracy thinking as the uninformed or the ignorant—perhaps even more so.

"Ironically, people who are highly intelligent are a lot better at rationalizing their own beliefs," he suggests. "They are much more sophisticated at locking themselves into the beliefs that they want to hold."[62]

Given this, Deakin University's Lydia Khalil cautions that arguing logically with people who have subscribed to conspiracy belief and misinformation is largely futile. The reason is that both sides consider each other "brainwashed" and incapable of independent or critical thought.[63]

As a result, ostracizing, mocking, or applying restrictions on conspiracy theorists only feeds the narrative and reinforces their assumptions. Even rational thought or evidence makes little difference. As economist and social theorist Thomas Sowell suggests, "It is usually futile to try to talk facts and analysis to people who are enjoying a sense of moral superiority in their ignorance."

Steven Novella illustrates this principle using the example of belief in moon landing conspiracies. Novella points out that "Pulling off a hoax to fake going to the moon was actually more complicated than just going to the moon. But this logic scarcely matters. To a true moon landing skeptic, there is almost no evidence that would convince them." You could show them live footage from a satellite currently taking pictures of the Apollo 11 landing site, astronaut footprints and all, and it would make little difference. "Well, NASA must have faked it," will be their response. Novella suggests that "even if we took that person to the moon and put them at the Apollo 11 site, they could say, 'Oh, they just mocked this up for me.' There's just no evidence that could possibly get them out of their mindset."[64]

It's a similar story when it comes to the issue of climate change denial. Numerous studies have found that someone who is politically conservative has a significantly higher chance of denying the reality of climate change—even if they are highly educated and intelligent. By the same token, research shows that liberal voters tend to reject reliable science regarding the safety of nuclear power and genetically modified crops because it doesn't gel with their existing ideology. The bottom line is that being well educated or highly intelligent matters little when it comes to our Instinctive Mind's capacity for ideology-driven thinking.[65]

Bearing this in mind, David Robson in his book *The Intelligence Trap* suggests we need to seriously rethink the widely held belief that a high IQ and rationality go hand-in-hand. "When it comes to analyzing evidence and thinking about it in a fair, even-handed way, IQ is really bad at predicting whether people can do that kind of thing," says Robson.[66]

In the words of legendary legal scholar Oliver Wendell Holmes, "The mark of a civilized person is their willingness to re-examine their most cherished beliefs." By this reckoning, modern humans are far less civilized than we'd like to otherwise imagine.

While identity and ideology play a key role in determining how open we are to new ideas, there's one final factor we must not underestimate—that of intuition.

3. Intuition

In the early 1780s, German philosopher Immanuel Kant set his formidable mind to the question of how humans come to understand themselves and the world around them. His conclusion was that there is much we know for no other reason than that we simply know—something he referred to as "a priori knowledge" (pronounced a-pry-oar-eye).[67]

We've all experienced the feeling of having absolute certainty about an issue or idea for no tangible reason. Sometimes it is something we feel "in our bones" or perhaps it's the vague inkling of something familiar such as déjà vu.[68] A more common way to describe this sort of knowledge is as a hunch, a sixth sense, or just plain old intuition.

Defined as knowledge that is unrelated to conscious thought, observation, or reason, intuition can be hard to pin down. Partly this is because it is metaphysical or spiritual in nature.[69] That said, even the staunchest humanist or devotee to rationality will acknowledge the times in their lives when they "just knew" something wasn't quite right with their child, or that something was amiss in a business deal and decided to ask some more questions. Experience tends to prove that these intuitions are a warning we ignore at our peril. When we've got bad vibes or get the strong sense that something is "rotten in the state of Denmark," we've learned to tread carefully.[70]

To this point, I've always found it fascinating how our Instinctive Minds often defer to intuition when making consequential decisions—while we tend to approach comparatively frivolous choices using more methodical logic. For instance, when it came to purchasing our family home a number of years ago (the biggest financial decision most people ever make), I spent far less time weighing the logical options than I had done in planning a four-week European adventure the previous year. In the end, while my wife and I had done a fair amount of homework, we ended up buying the house that just "felt right" when we inspected it. Whether the numbers stacked up or the building reports checked out scarcely mattered. Our Instinctive Minds had made a decision based on intuition and then all we had to do was look for Inquiring Mind logic to back up our choice.

A vibe has value

Interestingly, it's when the stakes are high and the pressure is on that our intuitive facilities are especially valuable. In a study reviewed by the *British Journal of Psychology*, researchers explored real-world case studies of intuition's power to help people make split-second choices. One example stood out in particular. It described the decision by a Formula One driver who braked sharply coming into a hairpin curve for no particular reason except that it just felt like what he needed to do. Unbeknownst to the driver, there was a pileup just around the corner and, had he failed to brake, he would have certainly made a bad situation considerably worse.[71]

In another example of how powerful intuition can be, consider the decision by a banking executive named Mike Smith in November 2008 that saved his life. As he was checking out of the Taj Mahal Palace hotel in Mumbai, India, Smith was informed he had ample time before his flight was due to depart and was invited to relax in the hotel bar for a complimentary drink. For a reason that even he couldn't describe, Smith reported having an uneasy feeling and so decided to head to the airport and wait for his flight there. He had only just got into the car and driven around the corner when terrorists stormed into the foyer where he had been standing moments before.[72]

Then there's the story recounted in Gary Klein's book *Sources of Power* that points to the role intuition played in famously saving the lives of a firefighting crew. In this particular instance, a fire chief had led his team into a blaze in a single-story house when he sensed that something wasn't right. With no tangible reason for his hunch, the lieutenant ordered the crew out of the building just a few moments before the floor they'd been standing on collapsed.

Only later was it discovered that the source of the fire was a basement beneath the house that the firefighters were unaware even existed.[73]

Some call this sort of insight "soul knowledge," others define it as spiritual discernment and sometimes it is described as premonition. But regardless of the label you use, these various expressions of intuition have a profound and powerful effect on the judgments our Instinctive Minds make.

The metaphysical mind

Acknowledging the role and reality of intuition does raise some interesting questions that scientists often struggle with.[74] At best, most neuroscientists put intuition down to a yet-to-be discovered brain mechanism that is responsible for immediate cognition without thought.[75]

After all, it is the spiritual or mystical elements of intuition that can be most difficult to make sense of. For instance, when someone describes an "aha moment" of revelation, there is often a sense of transcendent intuition involved.

The reflections of *New York Times* bestselling author and law professor Bob Goff struck me as especially insightful in this regard. As a committed Christian, Goff describes the importance of discerning the will of God. In his book *Love Does*, Goff admits that while "God doesn't speak to me with a voice that makes audio needles move, there are times when I've sensed something down deep, almost like a tuning fork has just been pinged in my soul."[76] This is a perspective on intuition that many people of faith can strongly relate to, myself included.

Similarly, the Islamic concept of intuition, often referred to as "hadas," is related to having prophetic knowledge. The twelfth-century Persian philosopher Siháb al Din-al Suhrawadi built on Plato's concepts of implicit knowledge to define intuition as insight that had come as a result of illumination or mystical contemplation.[77]

But even outside the spiritual realm, intuition is a force to be reckoned with. The famous Indian mathematician Srinivasa Ramanujan once said that he would "simply know" the solution to a complex equation or number problem, and it would then be a matter of proving why this was the case.[78] This sense of correctness or "knowing" isn't something that Ramanujan arrived at through a linear or methodical process of thinking. It was something his Instinctive Mind just knew with certainty and conviction.

Albert Einstein was famous for paying tribute to the often-overlooked role of intuition. "The intuitive mind is a sacred gift, and the rational mind is a faithful servant," said Einstein. "We have created a society that honors the servant and has forgotten the gift."[79]

While not diminishing the metaphysical nature of intuition, cognitive scientists George Lakoff and Mark Johnson in their book *Philosophy in the Flesh* suggest that much of our intuitive ability is driven by our physical bodies.[80] Neurologist Robert Burton agrees, suggesting that our bodies are "instrumental in imbuing our thoughts with a sense of their correctness or incorrectness."[81]

Listen to your heart

This idea of our bodies having a capacity to "think" ought not be such a revolutionary idea. For millennia, we have been told to "listen to our heart" and be guided by what it tells us. Interestingly, numerous scientific discoveries of late suggest that we ought not dismiss this advice as merely sentimental, poetic, or metaphorical.[82]

Researchers at Montréal's Hôpital du Sacré-Coeur have recently discovered that our hearts contain an intrinsic nervous system that consists of approximately 40,000 neurons. These "sensory neurites," as they are called, have been shown to play a key role in the forming and relaying of judgments.[83]

Further still, it has been discovered that the human heart contains cells that were previously only thought to exist as part of the central nervous system. This has caused scientists to reconsider the very nature of how we think and the function our physical hearts play. Even more extraordinary is the discovery that the human heart also releases the powerful hormone oxytocin, which we referred to earlier in this chapter. This hormone is an essential component in how we build trust and affinity, and it has now been shown to exist in the heart in similar doses to our brains.[84]

Perhaps seventeenth-century French mathematician and philosopher Blaise Pascal wasn't too far off when he observed, "The heart has its reasons whereof reason knows nothing." It would seem that our hearts have a way of making sense of the world that has little or nothing to do with rational consideration.

And it's not only our hearts that inform our intuitive faculties—our gut plays an important role too.

Go with your gut

Back in 2010, Duke University neuroscientist Diego Bohórquez stumbled upon a fascinating discovery while examining enteroendocrine cells through an electron microscope. Although the digestive function of these cells that line the human gut has been well understood for decades, Bohórquez noticed something that researchers had previously overlooked: these cells had "foot-like protrusions" that resembled neural synapses. Intrigued by his discovery, Bohórquez assembled a research team and commenced a series of experiments that eventually revealed our guts have a unique role to play in unconscious thought.[85]

This discovery was significant because it validated what humans have known for millennia: that "gut instinct" does indeed exist.

The area of brain-gut research represents one of the most fascinating frontiers in our understanding of human thought. For instance, numerous studies indicate that our guts contain 500 million neurons that have the capacity to process information, experiences, and ideas more rapidly than our brains. These gut reactions happen at a deeply unconscious level and have a powerful influence on the conclusions our Instinctive Minds arrive at.[86]

We all know what it feels like to "just know" something to be true due to a vague sense that we can't pin down. While nebulous, our intuition doesn't just contribute to our sense of certainty, but to our stubbornness too. It has a unique ability to make us mindstuck.

And this is the challenge that intuition poses in the area of influencing the Instinctive Minds of others. If someone intuitively feels something to be true, correct, or accurate, trying to persuade them to think otherwise can be a tough ask indeed. This challenge is not insurmountable, but it is also far from insignificant.

■ ■ ■

As we have explored in the previous pages, arriving at a point of certainty is far from the considered and rational process that many of us imagine it to be.

Although it may be natural to defer to identity, ideology, and instinct when exposed to ideas or information, doing so allows prejudice to powerfully shape our perceptions. This invariably results in us arriving at conclusions by impulse rather than rational consideration.

As a result, we need to realize that whenever we try to persuade someone to consider a new perspective or point of view, their Instinctive Minds are essentially asking one or all of these questions:

- **Is this idea SAFE?** – Does it threaten my sense of belonging? (Identity)
- **Is it FAMILIAR?** – Does it gel with and reinforce what I already believe to be true? (Ideology)
- **Does it FEEL RIGHT?** – Does it match up with what I unconsciously sense is true and real? (Intuition)

The significance of taking these questions into account in the process of changing minds is hard to overstate. As neuroscientist Robert Burton suggests, we must never forget that identity, ideology, and intuition have a unique capacity to "overpower and outsmart intellect."[87]

PART I

CLOSING REFLECTIONS

The comedian Stephen Colbert has repeatedly poked fun at the way in which people account for their opinions of what is right or wrong based on something he refers to as "truthiness." According to Colbert, truthiness describes how identity, ideology, and intuition have "become a preferred method of determining what's true or not—regardless of critical investigation or evidence."[88]

While this notion of "truthiness" started out as a piece of incisive social commentary on late night television, it struck such a chord that Merriam Webster's dictionary ended up listing it as one of their "words of the year."[89]

Although it's understandable to flinch at the suggestion that you and I are inherently irrational, the evidence is hard to ignore. Certainly our Inquiring Minds have the capacity for reasoned logic and careful consideration, but at the end of the day our Instinctive Minds tend to run the show. And so any meaningful persuasion must start here. The key is to work *with* human nature rather than against it. This is where we will turn our attention in Part II as we explore what it really takes to change even the most mindstuck people.

PART II
A TOOLKIT FOR PERSUADING STUBBORN PEOPLE

By all reports, my brother-in-law's initial assessment when I started dating his sister wasn't entirely flattering. "He's a great guy," Lynton had remarked, "but he's never going to be much use on the end of a shovel."

And he's not half wrong. Marrying into a family of tradesmen was an inspired move on my part given how unskilled I am with anything hardware-related.

Despite my lack of aptitude, however, I've always been willing to give odd jobs around the house a try over the years—often ill-advisedly. One such job was the erecting of a new wall-mounted clothesline a few years ago.

As I'd never done something like this before, my first port of call was the hardware store to invest in a new electrical drill and the highest quality drill bit on sale. I even purchased safety goggles and ear plugs for good measure!

Once I'd carefully measured where the mounting holes would need to be, I set about drilling into the rendered wall. Very quickly, I got the distinct sense that something wasn't right. The drill started making a strange droning noise and I detected the off-putting smell of burning electronics coming out the motor. Undeterred, I pressed on.

When I stopped to inspect my progress five minutes later, I was dismayed to find that there was hardly a dent in the wall. In fact, I'd made little more than a scratch. After a further ten minutes of drilling with little more to show for my efforts, I downed tools and Face-timed my father-in-law.

It only took a few moments to find out what the problem was. "You're using the wrong type of drill bit," he gently informed me. "That one is only good for timber. What you need is a masonry drill bit." After a quick trip back to the hardware store, I returned with the correct tool for the job and the clothesline was mounted in no time at all.

In many ways, this same principle applies to the process of persuading stubborn people. As we have seen, using the tools of logic and reason will hardly make a dent when identity, ideology, and intuition are at work. Pushing harder or giving better evidence will make little impact at all. What we need are different tools.

While people today may be more mindstuck than ever, the truth is that changing others' minds has never been easy. Many of humanity's greatest thinkers over the centuries have grappled with the question of what it takes to move others.

Almost 2,300 years ago, Aristotle's famed work *The Art of Rhetoric* was the first comprehensive attempt to understand the mechanics and methods of influencing people. According to Aristotle, effective persuasion was always a function of three things—something that became known as the rhetorical triangle. These are:

- Ethos
- Pathos
- Logos

It was these three elements that determined whether you and your ideas had any hope of influencing others—and they are a valuable starting point for examining what works in a modern era too.

Ethos

Sometimes described as "argument by character," ethos describes the ability to use personality, reputation, and trustworthiness to create affinity with those you are seeking to influence.

Who you are, not just what you say or how you say it, counts for a lot. As the old adage suggests, "A person's life persuades better than their word."[1]

Aristotle suggested that we have to be seen as worth trusting and worth listening to in order to have influence.[2] "We believe good-hearted people to a greater extent and more quickly than we do others."[3]

The key distinction here is that it's not enough to be sincere, honest, and well-intentioned—ethos is about an individual or audience *perceiving* you as such.[4]

To see how important credibility and trustworthiness are in the process of persuasion, consider the controversy that arose when Al Gore's film *An Inconvenient Sequel* hit screens in 2017. This film promised to continue the work begun a decade earlier with the launch of *An Inconvenient Truth* but hit a major speed bump when it was revealed that Gore's family home in Nashville, Tennessee, consumed twenty times more energy per year than the average American household. For a high-profile advocate of energy reform, this inconsistency did untold damage to Gore's credibility and significantly limited the persuasiveness of his message.[5]

Al Gore learned the hard way that none of us "own" our ethos. We don't create it and we cannot control it. Ethos is always in the eyes of the beholder and is a function of others' judgment.

We all give credence to book covers

We're warned as children not to judge a book by its cover. However, decades of research indicates that this advice is practically impossible to follow.

Consider the fact that while less than 15 percent of the male population is over six feet tall, roughly 60 percent of CEOs exceed this height. Obviously, this is not a coincidence, but neither is it a function of conscious decision-making. After all, it's not as if corporate recruiters are given the memo to go and seek out a tall leader to fill a vacant CEO position. Instead, our Instinctive Minds tend to have a subliminal bias that tall males are good leaders. As a result, we unconsciously gravitate towards people who match this preconception of who will best fill the role.[6] Ethos can indeed be an expression of prejudice.

In an interesting experiment that examined the powerful role of unconscious credibility cues, a team of Australian researchers introduced different cohorts of students to a supposed visitor from Cambridge University in England. The twist was that the perceived status of the individual was to be different for each class group. To one class he was introduced as a student; to another, he was a lecturer; to another he was a senior lecturer; and to a final group he was introduced as a professor. After the visitor left the room, each class group was asked to estimate the height of the man from Cambridge they had just met. With each increased level of status, the man's perceived height grew by half an inch—so much so that the "professor" was perceived to be a full 2 inches taller than the "student."[7]

This is significant considering numerous studies over many decades have found that taller people are perceived as more competent, authoritative, intelligent, and having better leadership qualities.[8]

Of course, height is only one factor that influences a perception of credibility and ethos. Research indicates that things such as charisma, posture, vocal quality, eye contact, dress, body type, and grooming also play an important role. Again, we know we ought not judge a book by its cover, but we all do it and we seem not to be able to help ourselves.

Expectation is everything

One of the curious elements of ethos is the degree to which it is based almost entirely on the expectations of the audience or observer. This was something the ancient Romans invented a word to describe: *decorum*.

As crass as it may seem, a big part of being credible is simply fitting in or fostering a sense of familiarity with those you are looking to influence. Twentieth-century American literary theorist Kenneth Burke defined the art of fitting in as the simplest path to persuasion: "You persuade a man only insofar as you can talk his language by speech, gesture, tonality and image."[9]

One of the chief criticisms leveled at anti-gun campaigners over the years, for instance, has been that they tend to lack ethos with the very firearm enthusiasts they seek to persuade. The pleas of gun reform advocates are simply too easy to dismiss when they use vague and ill-defined terms like "assault rifles" and "high-capacity clips." Psychologist Joe Pierre suggests that simply using the correct language would go a long way to giving anti-gun arguments weight and credibility. "To engage in meaningful discussion, it'd pay to know the difference between semi-automatic and fully automatic weapons, the difference between magazines and clips and how hollow-point jackets differ from full-metal jackets."[10]

Naturally, there must be substance behind a perception or appearance of trustworthiness and credibility. It must be more than simply using the right terminology, looking the part, or fitting the bill. In the irrefutable words of Abraham Lincoln, "You can fool some of the people all of the time, and all of the people some of the time, but you cannot fool all of the people all of the time." Substance is the only sure path to genuine ethos.

While ethos is about people's perceptions, the second element in Aristotle's triad has to do with their emotions.

Pathos

Persuasive people know that emotions are what move others. In fact, the original Latin word for emotion, *emovere*, means exactly this—*to move*. As my colleague, advertising executive Adam Ferrier, suggests, "Emotions are one of the most powerful ways to cut through and connect with someone."[11] Neuroscientist and researcher Bridget Queenan agrees, saying, "It is emotion, not evidence, that changes minds."[12]

This insight lies at the heart of Aristotle's concept of pathos.

While we tend to be wary of being manipulated by people who play to our emotions, pathos is more than simply relying on vague sensations or feelings as a tool of influence. After all, emotional reactions are fleeting and rarely result in sustained change.

Instead, pathos is about understanding that emotions play a powerful role in the perceptions we draw about events, ideas, and the world around us. As Andrew O'Keeffe suggests in his book *Hardwired Humans*, people make sense of experiences and information based on how it makes them feel. "Our brains are wired to process emotions before reason."[13]

This perspective challenges the common tendency in Western culture to see emotion as the poorer cousin to logic. We tend to assume that using an emotional argument, or being swayed by one, somehow denotes lesser intelligence. But attitudes toward emotional arguments are changing as psychologists learn more about the vital role emotions play in our thinking. Rather than seeing emotions as opposed to rationality, psychologists frequently describe them as vital components of reason. Contrary to centuries of prejudice, an "emotional thought" isn't necessarily an irrational one.[14]

A few years ago, change management gurus John Kotter and Dan Cohen conducted a global study in partnership with Deloitte examining this very principle. In studying the success and/or failure of change initiatives in over 130 companies, Kotter and Cohen found that meaningful change only ever happens "by speaking to people's feelings." They discovered that this is the case "even in organizations that are focused on analysis and quantitative measurement." Their conclusion was that "In highly successful change efforts, people find ways to help others see the problems or solutions in ways that influence emotions, not just thought."[15]

Not all emotions are created equal

The question then is, which emotions tend to be most effective in the process of changing minds? What's clear is that not all emotions are created equal.

According to eminent American psychologist Robert Plutchik humans have eight primary emotions:[16]

1.	Joy	**5.**	Fear
2.	Sadness	**6.**	Anger
3.	Trust	**7.**	Surprise
4.	Disgust	**8.**	Anticipation

When I first came across Plutchik's research and read the above list of emotions, I was struck by how decidedly skewed toward negativity it is. Of this list of eight primary emotions, only one is positive (joy), three are neutral (surprise, anticipation, and trust) and the remaining four are decidedly less than rosy.

From the perspective of persuasion, it's hard to overlook the fact that negative emotions do pack a more immediate punch than positive ones. In fact, the University of Pennsylvania's Paul Rozin suggests that we are intuitively wired to respond to negativity. As Rozin points out, a single cockroach will completely ruin a bowl of cherries but one cherry on top of a pile of cockroaches does little to improve their appeal. Put simply, "negativity trumps positivity."[17] Advertisers and politicians know this all too well and play to our fears, dislikes, and aversions masterfully.

But this is not to say that negative or fear-based emotions are necessarily the most persuasive.

Research by psychologist Barbara Fredrickson shows that while negative emotions can be effective in spurring change, we need to consider the *type* of response we're aiming for. She argues that negative emotions have a "narrowing effect" on our thoughts. In the same way our body will tense up when we're afraid, so our brains tend to become hyper-focused when triggered by negative emotions like fear, anger, and disgust. In contrast, positive emotions like joy open our thinking and spark creativity and hope. The bottom line, then, according to Fredrickson's research, is that positive emotions are more likely to draw out the kind of thinking that helps people embrace situations that are vague, ambiguous, and evolving—which are, after all, the bulk of the problems we all face in a modern age.[18]

Wearing your heart on your sleeve

While tapping into the emotions of others can be a powerful path to persuasion, leading with our own emotions is equally important. In his book *Think Again,* Adam Grant points to numerous studies that indicate when people show their genuine emotional commitment to a viewpoint—rather than emphasizing their logical conviction—their opponents were more likely to see them as a real person rather than an ideological adversary. They were therefore more likely to engage in conversation more generously and openly.

As Grant observes, "even if we disagree strongly with someone on a social issue, when we discover that she cares deeply about the issue, we trust her more. We might still dislike her, but we see her passion for a principle as a sign of integrity. We reject the belief but grow to respect the person behind it."[19]

The important caveat here is that our emotions need to represent the full range of our nuanced perspective. Variety of experiences may be the spice of life, but variety of emotions is the secret to meaningful engagement with others.

Simplistic emotions derail a conversation as quickly as simplistic viewpoints—and for the same reason. In Grant's words, "What stands in the way of rethinking isn't the expression of emotion; it's a restricted range of emotion." The key then is to "infuse our charged conversations with greater emotional variety—and thereby greater potential for mutual understanding." Rather than simply being "angry" or "offended" when presented with a confronting view, acknowledge and share the fact that you are also "afraid," "intrigued," and "hopeful" for the future of your relationship with your opponent, for instance.[20]

But pathos isn't just about sharing emotion or engaging the emotions of others, it's also about "reading the room" and matching the mood of those you are looking to influence.

Matching the mood

Understanding the emotional state of the individual or group you are seeking to persuade is essential if you want your message or point of view to resonate. An idea presented in a way that's jarring will be rejected almost immediately—no matter how sensible it is, or how credible you are.

The importance of resonance is something that sound engineers understand well. Any audio technician knows that in order to produce a clean sound that gets cut-through in a room, you must account for the resonant frequencies of the space.

Whether you're aware of it or not, every room you've ever been in has a tone or a frequency range at which notes will ring out. This is something that can be calculated mathematically and is typically caused by the dimensions and shape of the space. Put simply, the resonant frequency is where sound waves bounce off hard surfaces in the room and collide with each other causing a hum or a booming sound.

The trick for audio engineers is to figure out what this frequency is for any given room they are EQ'ing and then adjust the sound mix accordingly. Failing to do this will muddy the sound and significantly affect clarity.

In much the same way, it's essential for us to discern the resonant emotional frequency of a situation, audience, or environment. Some words or tones will strike a nerve in all the wrong ways, jarring our audience and detracting from the clarity and impact of our message. We need to understand the culture, context, and circumstances of those we are looking to persuade lest we appear tone deaf in the message we are trying to get through.[21]

Once you have established your credibility (Ethos) and allowed for emotion (Pathos), only now is it possible to engage someone's faculties for rational logic (Logos).

Logos

At the core of Aristotle's concept of logos was a firm belief that humans are reasonable and that they will tend to make sensible choices based on proof, evidence, and reason.

Logic and reason may be the native language of our Inquiring Minds, but as we have already established, our views and opinions are far less persuaded by evidence than we'd like to assume. The simple truth is that our Inquiring Mind generally struggles to have the loudest voice at the cognitive table. It was Scottish philosopher David Hume who put it best when he observed that "Reason is the slave of the passions."[22]

You may wonder how this accounts for those who have a natural bent toward dispassionate rationality? We can all think of people who seem naturally level-headed and evidence-driven. Well, you may be surprised to learn that even in typically rational disciplines such as science, medicine, and economics, logic and facts are far less persuasive than we may otherwise think.

As Edward De Bono suggested in his book *I Am Right, You Are Wrong*, most scientists believe that the analysis of data will inform thinking and lead to breakthrough new ideas. "Unfortunately, this is not so," according to De Bono "The mind can only see what it is prepared to see. That is why after a breakthrough in science, we look back and find that all the needed evidence had been available for a long time."[23]

De Bono further suggests that even supposedly rational and logical people can't help but view new ideas through the lens of an existing belief system—the very idea at the core of Kuhn's paradigm shift theory we explored in chapter 2.[24]

The work of nineteenth-century Hungarian doctor Ignaz Semmelweis is a case in point. Semmelweis worked at a teaching hospital where doctors constantly swapped between handling cadavers and delivering babies without any awareness of the importance of washing their hands in between.

Semmelweis noticed that the death rate of mothers who gave birth in his part of the hospital was roughly 10 percent—a rate that was over double that of mothers whose babies were delivered by midwives in a different part of the hospital.

After examining all the variables, Semmelweis concluded that the difference in mortality rates was that midwives did not come in contact with cadavers. In response, he instituted the practice of requiring all doctors to wash their hands in a solution of chlorinated lime before entering the delivery rooms.

The death rate of new mothers immediately dropped to 4 percent—on par with those whose babies were delivered by midwives. Despite this clear evidence that Semmelweis was onto something, his logic was completely rejected by the medical community at large. Many doctors were offended by the idea that they were responsible for the death of their patients. Others poked holes in Semmelweis's theoretical explanation.

Semmelweis died a few years later, unfortunately not living long enough to see his theory vindicated. It was only once Louis Pasteur's concept of germ theory became widely accepted that the medical community reconsidered Semmelweis's ideas. While he hadn't gotten everything right in his assumptions, Semmelweis's explanation was sensible, logical, and ought to have prompted further inquiry. Instead, it was rejected outright merely because it did not line up with the accepted and conventional thinking—a dynamic that has become known as the Semmelweis reflex.[25]

While logic and rationality are less persuasive than we've long been taught, this ought not discount the role that logos can play in the process of persuasion. We do love evidence, data, and proof—it's just that we tend to use these to justify the conclusions our Instinctive Minds have already arrived at.[26] So, while logic and rational arguments can play a role in changing minds, these mustn't be the first tool in our influence toolbox that we reach for.

Given this reality, the remainder of this book will explore the factors that *do* work in influencing people's Instinctive Minds. We will explore a range of simple and proven techniques for persuading stubborn people. In many cases, these are age-old approaches to influence that we need to re-learn and apply in a modern context.

In extending the toolbox metaphor, consider each of the five remaining chapters as five different trays or sections of a toolbox that each contain tools designed for different purposes or different contexts.

While changing stubborn thinking has never been easy, it need not be complicated or onerous. But as I learned in the process of trying to mount our clothesline, all the tenacity in the world will be of little help unless you are using the right tool.

CHAPTER 3
RELATIVITY

A few years ago, a logic puzzle became an unlikely internet sensation. What was most intriguing about this puzzle was that although adults found it tremendously difficult to solve, most children could do so in less than twenty seconds.

See if you can solve it:

There are 6 parking spaces in a numbered parking lot and one space has a car in it obscuring the number (represented by X).

16, 06, 68, 88, X, 98

Which number is the car obscuring?

If you're anything like me, five minutes of attempting to solve the puzzle got me nowhere. The numbers themselves don't seem to follow any discernible pattern.

If you can't figure out the answer either, don't be too dismayed—most adults are the same. The reason is that anyone over the age of about twelve tends to overthink the puzzle and assume the solution will involve some sort of algebraic prowess.

On the other hand, children approach the puzzle with a very different perspective. For them, it is obvious that the answer is 87.

How? Well, all it takes is to turn the image upside down and the pattern becomes immediately apparent. As soon as you realize you are viewing the parking spaces from behind them rather than in front of them, the answer is obvious.[1]

Herein lies an important principle. Much of what we see and perceive in the world around us is a function of relativity. In the timeless words of French-born writer Anaïs Nin, "We don't see things as they are, we see them as we are."[2]

Even the substance of our sensory perceptions can be highly subjective. In the words of British doctor and author James Le Fanu, "while we have the overwhelming impression that the greenness of the trees and the blueness of the sky are streaming through our eyes as through an open window, yet the particles of light impacting on the retina are colorless."[3] Our very perception of color, like beauty, is in the eye of the beholder. If in doubt, just ask someone with color blindness.

Given the nature of relativity, one of the most effective strategies for unlocking people's thinking is to change their perspective or point of view. As the inspirational American author Wayne Dyer once said, "When we change the way we look at things, the things we look at change."

The Overview Effect

This dynamic has been studied for years in astronauts who report having a shift in their worldview—both literally and philosophically—when they see Earth from space for the first time. Psychologists have noted that after returning from a trip to space, astronauts tend to be less focused on individual achievements and instead are more concerned about the collective good. So prevalent is this phenomenon, it even has a clinical name: the Overview Effect.[4]

First coined in 1987 by space exploration author Frank White, the Overview Effect describes the overwhelming and even transcendental shift in perception created by seeing the finiteness of our world. It is typically characterized by a new sense of how precious and interconnected all of life on Earth is.

As Frank White suggests, "Our 'world view' as a conceptual framework depends quite literally on our view of the world from a physical place in the universe." When we shift the way we see the world around us, our assumptions get challenged.[5]

More than simply inspiring a sense of awe and wonder, this shift in vantage point can have a profound impact on the way individuals live life thereafter. Cosmonaut Boris Volynov reflected on this in 1999 when he said, "During a space flight, the psyche of each astronaut is reshaped; having seen the sun, the stars, and our planet, you become more full of life, softer. You begin to look at all living things with greater trepidation, and you begin to be more kind and patient with the people around you."

It's one thing to have our worldview changed by rocketing into space or rotating a parking lot image. However, it's another thing to change someone's perceptions in a way that fundamentally alters their thinking.

And that is the focus of this chapter. We will explore how to shift an individual or group's frame of reference in order to change their mind. In the words of Albert Einstein, "We can't solve problems with the level of mind that created them." Changing people will always start with trying to shift their level of mind.

Often described as "reframing," the simple power of shifting perceptions is illustrated well by Harvard professor Deepak Malhotra. "There's an old anecdote about two monks," says Malhotra. "The first says, 'I asked if I could smoke while I prayed and was told no.' 'That's strange,' said the second Monk, 'when I asked the Abbot if I could pray while I smoked, he said yes!'"

When you put it that way

I vividly remember the power of reframing and how it fundamentally shifted my approach to disciplining as a parent. Having grown up at the tail end of the era when parents believed that "sparing the rod" would "spoil the child," it was not unknown for my four brothers and I to "cop a hiding" on the odd occasion. When we did something particularly rebellious, we knew that the wooden spoon, a good old-fashioned smack, or even the cane could be coming our way (my dad was a schoolteacher after all).

This punishment was never overly harsh, abusive, or unwarranted. And truth be told, we often deserved worse than we got. So, I imagined that I'd adopt a similar approach when I became a parent. I was well aware that times and attitudes had changed and that any hint of physical punishment was now frowned upon (or in some countries deemed illegal). And yet, I riled against what I dismissed as a coddling approach to parenting and boasted to friends that I felt proud to be an "old school" type of parent. Loving, but firm.

When my friend and world-renowned parenting expert Dr. Justin Coulson mailed me a copy of his new book *10 Things Every Parent Needs to Know*, I was curious to see what his take on the topic would be.

In honesty, I assumed Justin would be an "old school" pragmatist like me when it came to discipline until I came across these words: "Too many parents believe that hurting and punishing children will make them better, wiser, more patient, considerate, and compassionate. It does not. Instead, it damages them... In short, kids learn to hate their parents when their parents hurt them. It seems clear that smacking does for your relationship with your child what hitting your partner might do for your marriage."

It was this last sentence that stopped me in my tracks. I had never equated disciplining a child to domestic violence and yet, here was someone I respected telling me that the two acts had a lot in common.[6]

As I placed down the book and reflected on what I had just read, I knew that my previous assumptions and attitudes needed to be re-examined. While my Instinctive Mind was tempted to dismiss Justin's words as yet another "fashionable" parenting approach, I knew him and his research well enough to know I couldn't do this in good conscience.

I felt convicted. I was convinced. Never after that moment did I use any form of physical punishment to discipline my son. Not because of a logical argument or even an emotional plea, but because I now saw violence toward my child to be the same thing as violence toward my wife—something that was unthinkable.

Change the category to change the conclusion

In a similar example of how the relativity of an issue can shift based on the way it is framed, one political commentator made a powerful point when reflecting on the appointment of conservative justice Amy Coney Barrett to the U.S. Supreme Court in October 2020.

"Imagine if, rather than being Catholic, Amy Coney Barrett was a devout Muslim woman who belonged to an extremist Muslim organization that demanded a lifelong covenant, professed a belief that women should be subservient to their husbands, taught at a madrassa, and once said that she viewed her participation in the legal profession as a way to bring about the Kingdom of Allah... The conversation surrounding her appointment to the United States Supreme Court would be very different."

While equating Barrett's conservative Catholic affiliation with Muslim extremism might be something of an overreach, it's hard to ignore the way a perspective like this shifts the tone of an issue.

Context is king

Reframing is all about context and delivery. It can be as simple as how a statement or question is posed, or as complicated as using unconscious cues that alter our perception of what is being communicated.[7] The power of reframing is that it forces us to confront the relativity of reality and consider whether our biases and assumptions offer a complete version of the truth.[8]

After attending a high school reunion a few years ago, it was great to reconnect with scores of friends I had lost touch with entirely. One such friend was a guy named James. While James and I had not been particularly close back in our school days, we had a great conversation at the reunion and subsequently connected on Facebook.

As I followed James's posts over time, it became pretty clear just how left-leaning he was politically. While I have struggled to identify with many of the views and ideas he shares online, I've come to really appreciate James's posts because they often frame ideas and issues in entirely new ways and cause me to pause and think.

Here are just three of the more impactful posts James has shared recently:

- A mocked-up headline from satirical newspaper *The Betoota Advocate* addressing the issue of rising interest rates saying: *"Local Landlord Furious He's Gonna Have To Chip In And Help Tenants Pay His Mortgage."*
- A 1950s-style poster advertisement that declared: *"Philanthropy exists to launder the reputations of the rich and serves to replace public institutions with private ones."*
- A quote that simply read: *"If free public libraries didn't already exist and someone tried to invent them, it'd be condemned as a communist plot."*

While you could easily argue with the premise and bias of these posts, it's hard to ignore the fact that they powerfully reframe some of the important issues and ideas of our day.

In a similar way, I was struck recently by a meme a colleague shared on Instagram that quoted Jay Z saying, "Don't tell me what they said about me, tell me why they were so comfortable to say it around you." What a powerful way to think about gossip and slander—not as an indication that the gossiper lacks integrity but that the reporter of it does.

Rethinking road rage

In a great nonpolitical example of reframing, consider attempts in recent years to defuse the common hostility felt and expressed toward motorbike riders who split or filter between lanes of traffic. While the behavior itself is entirely legal, many drivers feel anger and resentment at bike riders on the roads when they do it.

Rather than simply educating drivers about the law or appealing to their sense of common decency, motorcycling groups have had great success in changing public attitudes by communicating clear evidence that lane filtering actually eases congestion on the roads—therefore reducing commute times for car drivers. One Belgian study found that average trip duration for car drivers could be reduced by up to eight minutes per journey due to lane splitting by motorcyclists.

This reframing of the issue as one that benefits car drivers shifted sentiment almost overnight.[9]

To this point, how we present numbers and data can be a powerful framing tool.

Consider how much more attractive it sounds to purchase 94 percent fat-free milk as opposed to picking up a carton of milk that is described as 6 percent fat.[10] Or imagine how many people would eagerly purchase a lottery ticket if they were informed that they must successfully pick a random number between 1 and 300 million in order to win?

This technique is also routinely used in legal settings by attorneys looking to cast doubt about the validity of evidence. For instance, rather than informing a jury that the chances of DNA evidence leading to a false match is 0.1 percent, they will point out that false matches based on DNA occur in one of every 1,000 cases. This figure, while exactly the same as the percentage, is more concrete and is more likely to persuade a jury to raise the threshold of reasonable doubt. After all, a single wrongly convicted criminal takes on a personality, face, and an imagined identity. In contrast, prosecutors will work equally hard to make the same statistic sound as abstract as possible.[11]

As we saw in chapter 1, numerical reframing tends to be highly effective because our Instinctive Minds are notoriously bad at making judgments when it comes to scale and probability.

The emotive power of perspective

To see the evocative power of relativity and framing, consider Florence Nightingale's famous "Rose Diagram" by which she persuaded a Royal Commission to prioritize funding for nurse training following the Crimean War.

While Nightingale could have simply shared raw data on how many British soldiers had been killed both in combat and in hospital during the war, the rose diagram visually highlighted the grim fact that ten times more soldiers had died from sickness than from battle wounds. In effect, soldiers were more at risk in a hospital than on the front lines. Not only was the Commission moved to act, but this approach so shocked the British public that donations poured in to help establish the world's first dedicated nursing school.[12] This was the power of pathos at work.

Misinformation researchers, John Cook and Stephan Lewandowsky, suggest that Nightingale's approach is one worth considering in any persuasive effort. They argue that graphics are uniquely effective in framing an idea in a way that speaks to people's Instinctive Minds. "When people read a refutation that conflicts with their beliefs, they seize on ambiguities to construct an alternative interpretation. Graphics provide more clarity and less opportunity for misinterpretation."

In an example of this very dynamic, Cook and Lewandowsky point to research showing that a significantly higher percentage of climate change skeptics were willing to reconsider their beliefs when shown a graph of temperature trends compared to those who were given a written description of the trend. "If your content can be expressed visually," they recommend "always opt for a graphic."[13]

Speaking to this principle, the behavioral economist, Aner Tal, suggests, "the presence of even trivial graphs significantly enhances the persuasiveness of the presented claims."[14]

The news is what you make it

In one memorable example of the power of framing and relativity, I vividly remember seeing newspaper headlines side-by-side in a store the day after France's shock loss to Italy in the 2006 World Cup. One newspaper stated the headline "France Loses" while another declared that "Italy Won."

In pointing out France's loss, the first newspaper put the spotlight on the French's failure while the second emphasized the positive triumph of the Italian team.[15] Both headlines were accurate but the inference of each was very different.

The underlying principle here is that the way news headlines are framed really does matter. In one study examining this, psychologist and misinformation expert, Ullrich Ecker, asked two groups of participants to read a newspaper article that stated burglary rates had increased by a relatively modest 0.2 percent in the previous year. The article pointed to the fact that this rise bucked the trend of a decades-long decline but that the overall trajectory in burglary rates was a downward one.

For half the participants the headline for the article was "Number of Burglaries Going Up" while the second group's article was headlined "Downward Trend in Burglary Rate." Although each headline was technically correct, Ecker found that the way the article was perceived and remembered changed dramatically. Reflecting on the findings, he said "A misleading headline impaired memory for the article and can thus do damage. The practical implications of this research are clear: News consumers must be [made] aware that editors can strategically use headlines to effectively sway public opinion and influence individuals' behavior."[16]

There's no value in a vacuum

Relativity is about more than simply our perceptions of concepts and ideas—it also shapes our more tangible judgments. As Loran Nordgren of the Kellogg School of Management suggests, "We understand the world in relative terms. Decisions aren't made in a vacuum."[17]

To Nordgren's point, relativity of expectations gives ample opportunity for changing the way someone approaches a decision. For instance, while spending $100 on healthy groceries can feel too expensive, it's amazing how spending the same amount on a dinner date seems reasonable. Or being asked to invest $1,000 in a college class or training course can feel like a rip off while we'd willingly spend that amount on a new smartphone without flinching. Or consider that most people would think more than twice before spending $130 on a much-needed session with a therapist but will eagerly drop the same amount on a new pair of shoes because they were "on sale."

Even in non-financial terms, relativity is a powerful reframing tool. Consider how the same people that will assure you they don't have time to exercise for forty-five minutes will joke that forty-five minutes simply evaporates when scrolling through Instagram.

I remember being challenged by this principle recently when my wife and I were in the market for a new mattress. As we agonized over the various options on sale, we weighed spending an extra few hundred dollars to buy the top-quality mattress as opposed to a cheaper option. In a masterstroke, the salesperson in the store said that he understood we wanted to make the right decision but reminded us that we'll probably spend 30 percent of the next decade of our lives sleeping on this mattress. He then quipped that most people spend more on a few weeks holiday than they do on a mattress. By chance, we were in the process of planning our annual family holiday at the time and this perspective shifted everything. I realized that I hadn't hesitated to spend whatever it would cost for our family to have a special and memorable time away but that I was willing to nickel and dime a purchase that could have a material effect on my quality of life in the long term. The decision to buy the more expensive and better-quality mattress became an easy one.

While our mattress-buying experience shows how effective comparisons and relativity can be in persuading people to spend top dollar, the same principle works as effectively in the world of discounting too.

The reason decision-making gets so tricky when relativity gets involved is because our Instinctive Mind gets activated. We lose all reason and perspective. Suddenly the purchase has the "gut feel" of something we'd be crazy to pass up.

We rarely experience what we don't expect

On a busy January morning in 2007, commuters at Washington D.C.'s L'Enfant Plaza subway station scurried past a violin-playing busker on their way to work. Anyone who has been to L'Enfant Plaza would know it is one of the busiest subway stations in the D.C. Metro and buskers are a pretty standard sight.

But this was no ordinary street performer. Despite being dressed nonchalantly in jeans and donning a baseball cap, the busker was in fact one of the world's most admired and revered violinists, Joshua Bell. And the instrument Bell was playing happened to be a $3.5 million Stradivarius.

Ordinarily it would cost many hundreds of dollars to be able to hear Bell perform live in one of the world's great concert halls where he typically plays to sold-out crowds. On this January morning, however, Joshua Bell was taking part in a *Washington Post* field study. As he played Bach's extremely challenging and exquisitely beautiful *Sonatas and Partitas for Unaccompanied Violin*, researchers were curious to see if anyone would notice.

Over the course of forty-five minutes, of the 1,097 people who walked by, barely any of them stopped or seemed to even notice the world class performance they were experiencing. There were no standing ovations or requests for autographs. Only twenty-seven people (roughly 2.5 percent of the passers-by) put money into Bell's open Stradivarius violin case and only seven stopped to listen for more than a minute.[18] Researchers reported that one of those who stopped had recognized Bell from his concert performance the night before. She stood watching in gaping disbelief. But no one else realized they were in the presence of greatness.

Reflecting on the study in their book *Sway*, Ori and Rom Brafman suggest the primary reason for this is that Joshua Bell didn't have any of the appearances of greatness. "He wasn't dressed in formal attire; he stood on no stage. For all intents and purposes, Bell looked like your average, run-of-the-mill street performer. Even though he didn't sound like a mediocre violinist, he looked the part. Without realizing it, the commuters attributed the ordinariness of what they perceived—the baseball cap, the jeans, the subway venue—to the quality of the performance. As they passed by Bell, most subway riders didn't even glance in his direction. Instead of hearing an outstanding concert, they heard street music."[19]

Shortly after the experiment, behavioral economist Dan Ariely interviewed Joshua Bell to ask what his experience of the busking experiment had been. He responded that he was "not all that surprised," and admitted that expectation is an important part of the way we experience music. "It takes an appropriate setting to help people appreciate a live classical music performance—a listener needs to be sitting in a comfortable, faux velvet seat, and surrounded by the acoustics of a concert hall. And when people adorn themselves in silk, perfume, and cashmere, they seem to appreciate the costly performance much more."[20]

This theme of expectations played a key role in people's response to Bell's "performance." When researchers interviewed commuters who had obliviously walked right by, these individuals were shocked that they had not been more perceptive—especially classical music fans. In explaining why they had failed to notice the virtuoso in their midst, most commuters simply said they didn't expect to encounter a world class musical performance in a Metro station. Put simply, they didn't expect it and so they didn't experience it.[21]

Our perceptions of value may be unconscious, but they are extraordinarily powerful. Once we have an established notion of something, everything we see, hear, or learn afterwards is colored by that assumption.

In much the same way that our mindset, belief system, or paradigm influences what we perceive in the world around us, so expectations mold our perceptions. They can even shape our felt experiences too.

Consider a study by Stanford University's Baba Shiv who used brain activity monitors to show how expectations influence people's experience of pain. When one group of participants were told they had received a $2.50 per-dose pain killer, they reported an 85 percent decline in pain. In contrast, a second group who were informed that the pill only cost $0.10 only saw their pain reduce by 61 percent. Significantly, neither of the pills in question had any active ingredient regardless of their perceived price.[22]

While framing can be an effective way to shape people's perceptions, judgments and experiences, it is the power of using relativity to shift stubborn mindsets and opinions that we will explore in the coming pages.

TAKE THE TIME TO PRIME

When you look at this image, what do you see? A bunny or a duck?

It may surprise you to learn that today's date could have more of an influence on what you see in this picture than you might otherwise imagine.

For instance, when people are shown this image on or shortly before Easter Sunday, 82 percent immediately see a bunny. However, when the same image was shown to people on a Sunday in October, 90 percent immediately saw a duck or bird.[23]

The influence of dates and seasonal associations in this example is a case of something known as "priming." In a more practical example of how priming works, consider that when a Pringles advertisement tells us "Once you pop, you can't stop," it's little wonder that eating a whole can of salty carb goodness seems reasonable, normal, and even to be expected. We've been unconsciously conditioned to do so.

Our Instinctive Minds are naturally associative and so initial inputs or information tends to influence our perceptions of what follows.

A study by the San Francisco Exploratorium examined this principle by asking a sample group of people to guess the answer to two questions:

1. *Is the height of the tallest redwood more or less than 1,200 feet?*
2. *What is your best guess about the height of the tallest redwood?*

A second cohort were asked two slightly different questions:

1. *Is the height of the tallest redwood more or less than 180 feet?*
2. *What is your best guess about the height of the tallest redwood?*

For those who were given the first scenario, the average estimate of the tallest redwood's height was 844 feet. In contrast, those who were asked the second set of questions guessed it was 282 feet—a variance of over 560 feet.[24]

In a similar experiment, the Exploratorium team surveyed visitors to gauge their willingness to make an annual donation to save 50,000 seabirds from offshore oil spills. When an initial group was asked how much they might be willing to donate, the average was $64. When a second group was given the donation request with the accompanying question "Would you be willing to pay $5?", the average contribution figure came down to $20. Interestingly, when the initial number was dramatically raised from $5 to $400 for a third group, the visitors indicated they would be willing to give $143 on average.[25]

What is perhaps most significant about studies like these is that even when researchers told participants about the research they were doing, and that the numbers being used were designed to sway their answers, the power of relativity to influence people's Instinctive Minds remained.[26]

While the above examples are interesting from a theoretical standpoint, priming can also influence our perceptions and choices when the stakes are much higher.

Consider a study conducted in Germany with a group of courtroom judges. After being handed the description of a woman who had been arrested for shoplifting, each judge was asked to roll a loaded dice that always landed on either a 3 or a 9. After rolling the dice, each judge was asked whether they'd give the women a prison sentence greater or lesser than the number on the dice they had just rolled. Then the judges were asked to forget the dice roll and share what prison term they would give the defendant based solely on the description of her crime.

It's important to point out that the judges were highly experienced with each boasting an average of fifteen years or more on the bench. And yet, their Instinctive Minds were no less prone to the effects of priming than the rest of us. In fact, judges who had rolled a 9 gave an average sentence of 8 months while those who had rolled a 3 indicated they'd sentence the woman to 5 months in prison.[27]

Looking at more trivial applications of this principle, various studies have demonstrated just how powerful priming can be in guiding perceptions and behavior. Consider that:

- Shoppers are more likely to purchase a bottle of French wine if French music is playing in the background,
- People are more willing to offer help and assistance if they have just viewed a photo in which people are standing close together, and
- Showing someone a picture of Auguste Rodin's *The Thinker* will prompt them to think more carefully about a decision they are going to make.[28]

Interestingly, our perceptions can also be primed by ideas and information that may seem irrelevant to the topic at hand.

Consider the fact that:

- People are willing to pay more for a meal at a restaurant named Studio 97 than one called Studio 17,
- You're more likely to pay more for a box of Belgian chocolates if you have just written down a high number (rather than a low one) on a piece of paper, and
- Spectators unconsciously expect an athlete with a high number on their jersey to perform better than one with a low number.[29]

While priming can sometimes be gimmicky and peculiar as in these examples, the principle remains true that the perceptions of our Instinctive Minds are largely relative and context-driven. This can have a significant influence on not just our thinking and behavior but also our emotional state.

Priming emotion

Consider one experiment where college students were asked two questions:

a. How happy are you?

b. How often are you dating?

When asked these questions, the correlation between the answers was quite low (0.11 to be precise). In other words, many people answered the first question saying they were generally happy but then admitted that they didn't have an especially active dating life.

However, this is where things got interesting. When the order of the questions was reversed and people were asked how often they were dating before being asked how happy they were, the first answer had a significant influence on their second one. In fact, the correlation was 0.62. In other words, if the respondent's first answer was a positive one because they were dating frequently, they were far more likely to report that they were happy.

The fact that the results varied so dramatically, depending on the order of the questions, shows that the relationship between dating and happiness was not causal or even correlated. Rather, one answer had become a primer for the other.[30]

Similar studies have found that reminding people of a happy experience in their lives or a time they felt powerful and in control will tend to make them more open to whatever idea you are presenting.[31]

What this means for you and me when it comes to influencing others is that sequence matters. The order in which we present ideas or information can make all the difference.

When is it worst to go first?

Back in 1962, a psychologist named Bennett Murdock became curious about the role that sequence plays when it comes to our perceptions. The implications of what Murdock discovered are many and varied.[32]

For instance, consider what happened when research participants were asked to guess the answer to the mathematical problem below:

$8 \times 7 \times 6 \times 5 \times 4 \times 3 \times 2 \times 1 = ?$

On average, people's estimate is that the answer was 2,250.

It was very different story when the mathematical sequence is reversed like so:

$$1 \times 2 \times 3 \times 4 \times 5 \times 6 \times 7 \times 8 = ?$$

When presented in this sequence, the average guess was 512.

Of course, the answer to both equations is identical—40,320 in case you were wondering. However, the first number in the sequence has a powerful effect as a point of relativity.[33]

This principle has enormous implications whether you are being interviewed for a new job, pitching for a lucrative contract, or auditioning in a talent contest. The inconvenient reality is that whether you go first or last actually can make a big difference.

In examining how big this difference can be, research by Columbia University's Adam Galinsky found that those who appear earliest in competitive line-ups tend to be judged more harshly. This is because adjudicators or evaluators tend to under-rate early contenders in case the field improves as things go along. Galinsky also suggests that there is also a tendency for judges to evaluate early contenders against their "imagined ideal contestant," which is never a fair comparison.

To Galinsky's point, an analysis of Eurovision Song Contests clearly shows that those who feature latest in the competition are typically awarded higher marks than those who perform early on—a factor that has been similarly evident in talent shows including *The Voice* and *American Idol*. This also means you ought not peak too early in your own performance but leave the judges with the final impression that is impressive and memorable.[34]

This principle also matters when it comes to getting others to evaluate our ideas or perspective favorably.

Concessions shape perceptions

Robert Cialdini suggests that one way to leverage the power of sequence when persuading others is to use a priming tactic he calls "rejection then retreat."

This approach is characterized by asking another individual for a large favor, donation, or investment, for instance, fully expecting that they will say no. The idea however is to follow this rejection up with a more moderate and reasonable request—one which the other party is more likely to agree to. This second request tends to be closer to what the person making the petition was hoping for in the first place.

Cialdini first explored this approach in a 2006 study where he stopped random strangers on the street and asked them if they'd consider acting as a chaperone for a group of troubled youth on a one-day trip to the zoo. Just 17 percent of people agreed to the request.

However, Cialdini then tried a different approach. He and his research team began asking strangers whether they would be willing to donate two hours of their time each week to mentor disadvantaged youth. Predictably, no one jumped at the idea. However, when this request was immediately followed up with the invitation to help out with a day-trip to the zoo, a full 50 percent of people said they'd be happy to volunteer—a three-fold increase on the initial approach. Significantly, when the day for the trip to the zoo arrived, 85 percent of the people who agreed to volunteer actually showed up. In comparison, only half of the 17 percent who said yes to the initial request followed through on their commitment. As Cialdini concluded, the concession approach not only increased people's willingness to say yes but also their commitment to action.[35]

The power of concession was also evidenced in research by social psychologist Steven Sherman, who was seeking to increase donations for the American Cancer Society. Rather than simply going door-to-door in a traditional fundraising campaign, Sherman and his team phoned people in Bloomington, Indiana, a few days before a canvasser was scheduled to visit the householder. During the phone call, Sherman and his research team simply asked people to predict how they'd respond if they were asked to spend three hours collecting money for the charity. Naturally, the cause was so well known and well esteemed that the vast bulk of people said they would likely say yes if asked to volunteer.

When the canvasser did knock on the person's door a few days later collecting money, the donation rates jumped by 700 percent. After all, donating money felt like a significantly smaller ask to help out a cause the person had already convinced themselves was important.[36]

The priming power of recall

Our recollections can also have a powerful influence on our perceptions. In a study that examined this, a German psychologist named Norbert Schwarz set out to understand the power of memory and recall in shaping perceptions. Schwarz found that by simply asking a person to list the occurrences of them acting in a certain way, they adopted a frame of mind that matched their recollection. For instance, if you want someone to be open minded, or bold, or cooperative or decisive, simply ask them to list five or six times in their lives that they have been those things.[37]

According to Schwarz, the number of occasions that people list makes a difference. If it is too few, the other person will feel unconvinced. However, if you ask an individual to list too many experiences or instances of behavior, the fact that they may struggle to form a long list could mean that they'll draw the opposite conclusion to the one intended. For instance, asking them to list ten examples when they have been open-minded may mean they struggle with the last two and in doing so will draw the conclusion that they aren't so open-minded after all.[38]

Rather than simply an exercise in prompting memories, the power of recall is that it primes the expectations we have of ourselves.

People live up to expectations

Social psychologists Alice Tybout and Richard Yalch have long studied the degree to which human behavior and perception is shaped by our self-expectations. In one particular study, they interviewed a large cross-section of individuals in the lead-up to a U.S. election. They informed roughly half of the cohort that their responses identified them as being "above-average citizens that were likely to vote and participate in political events." The other half were informed they were ranked as "average" on political engagement scores. Come election day, those in the first group ended up being 15 percent more likely to vote.[39]

The opposite tactic is equally effective too. Rather than using expectations to prompt someone to be open to an idea or suggestion, it's helpful to overtly address expectations that might cause points of resistance.

In her book *Influence is Your Superpower,* Yale researcher Zoe Chance recommends doing just this. "If you think you know what the other person will object to or you sense resistance around a particular issue, put it into words before they do," says Chance. She goes on to offer some examples such as "You might be thinking we won't have enough time," or "This may sound like a lot of money," or "I may seem a little young to be in this role."

In summing up the power of this technique, Chance suggests that "By reading the other person's mind and articulating the objection, you free their attention from the voice in their head so they can listen to you. You've also shown yourself to be a smart and reasonable person since you see their point of view."[40]

No better than you expect

Not only does priming someone's expectations influence their behavior and choices, it has also been shown to dictate their judgments.

In one revealing study, researchers looked to examine whether an individual's expectation of how a glass of wine would taste influenced their experience of actually tasting it. To do this, they had a group of people sample a range of different wines while their brain activity was monitored. The wine tasters were informed that the drinks they'd be sampling would range from wines that cost $5 per bottle through to $90 per bottle.

Significantly but perhaps unsurprisingly, the measured degree of enjoyment each person felt while drinking the wine increased with the stated price tag of each bottle. The trick of course is that each of the wines they sampled was exactly the same.[41]

Along similar lines, a revealing study conducted by a team from Cornell University involved a large group of diners at a French restaurant in Urbana, Illinois. Each of the restaurant's patrons was given a free glass of Cabernet Sauvignon to accompany their meal. Half the diners were told that the complimentary glass of wine was from Noah's Winery in California, while the other half were informed that the wine was from Noah's Winery in North Dakota (a region not known for its wine growing prowess).

Although both groups were unknowingly consuming an inexpensive bottle of Charles Shaw wine, the priming influence of expectations was significant. Those who believed they were drinking a bottle of Californian Cabernet Sauvignon rated both the wine and food as tasting significantly better and consumed

11 percent more of their meal than their counterparts. They also became more loyal diners at the restaurant than those who had consumed the North Dakotan wine who rated not only the wine but also the food as being of lower quality.

Reflecting on the findings of the research, Cornell professor Brian Wansink suggested that people's expectations about the wine influenced their perception of the entire dining experience—either positively or negatively.[42]

While priming is an effective tool in shaping perceptions, judgments, and expectations, it can also be a powerful way to "inoculate" people's thinking.

Inoculation theory

The principle that underpins Inoculation Theory dates back to the 1940s when psychologist Carl Hovland discovered that the best way to guard against enemy propaganda was to deliberately expose soldiers to the enemy's claims. Hovland found that giving soldiers the opportunity to consider and then dismiss the other side's perspective made them far less likely to be swayed if they encountered it on the front lines.[43]

These insights were built on and refined in the early 1960s by social psychologist William McGuire who discovered that the information processing functions of our minds work in a similar way to the immune system of our bodies. The basic premise of medical inoculation is that our bodies develop immunity to a virus or disease if exposed to a weak version of it. Once our immune system defeats the virus, we are no longer susceptible to it. McGuire found that the same dynamic works with ideas and beliefs. His key discovery was that we can be inoculated against misinformation if we are exposed to a small or diluted version of it.[44] Something about this exposure has a priming effect on our Instinctive Minds.

Australian scholar John Cook puts it this way: "Much like vaccines train your immune response against a virus, knowing more about misinformation can help you dismiss it when you see it."[45] But it's not just about exposure. The key is that an individual must be capable of, or be given, the tools to refute the ideas or beliefs in order to become immune to them.[46]

Recent years have seen McGuire's work revisited as society has sought to counteract the dangers of radicalization, fake news, and the rise of conspiracy belief.[47]

Priming through pre-bunking

In the case of inoculating against misinformation, the work of Dartmouth College's Josh Compton has been significant. According to Compton, in order for inoculation against misinformation or conspiracy belief to be effective, the person being "inoculated" must be forewarned that what they are about to hear is untrue; and they must also be pre-armed with counterarguments (something Compton refers to as "prebunking").[48]

One study led by Cambridge University psychology researcher Sander van der Linden achieved extraordinary results in using this approach to address climate change-related misinformation. As part of his inoculation experiment, van der Linden deliberately exposed participants to ideas from the Global Warming Petition Project, which boasts 31,000 signatories who hold a bachelor of science or higher. In this document, which was the most shared climate article of 2016, signatories attest to the fact that there is no scientific consensus that humans are causing climate change. The immediate impact of the exposure to this information was that participants' confidence in the scientific evidence regarding climate change took a hit.

However, van der Linden pointed out that many of the signatories were indeed fake—even that one of the Spice Girls was falsely listed as a signatory. He also pointed out that while 31,000 signatories may sound like an impressive number, it represents less than 0.3 percent of all U.S. science graduates since 1970 and, more significantly, that less than 1 percent of the signatories had any expertise in climate science at all.

When participants were surveyed after digesting this additional information, their convictions regarding the reality of human-influenced climate change were reinforced. More importantly, follow-up research found that the participants had been effectively "immunized" against further misinformation.

Reflecting on the results of this research, van der Linden writes: "Practically, these findings suggest that, when possible, communicating the scientific consensus on human-caused climate change should be accompanied by information that forewarns the public that politically or economically motivated actors may seek to undermine the findings of climate science. In addition, audiences should be provided with a basic explanation about the nature of disinformation campaigns to preemptively refute such attempts."[49]

Prevention is better than a cure

It's significant that many of those in van der Linden's study were already open to the idea that climate change was both real and influenced by humans. But what about when someone is fully convinced that the opposite is true? What about when someone has fully bought into misinformation or "gone down the rabbit hole" of conspiracy belief?

In a sober assessment, van der Linden writes that once someone has become consumed by conspiracy belief or misinformation, "there's very little research that actually shows you can come back from that. When it comes to conspiracy theories, prevention is better than cure."[50]

This is not to say that all hope is lost. In order to side-step another person's immunity to an argument or idea, you will need to present a "mutated" form of the argument that they haven't considered or previously been exposed to. The key will be for them to recognize that your view is sufficiently unfamiliar and different from what they have already intellectually considered a closed case.[51]

As in the medical world, mental inoculations are never a set-and-forget thing. As ideas and arguments evolve with time, people need "booster shots" in order to remain immune. If you are looking to reinforce someone's protection against unhelpful or destructive ideas, it's necessary to introduce new variants of misinformation that they might need to mentally combat.

You may be glad to learn that the priming effects of intellectual inoculation are not only effective as a counterbalance to conspiracy belief, fake news, and misinformation. Recent research has also shown it is effective in reducing rates of smoking and binge drinking plus encouraging healthy exercise habits.[52]

Better yet, mental inoculation can prove highly effective in resolving more traditional disagreements as psychologist Peter Colman has discovered at his "Difficult Conversations Lab."

Inoculated by nuance

The Difficult Conversations Lab is a facility housed on the second floor of a nondescript building on the grounds of Columbia University. It is solely dedicated to the purpose of debate.

Participants at the Difficult Conversations Lab are matched up with an opponent with strongly different views on a polarizing topic of the day—be it abortion laws, the death penalty, or immigration, for instance. Each debater has a total of twenty minutes to present their case and discuss the issue. At the conclusion of the exchange, if both sides can arrive at an agreement of aligned views, each signs a joint statement to that effect and this statement is then posted to a public forum.[53]

But the Difficult Conversation Lab is more than a talk fest or forum for rhetorical showmanship. The purpose it serves is to examine how and why some arguments are persuasive while others are not.

Over the years, Peter Colman has examined this question carefully and experimented with different approaches that increase the likelihood of persuasion occurring. One of the most effective is to prime participants by exposing them to complexity and nuance.

For instance, if two individuals are about to engage in a conversation about abortion, Colman will first have them read a news article about another polarizing issue like gun control. This article goes into detail explaining both sides of the gun control debate while offering the pros and cons of opposing perspectives. Interestingly, when the debaters then begin to engage around the issue of abortion, they arrive at a point of agreement in 46 percent of conversations.

Even more impressive was what occurred when debaters read an article that not only explained the two opposing sides of a controversial issue, but went to great lengths to show that the issue was far from black-and-white. These articles outlined numerous viewpoints or shades of gray. Amazingly, after being exposed to these types of articles, 100 percent of Difficult Conversation Lab participants arrived at a point of agreement at the end of their conversation.

Wharton School psychologist Adam Grant argues that the reason this second approach is so successful is that it challenges the convenient notion of simple and opposing ideas. "Hearing an opposing opinion doesn't necessarily motivate you to rethink your own stance; it makes it easier for you to stick to your guns. Presenting two extremes isn't the solution; it's part of the polarization problem."[54]

Grant goes on to suggest that the key in overcoming stubborn thinking is to inoculate people by "complexifying" issues and ideas. "We might believe we're making progress by discussing hot-button issues as two sides of a coin, but people are actually more inclined to think again if we present these topics through the many lenses of a prism."[55]

■ ■ ■

While we are familiar with the notion that everything in life is relative, few of us recognize the degree to which this principle shapes the judgments of our Instinctive Minds.

Human perceptions are never made in a vacuum and every judgment we make is a function of relativity. Given that this is the case, priming can be an incredibly powerful way to influence the judgments and perceptions our Instinctive Minds arrive at.

Whether through the use of expectation, inoculation, or sequence, there's great power in creating points of reference that change our perceptions of reality.

PERSUASION TOOL #1 PRO TIPS

1. Remember that numbers and words can be a powerful prompt. If you are looking to have people think or act in a certain way, present them with information that will make this decision or perspective seem natural.

2. Our emotions and memories have a big influence on our current state when we are made aware of them. It's helpful to remind people of feelings and experiences that are congruent with the frame of mind you are hoping they'll adopt.

3. If you are pitching an idea or proposal, try to go last in the group. And make sure you don't peak too early—save some of your best ideas for the end of your presentation.

4. By starting with a big and unreasonable request, a subsequent and more reasonable request will be more readily considered.

5. We rarely experience what we don't expect. By setting high and aspirational expectations for individuals or ideas, you're more likely to get the response you are aiming for.

6. If you are wanting to prevent someone's thinking from being distracted or derailed by misinformation, try "inoculating" them with a diluted version of the ideas you want to protect them from. Or at least ensure they are well aware of how nuanced and complex the issues at hand are.

USE CONTRAST TO BRING CLARITY

Just as with the duck or bunny example at the beginning of this chapter, optical illusions are a powerful illustration of how our perceptions can be influenced.

In looking at the graphic below, which circle appears bigger—A or B?

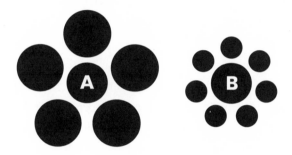

While you may have logically concluded that the two circles are actually the same size, this conclusion is far from instinctive. Even when we know there is no difference in the size of the two circles, our eyes still want to convince us otherwise.[56]

The reason for this comes down to the power of contrast. In the same way priming can shape our expectations and judgments, so contrast can influence our perceptions.

Resorting to extremes

When it comes to using contrast, bigger tends to work best. There is no place for subtlety when using contrast to inform perceptions. Instead, exaggeration and extremes are the name of the game.

The best way to do this is through a technique known as Paradoxical Thinking. Rather than traditional persuasion approaches that expose people to information and evidence that directly challenges or contradicts their worldview, Paradoxical Thinking presents someone with a concentrated form of what they already believe to be true.

This may seem counterintuitive. After all, we might assume that giving someone a more extreme version of a belief we're trying to shift them away from would cause them to become more mindstuck. However, the opposite is actually the case. The great Chinese strategist Sun Tzu picked up on this theme in his legendary book *The Art Of War* when he advised to "Use the enemy to defeat the enemy."[57]

Researchers suggest that by exposing people to extreme—but not absurd—versions of their view, their reasoning faculties engage while their defense mechanisms do not. This results in people being "open to reconsidering their views, and eventually (arriving at) the conclusion that their previously held narrative is illogical."[58]

Even if the Paradoxical Thinking approach doesn't convince someone that their previously held view may be an inaccurate or incomplete view of reality, it is likely to result in them being more open to considering a different perspective. This point of reflection gives people the opportunity to safely change their mind or at least consider views that they may otherwise have instinctively rejected.

Stopping smokers in Thailand

The persuasive power of contrast was demonstrated by a brilliant public health initiative rolled out a few years ago in Thailand.

One of the unspoken social norms for smokers worldwide is to readily comply with the question "Can I get a light?" In this particular experiment by the Thai health authorities, volunteers were sent out into the street to ask smokers for a light, but they were met with highly unusual responses. One smoker shot back "No way, I'm not giving it to you," while another lectured that "cigarettes contain poison." Some smokers replied with even more graphic and confronting responses such as "They drill a hole in your throat for cancer. Aren't you afraid of surgery?"

Almost without exception, the volunteers didn't "get a light" but were instead offered lectures on the evils and dangers of smoking. The eye-watering irony, of course, was that many of these smokers paused their rants only to take a puff on a cigarette.

The reason for this surprising turn of events was that the volunteers wandering the streets politely petitioning smokers were none other than children. As Jonah Berger writes it in his book *The Catalyst,* the typical volunteers in the program were "a small boy wearing a monkey T-shirt, or a girl in pigtails. Each no more than four feet tall and barely over ten years old."

After being rejected and scolded for their request, the children reached into their pockets and took out a small, folded note that read "You worry about me, but why not about yourself?" At the bottom of the note was the phone number for a hotline for helping smokers quit their addiction.

This particular hotline had been established years earlier and many millions of dollars had been spent promoting it to smokers but to no avail. That is, until the children in the street started giving out their folded notes. Calls to the hotline jumped 60 percent and filmed videos of the children's interactions with smokers went viral online attracting more than 5 million views in the first week. And this was more than a flash in the pan. Even many months after the beginning of the campaign, calls to the hotline remained 30 percent higher than they had previously been.

The "Smoking Kid" campaign, as it became known, was tremendously successful because it utilized the powerful dynamic of contrast. The initiative's creators realized that the most persuasive person for any smoker is the smoker themselves. Hearing arguments for quitting smoking coming out of their own mouths was always going to be more effective than even the most powerful information campaign.

Mind the gap

One of the reasons Paradoxical Thinking works so well is that when we are exposed to extreme versions of a view we hold, we often are confronted with the reality that what we've held to be true is actually at odds with what we believe to be important, reasonable, and fair. We're often not even aware of this inconsistency until contrast brings it to the foreground.

Consider how this approach persuaded surgeons and doctors to start washing their hands properly. As we saw with the story of Ignaz Semmelweis, the value of hand washing in a medical context has been well-understood for centuries. However, one of the persistent challenges has been to turn this awareness into action even in modern times.

Many doctors, nurses, and surgeons had persisted in not adhering to proper hand hygiene procedures despite knowing they should. This had been especially pronounced among surgeons who tended to wash their hands less than half as often as guidelines prescribed.

A few years ago, researchers Adam Grant and David Hofmann set out to address this. They examined each of the various interventions that had unsuccessfully changed the hand hygiene habits of surgeons over the years. What they discovered was that each of these initiatives had focused on educating, threatening, or pleading with surgeons to do the right thing.

Grant and Hofmann decided to try a new approach. In their experiment, they placed two different signs above various examination room soap and gel dispensers. The first of these said, "Hand hygiene protects you from catching diseases," while the second one read "Hand hygiene protects patients from catching diseases." Although the difference between the two signs was only a single word, the impact was remarkable. The first sign saw barely any difference in the rate of hand washing while the second sign resulted in a 45 percent increase.

Why was this the case? The researchers concluded that the suggested change tapped into the doctors' deeply held values while exposing how their past behavior was out of sync with their ideology. The reality is that most surgeons enter the medical profession with a passion for helping patients. Being confronted with the reality that failing to wash their hands stood in stark contrast with their commitment to patient safety demanded a response. In this instance, the response was to start doing the right thing.[59]

The bottom line is that in order to influence someone to change, it's helpful to identify where and how their beliefs are at odds with their actions and then show how what you are wanting them to consider will help close the gap.[60]

Susan Weinschenk suggests that this approach is incredibly powerful in a variety of contexts. "If you understand what stories people tell themselves about who they are, then you can communicate in a way that matches those stories and thereby get people to do stuff."[61]

In addition to highlighting the gap between behaviors and beliefs, another powerful contrast technique is to identify where someone's conduct is at odds with the commitments they have made—to themselves and others.

The compelling power of congruence

If an individual's publicly expressed commitments don't line up with their private behavior, the discomfort this creates can offer fertile soil for change. The reason for this is that decades of research reveals that people will almost always adjust their behavior rather than abandon their publicly stated commitments when the two are misaligned.

This impact of public commitments on behavior is precisely why accountability in weight loss programs is so important. By telling friends your weight loss goals and the commitments you've made to get there, you are far more likely to follow through. However, this is about more than mere accountability. Even making a commitment in front of complete strangers who have no ability or interest in holding you to account has a similar effect.

Consider how the power of public commitment has played out in a series of real-world cases:

- Car insurers have been successful in reducing the likelihood of people lying on odometer readings by placing an "honesty pledge" at the beginning of the reporting form instead of at the end.[62]
- Brands can achieve greater loyalty from existing customers by asking them to refer the brand to their friends. The very act of referral is a statement of public belief—even if it is only to a handful of people.[63]
- By calling a potential car purchaser and asking if they intend to buy a vehicle in the next six months, purchase rates increased by 35 percent.[64]

The implications of this principle are clear. If you can get someone to make some degree of public commitment or statement of belief, they are far more likely to follow through with actions that align with what they have committed to.[65]

In a great example of this, I recently had to phone our health insurer to make a change to our policy. After making various selections indicating the reason for my call, there was one final step. The voice recording said, "Before we connect you to an assistant, would you be willing to help us by sparing a minute after the call to answer a few questions about how we can serve you better? If yes, press 1, if no, press 2."

This request was by no means new or unique but the fact that I was forced to make a selection *before* I would be connected was something I had never come across before. On this particular day, I was in a rush so I declined the request to complete the survey. But I remember thinking that if I had pressed 1, there's no doubt I would have followed through with the commitment. And I'm sure others who call this customer service line are much the same. Better yet, by pre-committing, the people giving feedback would not just be those with a grievance to air as is so often the case with customer satisfaction surveys. This would mean the data would be far more moderate, representative, and helpful.

The persuasiveness of a pledge

Social scientist Anthony Greenwald discovered the power of making pledges in a study designed to increase voter turnouts at U.S. elections. On the eve of the election, Greenwald and his team surveyed a group of potential voters and asked them to predict whether they would vote on Election Day. However, after people rated their likelihood of voting, Greenwald also asked respondents to specify a reason for why they would be casting a ballot.

When polling opened the next day, it turned out 86.7 percent of those who'd explained why they would vote did indeed do so—compared with the control group of 61.5 percent who didn't make a prediction. In examining why there was such a significant variation, Greenwald concluded that the very act of offering an explanation for why they would vote became a form of commitment. This in turn compelled people to act in a way that was consistent with what they had said was important to them.[66]

This pledge-making principle works in a variety of settings. Consider the difference it made when a blood donation service changed the final sentence in their appointment confirmation phone calls from a statement to a question. Instead of wrapping up a booking call saying "We'll mark you on the list as coming then. Thank you!", the admin team began saying "We'll mark you on the list coming then, okay? (Pause for confirmation) Thank you."

This simple tweak increased the likelihood of people showing up for their appointments from 70 percent to 82.4 percent.[67]

It was a similar story for a restaurant chain that wanted to address the common problem of no-show guests who fail to call and cancel their booking. Previously the restaurant's reception had signed off from reservation phone calls saying, "Please call if you have to cancel." However, they then rephrased this as the question "Would you mind please calling if you have to cancel?" and then waiting for the predictable "Yes" response. After implementing this simple commitment-inducing change, the no-show rate dropped from 30 percent to 10 percent.[68]

Raising the cost of inconsistency

In a particularly powerful example of leveraging public commitments to drive behavior change, consider the successful tactic used to address the issue of over-prescribing antibiotics in doctors' clinics.

Given that recent years had seen American adults being given an estimated 41 million unnecessary courses of antibiotics annually at a cost of over $1 billion, the need for change was significant.

To combat this, a team of doctors and behavioral scientists decided to trial an initiative that would encourage doctors to think twice before writing an antibiotics prescription. Recognizing the power of public commitments, the idea was to ask doctors to sign a pledge to not prescribe unnecessary antibiotic treatments and then to have doctors display this pledge publicly in the clinic waiting room.

The psychology behind this approach was that once a doctor had made this public pledge, they had "created a mental cost for writing an unnecessary prescription," and that breaking their word meant "the 'price' of prescribing an unnecessary antibiotic has gone up."

Researchers initially trialed the technique at a selection of busy clinics in Los Angeles where some doctors were asked to sign the pledge while others were not in order to act as a control for the experiment. And the results were remarkable. When 1,000 patients presented and complained of the same symptoms, those doctors who had signed the pledge were 30 percent less likely to prescribe unnecessary antibiotics as a treatment.[69]

This example also points to the fact that while verbal or demonstrated public commitments are effective in influencing us, there is something uniquely powerful about commitments that are written down. The significance of having people writing down a commitment is that it makes the process one that is active rather than passive.

In considering why pledges are so persuasive, the role of contrast is hard to ignore. When people realize that there is a gap between their current actions and the things they've previously committed to, something invariably needs to give. If our idea, suggestion, or request helps close the gap, it will be more readily considered.

Clarifying what really counts

I found this principle helpful a few years ago when speaking at the Rotary International global convention in Hamburg, Germany. Like many volunteer organizations, Rotary is full of passionate members with clear opinions of how things should be done. The challenge is that many of these ideas are strongly informed by the way things have been done in the past and what suits the needs of current members. This is not a problem of course until some of those very traditions become barriers that put off new members. When this happens, Rotary clubs become a hostage to their own heritage and the future of the organization is threatened.

As I implored Rotarians to be open to stepping out of their comfort zones and embrace new ways of doing things, I could sense the push-back. In an effort to acknowledge and address this resistance, I gently reminded audience members of the core ethos of the organization to which they belong: *Service Above Self*.

While this was far from a silver bullet, it certainly worked. Resistance quickly dissipated as the meaning of what I had said sank in. After all, this is a motto that goes to the heart of a Rotarian's values system and paradigm. When even the toughest stalwarts recognized that demanding the organization cater to their needs and preferences at the cost of achieving the greater vision, there was a fresh openness to consider the value of change—no matter how uncomfortable it may be.

Naturally, when trying to use commitments to compel change, it's important to remember that we must allow the other person to save face. As we will see in chapter 5, others need to feel that changing their behavior is not an indication that they were wrong in the past but that rather they now know something they didn't know before.

It's about acknowledging that they likely made the "best decision" available to them at the time based on what they knew. This allows the other person to not feel that change is hypocritical, while also freeing them to embrace the new behavior, perspective, or idea.[70]

Contrast brings clarity because it gets our attention. It shocks us into thinking and rethinking. While exposing people to extreme versions of their own ideas or pointing out areas of inconsistency can be a great way to do this, another strategy can be to simply draw another individual out and have them follow their views to their logical conclusion.

It's a little bit like...

The truth is that some of our strongest views are quite ludicrous but we can doggedly hold on to them so long as they remain unspoken hunches and deeply held convictions. But drawing people out and encouraging them to share why they believe what they do, tends to see things quickly shift.

Adam Grant describes how he used this approach when engaging with a friend who was a vaccine skeptic. In making his argument, Grant's friend was trying to use a chart implying a weak correlation between vaccination rates and mortality to debunk the results of multiple randomized controlled trials. He said the results of these trials could be exaggerated by scientists who had the incentive—financial or otherwise—to promote vaccines and minimize the potential adverse reactions.

Grant acknowledged that this was a perspective he probably hadn't sufficiently considered when forming his pro-vaccination views. But it was his friend's own line of reasoning that Grant then used as a point of rebuttal.

"I asked if he believed the Earth is round. He said yes," Grant recounts. "I asked him to consider what it would look like if he evaluated evidence on the shape of the Earth the same way he does vaccines. He might say physicists are biased and astronauts are paid to lie. He might insist on seeing it with his own eyes."

Grant then followed up with another question. "Even if he could see a round Earth from space, who's to say it isn't an optical illusion? The Earth is spinning, but your eyes (and inner ears) tell you it's standing still." While Grant went on to acknowledge that he shared a few of the common vaccination concerns that his friend held, he suggested that the line of argument that his friend had used was causing the friend to approach the question like more of a "Flat Earther" than a scientist. But it's how the exchange concluded that offered the best hint at how powerful this approach is. "For the first time in our thirty-year friendship, he said: 'I see what you're saying.'"

In reflecting on the interaction, Grant observed "I didn't have to attack my friend's conclusions, I just had to help him reflect on his own thought process." He continued, saying, "The highest compliment from someone who disagrees with you is not, 'You were right.' It's 'You made me think.' Good arguments help us recognize complexity where we once saw simplicity."[71]

Say it out loud

In a similar vein, Yale University's Frank Keil suggests that the best way to help people see that a belief they hold may be silly is to have them express it out loud.

One way to do this is to ask others to explain their beliefs in depth and detail. Often, explanations start out as confident and coherent but quickly get to a point where they become so convoluted, extreme, or irrational that the ideas collapse in on themselves. As Zig Ziglar was famous for saying, the problem with closed-minded people is that their mouth is always open.

Keil defines this as the "Illusion of Explanatory Depth." As he describes it, when people are encouraged to explain why they hold an opinion or belief, they quickly recognize the limitations of their understanding. Keil's research indicates that this moment of realization tends to also result in that person becoming less confident in their assumptions.

Beyond having others consider the "why" of their beliefs and assumptions, there's also great value in focusing on the "how." The limitations of our opinions tend to become quickly apparent when we are asked to explain how our views translate to reality or what they look like in practical terms.[72]

Transcend the theoretical

In an article for the *Harvard Business Review,* science writer Matthew Hutson explores this theme, saying "We often overestimate our ability to explain things."

Hutson cites one particular study where people rated their understanding of various devices and natural phenomena such as zippers and rainbows. After trying to explain how these things worked, the study participants quickly grew less certain about their understanding. People's rates of assuredness "dropped precipitously once (they) had confronted their own ignorance."

In a similar vein, Brown University cognitive scientist Steven Sloman suggests that asking people to explain the practical outworking of their ideas can be particularly effective in addressing political polarization. In Sloman's research, participants rated their understanding and convictions about policy issues ranging from health care to taxation and then were asked to explain the policies they felt so strongly about. Consistent with previous research, Sloman found that the more people tried—and failed—to explain political policies, "the less extreme their positions became." As Sloman summarized, "You can't take a firm stand on shaky ground."[73]

Reflecting on this research and Sloman's subsequent book *The Knowledge Illusion*, Elizabeth Kolbert writes for *The New Yorker*, "If people spent less time pontificating and more time considering the practical implications of their views, there may well be some hope of moderating views and changing attitudes."[74]

If we can't easily explain what we think we know about a given subject, we may need to confront the reality that there is a gap between our confidence and our competence. Helping others to become aware of this gap can prompt them to consider it might be time to reflect or rethink.

Asking people to explain the details or practicalities of their ideas can be a uniquely effective reframing tactic because this creates a contrast between what people think they know and what they actually understand. Naturally, this must not become a "got ya" moment lest the Backfire Effect kick. As Keil suggests, "If you ask them gently and non-aggressively to walk you through their point of view, they'll likely see the holes more."[75]

What comes to mind when you think of...?

Another way to use contrast when trying to persuade another person to consider a new perspective is to address the imagined reality that's underpinning their existing beliefs and assumptions.

This can be as simple as asking someone to clarify for themselves—or out loud—what they imagine to be real or true.

Take the example of abortion, for instance. One of the reasons it is such a hotly contentious issue is that it is deeply imagination-driven. When a staunch pro-lifer imagines the very notion of abortion, they invariably go straight to images of fully formed fetuses having their lives snuffed out violently and unjustly.

Their minds conjure up the images and stories of horrific "partial-birth" abortions such as those conducted by infamous Pennsylvania doctor Kermit Gosnell. Perhaps they picture a selfish and uncaring would-be mother making the decision to abort a pregnancy as flippantly as if they were deciding on a new hairstyle. Then there is the imagined abortion clinic that they picture as an outpost of evil run by doctors and nurses without a conscience.

To this point, one Facebook post from a pro-life colleague of mine lamented the fact that "In the past 12 months, Planned Parenthood stopped the beating hearts of 354, 871 boys and girls." When the issue is described this way, it's very hard to remain emotionally detached.

While there must be some would-be mothers who fail to appreciate the gravity of the decision to terminate a pregnancy, the reality is that most women agonize over and are haunted by the decision to abort a pregnancy for many years. It is not a decision many women make lightly.

And while there are perhaps some abortion providers and health care operators that are motivated as much by politics or ideology as the needs of an expectant mother, again these are undoubtedly a tiny minority. The overwhelming majority of medical practitioners in the field take their responsibility of informing and supporting women very seriously.

Then finally there are the babies themselves. While there are truly heart-breaking stories of late-term abortions that would make even the staunchest pro-choice advocate mildly nauseous, the reality is that these partial-birth, late-term abortions account for just 0.017 percent of terminations performed each year.

By the same token, the way pro-choicers imagine their ideological counterparts is just as prone to inaccuracy. They likely picture red-faced, hate-filled zealots who picket clinics carrying furious signs and shouting obscenities at those who enter. Or they imagine religious leaders fixated uncaringly on the issue with no sympathy or concern for the particular circumstances of individuals who may consider an abortion. Or perhaps they picture portly, white-haired male politicians in their 60s casting aspersions and judgments while voting for laws that impact people whose lives are very different from their own.

Again, the vast majority of pro-lifers don't fit any of these stereotypes. Most are measured, thoughtful, and deeply compassionate individuals. They care about the next generation and the lives of innocent children. Their hearts break at the breathtaking numbers of abortions performed each year and worry that any society willing to endorse this unthinkingly has lost its moral compass. However, they are equally moved with compassion for mothers in need and willing to donate their time and money to women's shelters, orphanages, and support services designed to help women make the often-difficult choice to keep a baby.

In the case of abortion or countless other hot-button issues, trying to persuade an individual to consider a different view must start by addressing the imagined realities that have formed their beliefs. We must start in the realm of imagination as that is where our deepest and most unconscious thinking occurs. By creating contrast or pointing out the gap between what people imagine to be true and what is more likely to be true, we give them the opportunity to reconsider their assumptions.

■ ■ ■

Contrast has a unique ability to bring clarity to ideas and issues. By highlighting where there is a misalignment of behavior and values, a disconnect between philosophy and practicality, or a mismatch between strong convictions and real understanding, creating points of contrast can be a powerful way to influence perceptions and change minds.

PERSUASION TOOL #2 PRO TIPS

1. Many of our opinions are not illogical as much as they are an inaccurate or incomplete view of reality. The best way to encourage people to consider this fact is to present them with an exaggerated or extreme view of what they already believe to be true.

2. Humans have a natural impulse for congruency. As such, a powerful approach is to help people identify where their behavior is at odds with their deeply held beliefs.

3. Pledges are highly persuasive. By having people make a commitment (publicly or privately) to a certain action or idea, they are more likely to follow through. Better yet, written pledges are uniquely effective.

4. Our views tend to be strongest when they remain unspoken hunches and deeply held convictions. Getting others to explain their opinions out loud and in detail creates a contrast between what they think they know and what they actually understand. This can be a great way to prompt reflection.

5. Our imagined realities have a powerful sway over our perceptions. By creating a contrast between what people imagine to be true and what is more likely to be true, we give others the opportunity to reconsider their assumptions.

PERSUASION TOOL #3
LET YOUR WORDS DO THE WORK

When reflecting on his fifty years of interviewing thousands of famous and infamous people, Larry King was asked to select just one interview that stood out from the rest. He didn't hesitate in his response. "It was with Martin Luther King Jr. in 1961."

Recalling the civil rights leader's account of being arrested in Tallahassee, Florida, a few years earlier, Larry King explained, "He was trying to integrate a hotel. The hotel won't give him a room even though he had a reservation, and the police squad cars are coming because he's blocking the entrance. He knows he's going to be arrested. So, King sits down on this porch in front of this small twenty-room hotel. The owner of the hotel comes out, very straightforward but not belligerently, walks up to King and asks, 'What do you want?' King says nothing, so the owner asks again in the same direct tone, 'What do you want?' And Martin Luther King just looked up at him and said, 'My dignity.' And that word has stuck with me to this day."[76]

Language can be an incredibly valuable trigger for change. Wharton School professor Jonah Berger suggests that too many of us waste time trying to force, coax, or push people rather than employing tactics that will remove their resistance to the change we're promoting.

According to Berger, using language to shape perceptions is the best catalyst for persuasion. He suggests that the key is to remove the barriers or roadblocks to change occurring. "Sometimes change doesn't require more horsepower. Sometimes we just need to unlock the parking brake."[77]

Examples of this in recent decades prove Berger's point well. When "gambling' became "gaming," "abortions" became "terminations," "mining" became "resource exploration," the meaning behind the idea changed along with the words. Then there's the case we explored in the opening pages of this book of "recycled wastewater" becoming known as "reused" or "purified" drinking water and how important this was in shifting people's mindsets.

To this point, I've often wondered what difference it would make to the sustainability agenda if it was talked of in terms of "planet health" rather than "climate change."

Terminology as a tool

While language is often used to smooth off the rough edges of an issue or idea, it can be used to shape perceptions in the opposite way too. In a powerful illustration of this principle, consider the work that branding strategists Dan Gregory and Kieran Flanagan have done with the United Nations to address the issue of human trafficking.

In 2012, Dan and Kieran were commissioned by the Singaporean Government and the United Nations to address the issues of exploitation and trafficking in Southeast Asia. In a wealthy country like Singapore, even discussing human trafficking is difficult as the issue is largely hidden beneath polite sensibilities.

As such, the suggestion was made that an important first step in addressing the issue was to recast the language used to describe it. Dan and Kieran recommended redefining "human trafficking" as "slavery," and referring to the "sex industry" as "organized mass rape."

While the genteel bureaucrats tasked with addressing the issue found this terminology unsettling and confronting, they also had the foresight to see that such a change was exactly what was required.[78]

Similarly, the arrest of Jeffrey Epstein in July 2019 on sex trafficking charges sparked a discussion about the need to reframe the language used to describe his crimes.

One article in *The Atlantic* called for a new degree of candor and honesty in the way we describe crimes against young women. "There is no such thing as an 'underage woman,'" the article's author proclaimed. "Instead of describing Epstein's victims as such, they should be described as exactly what they are: girls, children. And that is the beginning. If children cannot legally consent to sex, the term 'child prostitute' is a misnomer. They ought to be referred to as 'rape victims' or 'victims of sexual assault.' And while we're on the topic, let's call 'non-consensual sex' what it really is: 'rape.'"[79]

Strategic semantics

Beyond the legal and social arena, corporations often use language deliberately to shape people's perceptions of well-understood concepts. A car isn't "used," it is "pre-owned." The price tag of a product or service isn't described as a "cost" but an "investment."

In the same way, sales experts know to avoid using the word "problem" because it establishes a negative frame for the conversation. It can even prompt people to formulate problems that didn't exist. Using words such as "issue," "challenge," or "consideration" shifts the frame and tone of the conversation entirely.[80]

While this may all sound a bit silly and semantic, the reality is that it actually works. For instance, in one energy conservation campaign, government officials informed citizens that using certain conservation methods would save them $350 per year. To test the reverse frame, the officials experimented by communicating that if citizens did not use the conservation methods being suggested, they'd lose $350 per year. The results were startling. The campaign communicated with "loss" language was significantly more effective than the "save" campaign.[81]

Using language to shape perceptions is not a one-size-fits-all approach. Instead, it works best when we know what will most effectively resonate with the person or people we are looking to influence. This is the basis of the Moral Foundations Theory framework developed by social psychologist Jonathan Haidt.

The Five Moral Foundations

According to Haidt, the five moral foundations that influence an individual's perceptions of issues—especially political ones—are:

1. **Harm**—the priority people place on preventing suffering and empathetically caring for others.
2. **Fairness**—the notions of justice, inequality, and prejudice.
3. **Loyalty**—the emphasis placed on belonging to a collective.
4. **Authority**—the degree to which authority figures, institutions, and traditions are valued. This extends to ideas about the role of personal responsibility and duty.
5. **Purity**—the concern of cultural sacredness and a sensitivity to disgust or immorality.

The reason these five "dimensions" matter is that they have a huge influence on the type of language and framing that works best with particular individuals. Language is leverage. As such, the key is to present an issue or idea in a way that will resonate with the moral foundations that a person holds.

At a base level, whether someone is ideologically "liberal" or "conservative" has an enormous influence on the moral foundations that shape their worldview. For instance, liberal individuals tend to place a strong emphasis on the first two moral foundations of *harm* and *fairness*. As such, the most effective approach would be to communicate an idea as something that will cause or alleviate damage and unfairness. The plight of the marginalized, disadvantaged, and disaffected is close to their hearts.

When it comes to conservatives, however, the *loyalty, authority,* and *purity* moral foundations resonate most strongly. Ideas and issues that get traction with conservatives tend to emphasize notions of loyalty or belonging along with the preservation of tradition and social virtue. Motivating a more conservative individual to change will be easiest if the change is described as a return to a better and more moral era, an assertion of autonomy, or reinforcing the great and glorious collective.

Of course, this is not to say that liberals aren't interested in their personal rights and shared history, or that conservatives are disinterested in social justice causes. However, the Moral Foundations framework does give powerful hints as to the sort of language that will most effectively resonate with people based on their ideological bent.

In looking at how this theory applies in practice, numerous studies have shown that conservative individuals were more willing to embrace the reality of climate change when it was described as something that would harm them, impact national identity or erode moral authority.

Likewise, liberal individuals were more open to the idea of engaging in international armed combat when the plight of those oppressed by the enemy was framed as an issue of fairness and equity. Research also reveals that liberal-minded individuals softened their stance on stricter gun control if the issue was described as something that limited people's ability to defend themselves against intruder violence.[82]

The bottom line is that a failure to understand the language that will press the right buttons when communicating an issue has a significant influence on your persuasive abilities.

Evocative vocabulary

Beyond changing the appearance of messages to make them relevant to an individual's ideology, Frank Luntz goes one step further and suggests that the best rule of thumb is to aim for language that prioritizes emotion over intellect. "What matters when it comes to word choice is emotion, not the giving of good reasons," according to Luntz. "Eighty percent of our life is emotion, and only 20 percent is intellect. I am much more interested in how you feel than how you think. Strong emotions are sometimes what animate us."[83] This insight takes on even greater significance when you consider that emotional processing tends to be done in the parts of our brain related to the limbic system.

Bearing this in mind, Kevin Hogan and James Speakman in their book *Covert Persuasion,* offer a revealing list of the words most likely to animate the emotions and influence the thinking of those we are looking to persuade. According to Hogan and Speakman, the twenty-four most persuasive words in the English language are: *You, Money, Save, Results, Health, Easy, Love, Discovery, Proven, New, Safety, Guarantee, Free, Yes, Fast, Why, How, Secrets, Sale, Now, Power, Announcing, Benefits, Solution.*

Of course, individual words on their own are only part of the equation when it comes to framing an issue or idea. Phrases and questions such as *I'm not sure if you've ever..., Would you be surprised if I told you that...,* or *Have you ever considered...* can go a long way to preparing people for the idea you're about to share with them.[84]

How you couch things counts

Underscoring the tangible difference that phrasing can make, psychologists Elizabeth Loftus and John Palmer conducted a landmark study where research participants were shown a video recording of a traffic accident. After watching the video footage, the viewers were asked to estimate how fast the cars were traveling at the time of the accident.

Participants were broken into five groups and asked to make this estimation in response to five questions that used different language frames:[85]

1. How fast were the cars going when they *contacted* each other?
2. How fast were the cars going when they *hit* each other?
3. How fast were the cars going when they *bumped* into each other?
4. How fast were the cars going when they *collided* into each other?
5. How fast were the cars going when they *smashed* into each other?

While the distinction between words like *hit, bumped,* or *smashed* may seem insignificant, the influence of this slight change was anything but. The speed estimate given by the different groups varied dramatically from 31, 34, 38, 39, and 41 miles per hour respectively.[86]

Similar research looking at the power of words has found that exposing an individual to words such as "flexible," "elastic," "rubber," and "change" has been shown to correspond with greater open-mindedness and malleability.[87]

In much the same way, people have been shown to be willing to wait longer in lines and be more polite after exposure to words such as "respect," "honor," and "considerate."

A 1996 study by Yale psychologist John Bargh examined exactly this phenomenon and arrived at some compelling conclusions. Bargh asked a group of university students to unscramble a series of five-word sentences under the pretense of wanting to test the student's language abilities. However, it was the impact of the words different students were unscrambling that he was more interested in.

For some of the participants, the unscrambled sentences featured aggressive or discourteous words such as "brazen," "disturb," and "bluntly." A second group's sentences included polite terms such as "courteous" and "behaved" while a third control group's unscrambled sentences included relatively bland or unemotional words.

Once the participants had completed the sentence decoding task, they were then instructed to approach the researcher to be given the second part of the assignment. This is where things got interesting.

When approached, the researcher was instructed to engage in deep conversation with an actor who was pretending to have trouble with an assignment.

They deliberately ignored the study participant for ten minutes or until the participant butted in.

The results were telling:

- Those who had unscrambled polite words waited on average for 9.3 minutes before interrupting and more than 80 percent waited the full 10 minutes without interrupting the researcher.
- Those in the neutral control group waited for an average of 8.7 minutes.
- Those who had uncovered rude words in their sentences waited just 5.4 minutes before interrupting.

Significantly, each participant's behavior appeared to be entirely unconscious. When interviewed afterwards, they could not pinpoint a reason for their decision to interrupt or not, and felt confident that they were not influenced by the words they had unscrambled—despite all evidence to the contrary.

In an interesting follow-up experiment, Bargh had participants unscramble sentences designed to influence their pace rather than their behavior. For instance, when participants decoded words that related to old age such as "retired," "wrinkled," and "bingo," the speed at which they walked to the front of the hall to find the researcher was considerably slower than their speed when they walked into the hall before the experiment had begun.[88]

Make your message memorable

Beyond using words as a way to "trick" people into acting a certain way, fascinating research indicates that what we communicate will have more impact if our language is poetic and memorable.

The reason for this is that humans tend to confuse fluency with accuracy. In other words, we invariably assume that if something is said well, it is likely to be true or worth taking seriously. In contrast, clumsy communication is dismissed as inaccurate, unreliable, and unpersuasive. Reflecting on this, Edward De Bono warned that "fluency of style can easily masquerade as integrity of thought."[89]

To explore this principle, a team of social scientists had two groups of participants read a series of statements.

The first group read a number of common aphorisms such as:

- Woes unite foes.
- Little strokes will tumble great oaks.
- A fault confessed is half redressed.
- What sobriety conceals, alcohol reveals.
- Life is mostly strife.
- Caution and measure will win you treasure.

The second group read statements that expressed the same sentiments but lacked the rhyming quality of the well-worn proverbs:

- Woes unite enemies.
- Little strokes will tumble great trees.
- A fault admitted is half redressed.
- What sobriety conceals, alcohol unmasks.
- Life is mostly struggle.
- Caution and measure will win riches.

When the groups were asked to judge how accurately the statements reflected reality, the results for each cohort varied dramatically. Despite each participant agreeing at the outset that the rhyming quality of a sentence shouldn't make any difference, those in the first group rated the statements as being "more true" than those who read the non-rhyming versions.

The researchers behind the study suggest that "rhyming phrases are mentally processed more easily than non-rhyming ones. Because people's (Instinctive Minds) tend to base accuracy evaluations, at least partly, on the perceived fluency of the incoming information, the rhyming statements are actually judged as more accurate."[90] As Daniel Kahneman recommends, "Put your ideas in verse if you can; they will be more likely to be taken as truth."[91]

There is a reason that marketers do this constantly. Whether or not Gillette really is "the best a man can get" hardly seems to matter. The rhyming elegance of the sentence lends it a ring of credibility and memorability that is hard to shake in the mind of a consumer. The same principle applies regardless of whether you're selling a product, an idea, or a point of view.

The element of surprise

When it comes to using language as a tool for shaping perceptions, sometimes the element of surprise or shock can work especially well. Massachusetts College of Liberal Arts professor, Timothy Jay, suggests that "Taboo words persist because they can intensify emotional communication to a degree that non-taboo words cannot."[92]

Validating this point, research has shown that mild swearing at the beginning or end of a persuasive speech is likely to cause an audience to warm to you and your ideas. The reason for this is that "edgy" language can powerfully communicate conviction, sincerity, and passion if used sensitively. We're not talking about gratuitous cuss words, but rather the sort of language that gets people's attention and causes them to lean in.

As an Australian, this is a technique I often use to build rapport when I am speaking internationally. For instance, the word "bloody" in Australian vernacular is colloquial and inoffensive, but I recognize that it can be seen as a bit edgy in other parts of the world. Because I am often presenting at large-scale events and the setting can tend to be quite formal, I will often use a sentence like "It's bloody great to be here..." during my opening remarks. This immediately grabs the audience's attention, disrupts their perception of me being yet another "corporate stiff" on the stage, and establishes a warm, playful, and humorous tone that allows me to speak directly to the pressing issues.

Make 'em laugh

The disarming power of edgy humor is far from new, of course. In the royal courts of old, one of the most influential and underrated figures was the jester. While not a member of the gentry or aristocracy, the court jester held significant sway over the sovereign because he had permission to do something others rarely could: tell truth to power.[93] The secret of course was to use humor to disguise otherwise jarring realities as entertainment. In doing so, the jester could often influence change in otherwise very difficult or delicate situations.

Rhetoric expert Jay Heinrichs suggests that humor "ranks above all the other emotions in persuasiveness." According to Heinrichs this is because it improves our credibility (ethos) in the eyes of our intended audience while also disarming or neutralizing their logic-based resistance.[94] As famed Canadian philosopher Marshall McLuhan put it: "Anyone who tries to make a distinction between education and entertainment doesn't know the first thing about either."[95]

Comedian and actor John Cleese put it well; "If I can get you to laugh with me, you like me better, which makes you more open to my ideas. And if I can persuade you to laugh at the particular point I make, by laughing at it you acknowledge its truth."[96]

Humorous language can indeed be a powerful tool of persuasion. It can break the ice and make the persuader seem more accepting, friendly, and approachable. But more significantly, humor bypasses a listener's logical faculties and taps directly into their Instinctive Mind. When people are laughing, they are less likely to analyze or critique the content of the message. Reflecting on this fact, cartoonist and playwright Herbert Gardner said, "Once you've got people laughing, they're listening, and you can tell them almost anything." It's little wonder that advertisers use humor extensively. In fact, a full 36 percent of television commercials in the UK are humor-based and almost a quarter of advertisements in the U.S. are too.[97]

Much like the use of swearing, humor must be used with discernment. While comedy can and often must be edgy, it's important to not risk going too far to the point of being considered "blue." In fact, the very term "blue humor," or ribaldry, can be traced back to the days of vaudeville comedy when a blue envelope would be sent backstage to the dressing room after a show if the content or language had been deemed too contentious.

Crossing the "blue humor" line means you'd gone too far and had lost the audience—and it's impossible to persuade an audience when you've lost them.

■ ■ ■

Whether by swearing, evoking emotion, or playing to deeply held values, using language as a tool for shaping perceptions is a powerful catalyst for change. As Polish-born novelist Joseph Conrad suggested, "He who wants to persuade should put his trust not in the right argument but in the right words."[98]

PERSUASION TOOL #3 PRO TIPS

1. Language can be an incredibly effective trigger for influence. Rather than wasting energy trying to force, coax, or push people to change, we'd be smarter to use words that create relevance while removing resistance.

2. Remember the 5 Moral Foundations that shape our ideological percep-tions (harm, fairness, loyalty, authority, and purity). The more you can frame your idea or perspective in language that resonates with another person's worldview, the more receptive they will be.

3. How people *feel* matters more than what they *think*. As such, we'd be wise to use language that speaks to people's emotions wherever possible.

4. Words can prompt certain mindsets and responses. Remember that exposing an individual to words such as "flexible," "elastic," "rubber," or "change" leads to greater open-mindedness and malleability—and vice versa.

5. Humans tend to confuse fluency with accuracy. If what we are communi-cating seems clumsy it is easier to dismiss as inaccurate, unreliable, and unpersuasive. By making our ideas rhyme or have a poetic simplicity to them, they are more likely to be taken seriously.

6. The element of surprise through the use of "edgy" language can work wonders as it gets people's attention and causes them to lean in.

7. If you can get people laughing, you'll be sure to have them listening. Humor is a powerful tool for persuasion but it must be used with sensitivity and discernment. Be careful not to cross the line because it's impossible to persuade an audience when you've lost ethos with them.

CLOSING REFLECTIONS
ON RELATIVITY

Former Associate Justice of the US Supreme Court Oliver Wendell Holmes put it well when he observed that "The human mind once stretched by a new idea never regains its original dimensions."[99]

By deliberately changing people's perspective through the use of priming, contrast, and language, we tap into the inherent relativity of life and irreversibly stretch the thinking of those we are looking to influence.

This doesn't mean the job of persuasion is complete. Rather it prepares the way, or tills the soil, for the seed of an idea to take root.

CHAPTER 4
AFFINITY

I have long been fascinated by the fickle nature of human helpfulness. Why is it that we will willingly offer our assistance in some situations, while at other times even the most reasonable request for assistance can be perceived as a rude imposition?

Certainly, things such as timing, our mood, and darker factors like prejudice can influence how congenial we are, but is there more to it than that?

A few years ago, Harvard Business School's Alison Wood Brooks was prompted to explore this very question. Brooks was curious to understand which situations would and would not result in someone willingly lending their cell phone to a complete stranger when requested.

She set up two different scenarios involving people standing in the rain at a train station. In the first scenario, a complete stranger approached one of the rain-soaked passengers and politely asked "Can I borrow your cell phone?" In the second scenario, a slightly different approach was used with the stranger asking, "I'm so sorry about the rain. Can I borrow your cell phone?"

While this second scenario in the experiment only added six seemingly meaningless words to the request, the difference was enormous. While the actual request itself was identical in both instances, the second scenario saw a 422 percent increase in the willing response rate.

Reflecting on the difference, Brooks points to the fact that while commiserating about the rain is only a simple thing, it plays an important role in establishing connection, trust, and above all else, affinity.

Dr. Gregory Walton of Stanford agrees: "These are massive effects," he wrote. Mentioning something as simple as the rain acts as a "little cue that signals a relationship. And this totally transforms the way people relate, how they feel, how they behave."[1]

At its core, affinity is about building genuine rapport to the point where people feel they know you, like you, and identify with you.

So important was affinity-building in Cicero's mind that he listed it as the first essential element in his famous Five Canons for Persuasion. In Cicero's view, until affinity (ethos) is built, pathos and logos are of little use or relevance. Once people like you, and identify with you as someone who shares their values, the way is paved for persuasion. If another person feels you care for them and have their best interests at heart, they will feel safe and be far more open to receive the ideas you want to share with them.[2]

Giving voice to unspoken views

Former FBI hostage negotiator Chris Voss suggests that Cicero's assessment is spot on. According to Voss, a key element in building affinity is truly listening to the other party and summarizing their perspective for them. "You especially want to focus on articulating any negative thoughts they have," says Voss. This can be as simple as acknowledging and articulating what the other person is probably thinking or saying to themselves. If the situation is already tense due to miscommunication and misunderstandings, for instance, Voss advises opening the conversation with something as abrupt as "Right now, you probably think I'm a jerk."

Articulating the very opinions and beliefs you are looking to challenge may seem counterintuitive, and Voss recognizes this. "Some people think that acknowledging how upset someone is allows them to dig in more. But it's the opposite. As soon as you articulate the other side's point of view, they are a little surprised. You've made them really curious to hear what you are going to say next. And you've made them feel that you are in this together."

Neuroscientists validate this principle showing that when negative emotions are identified and "brought out into the light," their power diminishes, and tension is defused. And this approach works not only at the beginning of a difficult conversation but throughout it as well. If an interaction gets heated or voices start getting raised, Voss recommends interjecting with an admission like "I am being an idiot." He suggests using "the strongest synonym you can: idiot, jerk, something stronger."

Naturally, this takes a good measure of humility and self-discipline. After all, you would probably quite like to justify yourself and make your point. However, doing so may see you win the point-scoring battle but lose the persuasion "war."

In any high-stakes interaction, it is vital to not deny or dispute the other person's position or opinion. Affinity is not about being heard by the other person, it's about them making sure *they* feel heard and understood. "And a person who feels understood is getting a feel-good wave of chemicals in their brain. Once they get a hit of oxytocin, everything is going to change. They'll feel bonded to you. And if they feel bonded, whether it's a little or a lot, that's to your advantage," says Voss.[3]

In order to endear others and build the sort of affinity necessary to influence others, there are three tools that can make all the difference. We will explore these in the pages ahead.

In the aftermath of what was arguably the most spite-filled and toxic election campaign in U.S. history, Joe Biden took to the platform in November 2020 to deliver his victory address. Against the backdrop of bitter division and with his predecessor still deeming his win illegitimate, Biden must have known how important his tone and wording would be. His speech was measured, calm, and sought to heal a divided nation. But it was one sentence that resonated with me most strongly when I heard it: "It is time to put away the harsh rhetoric, see each other again, listen to each other again. To make progress, we have to stop treating our opponents as an enemy."[4]

It was the contrast of these two concepts that I found most striking. Our opponents need not be our enemies. After all, while differences of opinion are completely inevitable, division is a choice.[5]

Meaningful engagement, constructive communication, and genuine persuasion can only occur when we can accept that those with whom we disagree need not—and must not—be considered our enemies.

And yet something about modern debate and dialogue has lost sight of this truth. Today we tend to define argument as being adversarial and oppositional. It is all too often a tool of power and coercion which comes at the cost of affinity.

This was not always the case.

How the ancients argued

The very principles, practices, and purpose of debate have changed so enormously over the centuries that the undisputed original masters of argument—Socrates, Aristotle, and Plato—would hardly recognize what we describe as debating today. For a start, the ancient concept of argument was far from a zero-sum game. It was not about winning or losing, scoring points, or ego strutting.

For Socrates and his contemporaries, losing an argument was not a failure or a source of shame and embarrassment. Quite the contrary. The feeling associated with losing or being tripped up in an argument was described as a moment of enlightenment, self-knowledge, and freedom.

They had a name for it: *aporia*.

According to modern philosopher James Garvey, the ancient notion of aporia was "a weightless moment as you float free of the mental rut you were in—you stop, your eyes narrow, and no words come to you." This feeling of aporia represented "a rare opportunity to move in new intellectual directions, grasp new possibilities."

Appropriately, the word aporia means "no path" and that's what losing an argument once represented. A liberating and exhilarating feeling of being in unfamiliar territory where the next step is unclear.[6]

In their pursuit of this experience of intellectual free-fall, the ancient Greeks would argue passionately for hours not with the intention of winning or dominating their opponent. Aporia was their aim.[7]

In pursuit of aporia

This philosophy of debate, known as aporetic argument, was focused on unearthing truth—even if that meant changing your mind or conceding defeat.

Interestingly, even countries like Japan that were not directly influenced by the Greek philosophies of argument developed their own way of ensuring that debates became a constructive exercise in exploration. Historically, arguments in Japanese culture were not about putting forward your ideas for debate. Instead, information and values were seen as inputs. As the argument or discussion unfolded, these inputs coalesced into an outcome or decision.

Regardless of the cultural background, what's clear is that for much of world history, argument has been an elegant and enlightened affair. This is perhaps best characterized by what became known as the Platonic Ideals: "To argue without quarreling, to quarrel without suspecting, to suspect without slandering."

The world's first lawyers

It should be noted that not all ancient Greeks were aporetic or altruistic debaters. The famed Sophists are a case-in-point. The original Sophists were a group of specially trained rhetoricians who played a key role in the early development of law—even generally being considered the world's first lawyers.

Where Sophists departed from the ideas of Plato and Socrates, was in the motivation of their rhetorical pursuits. While Socrates and Plato were solely focused on arriving at the truth, Sophists were more interested in proving a case—and teaching others how to do the same thing, at a price. In contrast with those who used rhetoric for philosophical purposes, the Sophists' pursuit of financial reward through rhetorical prowess was largely looked down upon. Even today the term "Sophism" is used disparagingly to describe an argument designed to mislead or deceive.

This contempt for sophistry is perhaps unjustified. Historians point to the fact that the Sophists played a key role in the development of public discourse and tolerance. In fact, the word "sophisticated" traces its roots to these ancient professional persuaders. Their liberal attitudes emphasized a tolerance of different beliefs and allowed unpopular or unconventional views to be heard in the public square.

In more ways than one, modern society is extraordinarily "sophisticated." The tools of rhetoric and persuasion today are often used for financial gain and establishing power or dominance.

Moreover, today we are generally more interested in making our point and arguing our case than genuinely seeking the truth in its varied and nuanced forms. As one meme I saw online recently joked, "I'm not arguing. I'm simply explaining why I am right."

In short, argument today would be better described as what ancient Greeks referred to as Eristic. Named after Eris, the Greek god of strife and discord, Eristic argument is characterized by the desire to win points rather than necessarily pursue truth.[8] According to Plato, the Sophists were the world's first Eristic arguers, but they'd be lightweights by today's standards.

Our adversarial age

Although Eristic debate is by no means new, recent centuries have seen it become the default mode of argument. It's hard to know exactly when this shift occurred but Edward De Bono suggested that the trend gathered pace by the late Middle Ages. According to De Bono, while Eristic or adversarial debate has served us well in areas such as science and law, it is an approach that has grown increasingly counterproductive and even dangerous in recent decades.[9] In effect, we have looked to revive Socrates's methods of argument but failed to maintain his motivations.

De Bono suggested that the problem with an Eristic approach to debate is that "the actual exploration of the subject starts to suffer: argument becomes case-making, point scoring, and ego-strutting. No person is going to bring to attention matters that would benefit the opposing side of the argument, even when such matters might greatly extend the exploration of the subject."[10]

Philosopher Martha Nussbaum equates our modern adversarial approach to public debate with a sporting contest. She suggests that this results in participants aiming only to score points, seeing those on the other side as enemies or opponents whom they hope to defeat by almost any means. No one is expected to seek common ground in a football match, and similarly, no one is likely to compromise or find room for give and take in a contest-like debate.[11]

Dan Pink in his book, *To Sell is Human,* highlights just how ingrained this competitive notion is in Western culture today. Pink describes how he will often give a live audience the challenge of breaking into pairs and instructs them to intersect their fingers so that their thumbs are in the air. The next step is for each participant to try and get their partner's thumbs down. As Pink describes, "Participants will assume that your instructions mean for them to thumb-wrestle. However, there are many other ways they could get their partner's thumb down. They could ask. They could unhook their own fingers and put their own down. And so on. The lesson here is that too often our starting point is competition—a win-lose, zero-sum approach. In most circumstances that involve moving others, we have several ways to accomplish the task, most of which can make our partners look good in the process."[12]

This activity is a powerful metaphor for how most of us engage in public dialogue today. It's about winning at all costs. It's about gaining the upper hand and dominating rather than the pursuit of truth. To be tripped up or one-upped in an argument is not equated with a weightless feeling of aporia where we feel free to change our views. Instead, when our opponent makes a point that challenges our truth, our Instinctive Minds double down on our ideology, retreat to outrage and offense, or we reach for the intellectually lazy escape hatch of "agreeing to disagree."

The novelist Robin Sloan describes how this radical perversion of the purposes of debate has caused our modern culture to give up on debate as "a tool for changing minds or achieving consensus. Instead, we use it as a stage for performance, for political point-scoring."[13]

Disagreeing without being disagreeable

If we have any hope of engaging constructively and respectfully with those we don't agree with, an important starting point is to learn to disagree well. Edward De Bono put it best when he observed that there is a big difference between disagreeing with someone and being merely disagreeable.

While many of us assume that being persuasive is about learning to present our arguments impactfully, the way we *respond* to individuals and ideas we disagree with is just as important.

Speaking to the theme, venture capitalist and author Paul Graham devised a spectrum for describing different forms of disagreement—from the toxic to the constructive.[14] Beyond safeguarding civility, Graham suggests that getting better at disagreeing well has other tangible benefits too. He suggests that while we all have a tendency to fall into intellectual dishonesty and toxicity, the biggest benefit of healthy disagreement is "not just that it will make conversations better, but that it will make the people who have them happier."

The Disagreement Hierarchy

Drawing and extending on Graham's ideas, below is a hierarchical model that characterizes the five common approaches to disagreement in modern discourse. At the top is genuine engagement with someone's viewpoint or argument, while the lowest levels resort to labeling, characterization and contradiction.

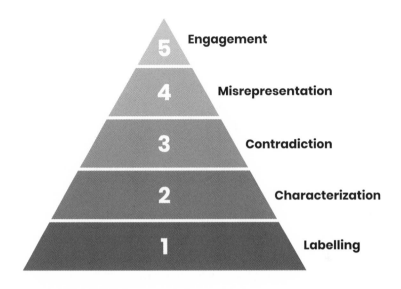

Level 1—Labeling

This lowest form of disagreement is also the most common. It relies on ridiculing or dismissing another individual in the most simplistic of ways: "You're a fool, a bigot, a moron, a socialist…" and the list goes on. As we explored in chapter 2, labels are invariably the vehicles of prejudice.

When we engage in labeling, the substance of another person's point of view or perspective is entirely ignored as we attack them as an individual. This is the realm of thrown insults, vented anger, and bitter contempt.

While hurling abuse at an adversary can feel good in the moment, it is ultimately unproductive and unpersuasive. The problem with making attacks personal is best typified by something called the "ad hominem fallacy." This Latin term, which means *to the person*, is akin to "playing the man, not the ball." Ad hominem arguments ignore the issue at hand and fall back on lazy and often cruel generalizations.[15]

In suggesting that labeling was a sign of intellectual laziness or defeat, it was Socrates who said, "When the debate is lost, slander becomes the tool of the loser."

Level 2—Characterization

The second level of the Disagreement Hierarchy centers on attacking the characteristics, title, or authority of another individual while ignoring their point or perspective. In other words, it is about undermining who the other person *is* rather than what their argument or ideas may be. "You would say that...you're a politician, a pastor, a labor unionist," etc.

Characterization tends to rely on the dismissal of another person as wrong simply because of who they are, or because of the group they belong to. In reverse, the characterization approach may see the responder bringing up their own credibility as a way to win the argument without actually engaging in it: "As a mother of four, I can assure you that..."

While uncharitable, the characterization approach is highly effective when it comes to point scoring. This is because attacking someone else's identity and credibility, or bolstering your own, can result in a perception that you've won an argument in the eyes of others watching on. If there is a sense that one person *seems* right or *sounds* right, they'll often be assumed to *be* right even if there is no real reason for this conclusion and vice versa. It is a common and effective strategy to discredit another person based on their background, race, gender, or associations even if these things have nothing to do with the argument they are making.

Characterization is not limited to identity but also includes tone. Often the disagreement is about taking issue with the perceived tone or temperament of the argument or perspective rather than the actual point of view itself.

While avoiding the trap of labeling and characterization is important in any context, it is perhaps most important when technology is involved. As Paul Graham reflects, "There's a danger that the increase in disagreement will make people angrier. Particularly online, where it's easy to say things you'd never say face to face."[16] It's worthwhile noting that Graham made this observation way back in 2008 when social media was still in its infancy.

Pointing to how challenging this dynamic has become in recent years, best-selling author Jon Acuff suggests, "The problem with social media is that it gives people the chance to be the worst version of themselves and then rewards them with the attention of other people who are doing the same."

Level 3—Contradiction

At this third level of disagreement, a response starts becoming related to the point or perspective of the other person. However, rather than engaging intelligently with the issue, the disagreeing party simply states an opposing view as if, in its own right, that was enough to nullify debate.

Sometimes contradiction goes one step further than simply stating the opposing argument and also adds cherry-picked evidence to back up that viewpoint. While these counterarguments can be a valid response in disagreement, the challenge is that they are often aimed at a tangent from the other person's argument. This often results in two individuals who end up arguing about different things.

Level 4—Misrepresentation

At this second highest level of disagreement, the disagreeing party looks to engage with the viewpoint or argument of the other but tends to do so narrowly. The focus is often on identifying the mistakes or shortcomings of another perspective while ignoring the broader context or nuance. Quotes taken out of context can quickly and effectively misrepresent another person and their argument.

The truth is that we're all prone to the trap of misrepresentation. This is simply because when we encounter ideas or worldviews we agree with, our Instinctive Mind is open and we scarcely evaluate what we are seeing and hearing. However, when we encounter confronting or unfamiliar ideas, we tend to be on the lookout for things to disagree with—even if substantial common ground exists.

Level 5—Engagement

The highest level of disagreement is where real thinking and intellectually honest debate takes place. This is where the guts of another person's viewpoint or perspective are challenged fairly and rigorously. To use the sporting analogy, this is where the ball gets played rather than the man or woman.

Step on the dance floor

While seeking to disagree well is an important factor in building affinity with those we are looking to influence, we'd also do well to re-think some of the unconscious assumptions we tend to hold about the nature of debate.

In their book *Metaphors We Live By*, Mark Johnson and George Lakoff suggest one of the biggest obstacles to changing others' minds is the very way we approach the exercise. Rather than seeing dialogue and debate as a constructive exchange, our modern approach to persuasion is shaped by a deeply held idea of it being a battle.

Consider how some of the phrases we commonly use in describing debates underscore this point:

* *Your claims are indefensible.*
* *He attacked every weak point in my argument.*
* *Her criticisms were right on target.*
* *I demolished his argument.*
* *She shot down all of my arguments.*[17]

As a compelling thought exercise, Johnson and Lakoff wonder how our approach to the idea of argument would change if we were to think of it as a metaphorical dance. "Try to imagine a culture where arguments are not viewed in terms of war, where there is no sense of attacking or defending, gaining or losing ground. Imagine a culture where an argument is viewed as a dance."[18]

Adam Grant picks up on this theme in his book *Think Again*, saying "A good debate is not a war. It's not even a tug-of-war, where you can drag your opponent to your side if you pull hard enough on the rope. It's more like a dance. If you try too hard to lead, your partner will resist. If you can adapt your moves to hers, and get her to do the same, you're more likely to end up in rhythm."[19]

As Grant observes, the single goal in warfare is to gain ground at all costs and never surrender a battle. In contrast, dancing means stepping back from time to time—conceding ground and accepting when your counterpart presents an idea you agree with. "We can demonstrate openness by acknowledging where we agree with our critics and even what we've learned from them.

Then, when we ask what views they might be willing to revise, we're not hypocrites."[20] Author and academic Neil Rackham has examined this very dynamic and how it plays out in negotiations. In studying the planning methodology of highly effective negotiators, Rackham notes that they approach the bargaining table with a clearly mapped-out series of "dance steps" designed to direct their discussions. Significantly, these experts devote over a third of their planning time to identifying what they expect to be common ground with their opponents.

In comparison, the less effective and experienced negotiators that Rackham studied did the opposite. They went in armed for battle with little attention to, or interest in, identifying points of commonality or agreement.

According to Rackham, the difference between the mentality of highly effective negotiators and their less effective counterparts became even more stark once the negotiation or exchange had begun. Whereas the highly effective group rarely adopted offensive or defensive tactics, the novice negotiators readily engaged in "defend-attack spirals." They would aggressively shoot down their opponent's positions while stubbornly defending their own at all costs. Naturally, this resulted in neither side adopting a posture of openness or congeniality. Each dug their heels in.[21]

Of course, seeking to argue without being adversarial isn't a guarantee of non-toxic interactions. Some people don't want to dance, no matter how often or how nicely we ask.[22] However, when we begin to see debates as a dance rather than a battle, the posture, tone, and purpose of the exchange will often change.

Do you want to make a point or make a difference?

In reflecting on the interpersonal cost of our modern adversarial debating philosophy, leadership author and pastor Andy Stanley puts it well when he suggests that "in any relationship, when one person wins, the relationship always loses." Founder of the Fuller Brush company Alfred Fuller knew this when he famously said "Never argue. To win an argument is to lose a sale."[23]

When we seek to persuade others to consider our ideas and opinions, the primary goal must not be the win. In the words of eighteenth-century French essayist Joseph Joubert, "The aim of an argument should not be victory, but progress."

The reason this matters is that although we may win the point or trump our opponent's argument in that moment, if our victory has come at the cost of affinity, ultimately we have both lost. Moreover, it's highly unlikely that genuine persuasion has occurred. As the American writer and columnist Tim Kreider observes, exhausting someone through argument is not the same thing as convincing them.[24]

The decision we all need to carefully make is whether we are more interested in making a point or making a difference. We can win an argument but lose the ability to influence depending on the way we engage with others.

While reframing arguments as a dance rather than a battle is a helpful start in fostering constructive interactions, psychologists also point to the importance of uncoupling our identity from our opinions—and doing that for our opponents.[25]

You are not your opinions

When we start to see ours or others' identities and opinions as one and the same, we lose the ability to constructively engage. As Paul Graham suggests, "People can never have a fruitful argument about something that's part of their identity. By definition, they're partisan."[26]

If we define ourselves by our opinions, we will resist changing our minds at all costs because rethinking our viewpoint becomes the same as having to relinquish who we are. Our Instinctive Minds will also automatically perceive any assault on our opinions as a personal attack. However, if we can separate our opinions from our identity, we have a better shot at calmly and genuinely considering new, different, and disconfirming ideas—and judging them fairly.

You or I are not the sum of our opinions and this is a foundational principle we must all work hard to keep front of mind. Even if someone holds a bizarre or irrational view, this doesn't make them a lesser person. We may lose respect for someone who is willfully ignorant, but we mustn't fall into the trap of losing regard for them.

If constructive debate is more of a dance than a battle, the way we approach the dance floor can make all the difference. In order to build the sort of affinity that enables persuasion, we must relearn the skill of disagreeing without being disagreeable and unlearn the battle tactics many of us have been taught over the years.

Ideally, this will come from both sides of any debate or exchange. As Dan Pink suggests in his book *To Sell is Human*, when it comes to arguing, "When both parties view their encounters as opportunities to learn, the desire to defeat the other side struggles to find the oxygen it needs."[27]

■ ■ ■

In his book *How to Argue and Win Every Time*, legendary trial lawyer Gerry Spence sums up the importance of prioritizing affinity when seeking to change minds. "What is winning an argument?" he asks "Is winning when we force the other to lay down his emotional and intellectual arms and surrender? Do we triumph when the other cries out, 'You win, I was wrong!' Do we envision winning as when the other hoists the white flag of capitulation?"

"If so, I have never won an argument in my career. I once believed, as most do, that if arguments are to be won, the opponent must be pummelled into submission and silenced. Argument is not the process by which we seek to destroy the Other; Argument is a tool with which we can achieve an end, satisfy a want, fulfill a desire. Argument is the mechanism by which we reveal the truth."[28]

Naturally, while we can't control the actions and behavior of others, we can always lay down our weapons and invite others to engage openly and wholeheartedly. With any luck, our "opponent" will step onto the dance floor and might even allow us to take the lead.

PERSUASION TOOL #4 PRO TIPS

1. Differences of opinion may be inevitable, but division is a choice. When interacting with people with whom we strongly disagree, never forget that our opponents need not become enemies.

2. In any debate, aim for what Socrates and his contemporaries referred to as aporia, where losing an argument was seen as a moment of enlightenment and freedom rather than a source of shame or embarrassment. Keep the pursuit of truth as your guiding principle even if it means changing your own mind.

3. Cultivate the skill of disagreeing without becoming disagreeable. This means avoiding the lower rungs of the Disagreement Hierarchy (Labeling, Characterization, Contradiction, and Misrepresentation) and instead aiming for sincere Engagement.

4. Something powerful happens when we approach arguments as a dance rather than a battle. Instead of seeing debates as an exercise in attacking and defending, approach any potentially tense exchange with carefully planned dance steps. This may mean conceding ground, taking the occasional backward step and looking for points of commonality or agreement.

5. Remember that when one person wins an argument, the relationship always loses. In order to preserve and build affinity, we need to decide whether we want to make a point or make a difference in the minds of those we are looking to influence. The aim of any constructive argument should be progress, not victory.

6. As challenging as it may be, work hard to uncouple your and other's opinions from identity. No human being is the sum of their opinions and acknowledging this allows us to engage with others respectfully while also freeing us to change our own perspective if need be.

PERSUASION TOOL #5
PUT YOUR WORST FOOT FORWARD

In his landmark book *The Trust Factor*, neuroeconomist Paul Zak explored the biological processes involved in establishing affinity in the minds of those we are looking to influence. Zak has spent years studying what builds rapport and intuitive trust between individuals and has come up with some remarkable but simple findings.

According to Zak, the most important element of gaining or regaining trust is to dial up our human-ness. Being real, vulnerable, and even fallible results in the release of the hormone oxytocin. As we have already explored, this is the neuro-mechanism humans have unconsciously used for centuries to determine who was safe enough to trust and work with.[29]

It's hard to overstate the importance of this dynamic. In order to be respected or seen as worth listening to, we often project sanitized and carefully crafted versions of ourselves. In the professional arena, spin doctors and corporate communications departments work hard to carefully craft messages to ensure our communication is predictable, reliable, and on-brand. And yet transparency, authenticity, and vulnerability are a much more effective strategy.

Picking up on this theme in his book *The Culture Code*, Daniel Coyle suggests that a posture of authenticity and vulnerability can work wonders when engaging with others. "You should open up, show you make mistakes and invite input with simple phrases like 'This is just my two cents;' 'Of course, I could be wrong here;' 'What am I missing?' 'What do you think?' This kind of signal is not just an admission of weakness; it's also an invitation to create a deeper connection, because it sparks a response in the listener: How can I help?"[30]

The value of being vulnerable

One of the legends of Roman persuasive speech, Quintilian, similarly believed that vulnerability was the most important factor in building affinity with those we seek to influence.

For Quintilian, one of the most powerful elements of transparency involved an openness about doubt and uncertainty. This idea came to be known as "dubitatio," from which we derive the modern English word "dubious."

Over the centuries, dubitatio has been used to great effect by many legendary leaders and communicators. In two of her most famous speeches, Queen Elizabeth I masterfully made use of it.

In her iconic address to troops at Tilbury in 1588, Elizabeth I directly called out the concern that a woman was not equipped for the rigors of battle. "I know I have the body of a weak and feeble woman; but I have the heart of a king, and a king of England, too!" The effect was immediate and reports from those in attendance were that the massed troops cheered so loudly and for so long that officers were forced to quiet the crowd so the Queen could continue.

Thirteen years later, Queen Elizabeth I again resorted to dubitatio in a speech that was so impactful and historic that it would later be dubbed her "Golden Speech." Addressing a fractious Parliament, the Queen proclaimed, "And though you have had, and may have, many mightier and wiser princes sitting in this seat, yet you have never had, nor shall have, any that will love you better." Historians recorded that members of the Parliament were so moved by the Queen's address that they left the hall "transfigured, many of them in tears."[31]

Abraham Lincoln was also a master of dubitatio and some have argued that it was the key to his election as President in 1860. In a fairly unkind assessment, Jay Heinrichs in his book *Thank You for Arguing* described Lincoln's many disadvantages in the presidential stakes. "What he lacked in background, he made worse in appearance: freakishly big hands, aerodynamic cheeks, a Western rube's accent."[32]

However, it was the way Abraham Lincoln leveraged these "disadvantages" that was the secret to his success. Heinrichs reflects, "When he addressed New York's elite, (Lincoln spoke) in his characteristic harsh whine and warned the crowd that they weren't about to hear anything new." According to Heinrichs, this approach was absolutely brilliant—a masterstroke. "His dubious opening set his highbrow audience up, not just by lowering expectations but also by conveying absolute sincerity. The speech was a smash. Without it, Lincoln likely would not have been nominated, much less elected, to the presidency that November."[33]

Own goals open minds

While transparency and vulnerability may make us seem more approachable or endearing, they are also powerful tools for persuasion. Nick Kolenda in *Methods of Persuasion,* examines research that shows that "presenting a little bit of negative information about your message can actually benefit you." Rather than trying to paper over weaknesses in your argument, Kolenda recommends we lead with them. Acknowledge them. Put them right out there. This seems to counter the conventional wisdom that we should put our best foot forward when looking to make a positive first impression.

Robert Cialdini similarly points to decades of research showing that "a communicator who references a weakness early on is immediately seen as more honest." This matters because once trust and affinity has been established, our ideas or arguments are more likely to be believed and accepted by others.[34]

Speaking to this theme, Wharton School psychologist Adam Grant argues that "Communicating your opinion with some uncertainty signals confident humility, invites curiosity, and leads to a more nuanced discussion. The natural starting point would be to emphasize your strengths and downplay your weaknesses. But this is unhelpful. An informed audience is going to spot the holes in our case anyway. We might as well get credit for having the humility to look for them, the foresight to spot them, and the integrity to acknowledge them."[35]

Beyond acknowledging weakness, Nick Kolenda recommends disclosing details that may otherwise undermine our position or perspective. This is due to the fact that "when a message contains only positive support, people tend to believe that the message is purposely excluding information, which causes them to be skeptical. On the other hand, when a message contains a small amount of negative information, people...believe that it is more complete."[36]

The power of this approach has been documented in numerous settings. Research by social psychologist Kip Williams found that jurors were more likely to view an attorney and their case more favorably if the attorney revealed weaknesses in their case before the opposition had the chance to do so. In doing this, the attorney established a perception of honesty. In fact, verdicts were statistically more likely to be given in favor of the party first to bring up the issue.[37]

A similar study by Duke University professor Chris Bail identified the Twitter posts from political leaders that proved to be most impactful and persuasive. What he found was that those who were willing to criticize their own side and acknowledge its shortcomings were more likely to be seen as persuasive. Bail's conclusion was that "Turning a critical eye on one's own party may convince people to open up the cognitive space necessary to begin listening, or see the possibility of compromise more clearly."[38] Put simply, being vulnerable and open-minded gives other people permission to follow suit.

This type of candor and transparency is especially important when an audience is already aware of a weakness or vulnerability. By calling out what is already front of mind for your counterpart, what could otherwise be a point of protest or objection immediately loses its potency.

When people persuade themselves

The unique power of honestly sharing the weak points of an idea or argument is that it invariably compels the listener to jump to your defense and even unconsciously start arguing your idea for you.

In one of the most thorough analyses of this principle Daniel O'Keefe from the University of Illinois, assembled over 100 studies on the use of one-sided and two-sided approaches in persuasive communication. These studies spanned fifty years of research and involved over 20,000 participants. The results of this meta-analysis were significant to say the least. The overwhelming evidence was that providing two-sided arguments was a far more persuasive approach than only presenting the arguments or evidence in your favor.

In the words of seventeenth-century French writer Francois de La Rochefoucauld, "We only confess our little faults to persuade people that we have no big ones."[39] While this may sound conniving or manipulative, it points to a powerful principle we ignore at our own peril.

One important caveat though is that it's not enough to merely acknowledge counterarguments or inconvenient evidence—these also need to be refuted or placed in context in order to not become a distraction. The key is to bring up opposing arguments and then address them. In doing so, our credibility and trustworthiness receives a significant boost—as does our persuasive power.[40]

Transitional statements or words are critical when leading with candor. Once points of weakness or vulnerability are highlighted, use words like "however," "but," and "yet" and then redirect the conversation to countervailing strengths. This may mean admitting that you lack skills and experience for a particular job "but are a very fast learner," for instance.[41]

Don't hide your doubts

In addition to being transparent or self-effacing, acknowledging any misgivings you may have can be a powerful way to build affinity. Just as scientists include caveats in research that give a nod to data that is inconclusive, we'd do well to not gloss over areas of nuance and uncertainty when presenting our ideas.

This dynamic was demonstrated in a series of experiments where psychologists shared scientific research with members of the general public and gauged their response. The first group read a summary of the research that examined the link between diet and aging but papered over areas of nuance and uncertainty. In comparison, the second group read about the same study but with the inclusion of a range of caveats. Interestingly, those in the second group were more engaged with the content and maintained more flexible beliefs and attitudes. The mere mention that the scientists were hesitant to draw definitive conclusions without conducting more research made people far more likely to consider the ideas they did present.[42]

Celebrate your shortcomings

In the world of product marketing, radical transparency has long been a powerful tactic for building affinity and trust. When a potential drawback or flaw exists, flagging it up front in marketing messages has been shown to significantly decrease buyer resistance and increase sales.[43]

Over five decades ago, the marketers in charge of launching the Volkswagen Beetle in North America knew that the car wasn't the most attractive vehicle on the market but that it was tough, cheap to buy, and economical to run. So rather than hiding the lack of aesthetic appeal or emphasizing only the car's selling points, Volkswagen practiced radical candor with slogans like "Ugly is only skin deep," and "It will stay uglier longer." The ad campaign propelled the Volkswagen Beetle to cult icon status and is recognized as one of the most successful advertising campaigns of all time.[44]

This same approach has worked wonders for countless other brands. Avis didn't try to inflate their image as a market leader but rather owned the fact that "We're #2, but we try harder." Similarly, Listerine billed its product as "The taste you hate three times a day" and L'Oreal touted "We're more expensive, but you're worth it."[45]

At an interpersonal or relational level, the affinity that comes through radical candor and transparency is just as important.

The endearing power of disclosure

In 2015, the University of British Columbia's Mandy Len Catron penned a piece for the *New York Times* that so captured the attention and fascination of readers that it became one of the most widely shared *Times* pieces in history. What's remarkable about this is that the article was not the type of characteristic elevated journalism that the newspaper is famous for. Instead it was featured in the Fashion and Styles section. It's title: "To Fall in Love with Anyone, Do This." The article promised a sure-fire way to create meaningful and lasting emotional bonds in less than forty-five minutes.

Catron's piece was based on her own personal experience coupled with research by psychologists Arthur and Elaine Aron who have spent years studying the dynamics of relationships. The article's advice on creating a unifying love that lasts? Personal self-disclosure. The Arons' research exploring the significance of this had involved pairing up strangers who took turns reading thirty-six questions to their partner—questions their counterpart was strongly encouraged to answer openly and honestly. The initial questions were fairly simple and superficial like "What would constitute a perfect day for you?" or "Who would you like to have as a dinner guest?" As the questions progressed, they became more probing and philosophical, e.g. "What do you value most in a friendship?" or "When was the last time you cried?" As the questions neared the end of the list, they got very deep: "Of all the people in your family, whose death would be the most disturbing?"

As the questions unfolded, the connection between the parties became noticeably stronger. Even though they had started out as complete strangers, there was a palpable bond and closeness that developed within the promised forty-five minutes—one that has been repeated hundreds of times over. Many of the individuals who have taken part in Aron's experiments have even gone on to marry.[46]

■ ■ ■

While it's only human to want to present ourselves and our ideas in the best light, doing so is both unproductive and unpersuasive. In order to build trust and affinity with those we are seeking to influence, it is vulnerability, self-deprecation, and self-disclosure that are more likely to shift the dial.

PERSUASION TOOL #5 PRO TIPS

1. Rather than projecting a sanitized and carefully curated persona, lead with radical transparency and vulnerability. Not only does this result in a release of the trust hormone oxytocin, but it encourages others to be more open and honest as well.

2. Acknowledge your doubts and inadequacies through the use of dubitatio in order to have others warm to you and your ideas.

3. Proactively point out the weaknesses and shortcomings of your argument before the other party gets the chance to. This signals that you are informed, fair-minded and forthright.

4. Don't be afraid to share information or disclose details that may undermine your position. By acknowledging both sides of an argument, you show that you have an appreciation for complexity, which will result in your counterpart being less skeptical and guarded.

5. When in doubt, err on the side of honesty. Open up, be transparent and don't be afraid to confess your doubts. Sometimes it even pays to poke a bit of fun at yourself and those on "your side" of an issue. Being self-effacing in this way can make all the difference.

PERSUASION TOOL #6
CONCENTRATE ON COMMONALITY

A few years ago, I was struck by the perspective and insight of chemical industry mogul Charles Koch as he was interviewed by Tim Ferris for Ferris's podcast. Widely regarded as a hawkish and divisive right-wing power broker, Koch came across as anything but. He was measured, magnanimous, and deeply sincere.

Of all the topics that Koch covered in the wide-ranging interview, it was his work in criminal justice reform that was most compelling. Having made a series of failed attempts at reform over the years, Koch admitted that one of his biggest mistakes had been to define "partnership" too narrowly. To make real change, he realized that he needed to work with and engage with people he had traditionally considered his enemies.

Koch described how his process of redefining what made a good ally had come back to the one essential ingredient: that of shared vision. Whether another individual or group held the same political views was nowhere near as important as whether they could rally behind a common vision of what was possible.

This shifted everything and, over time, an unlikely coalition was formed, which included CNN's Van Jones, and the left-leaning George Soros—both of whom had famously clashed with Koch for years. Despite their differences, each individual shared the same passion for criminal justice reform, and that's all that counted. The success of their efforts to date has been nothing short of remarkable and inspiring.

Starting with what we share

In theory, points of commonality with others ought not be that hard to find. From a genetic standpoint, we share 99.8 percent of our DNA with every other human being on the planet. In the most literal sense, what we all share in common far outweighs what divides us. And yet, as award-winning advertising executive Jason Harris observes, "we spend a whole lot of time and energy fixating on the 0.2 percent that makes us different."[47]

Oscar-winning producer Emile Sherman recently embarked on a journey to discover what it might take to get ideological opponents to find meaningful common ground. When he launched his podcast *Principle of Charity*, Sherman set the goal of finding a way to be "more generous" when engaging with people who held opposing views. "What would happen," he wondered, "if we went in seeking to understand the strongest version of the other viewpoint, in search of the truth of a matter, instead of going in combatively to 'win'?"[48]

Each episode of *Principle of Charity* teams up experts with opposing views to discuss various topics. The catch, however, is that each expert must present the most generous version of the other side's viewpoint.

In one episode, for instance, Sydney University professor of media Catherine Lumby was teamed up with ethics professor Clive Hamilton to discuss whether pornography has any redeeming characteristics or whether it is "inherently demeaning to women." Both parties had clashed publicly in the past over the issue. Lumby said that prior to the *Principle of Charity* conversation, she'd felt "misunderstood, misrepresented, and that (Hamilton) had no respect for me." This perspective was understandable considering Hamilton had once described Lumby as being "naive" and "so enamored with the liberating possibilities of porn that she refuses to recognize its dark side." For her part, Lumby admitted that "I had pigeon-holed Clive as someone who was very polemic and had a paternalistic view of women and children."

Following their podcast episode exchange, Lumby felt very differently about her former opponent. "What surprised me is I think we largely agree," she said. "We both agreed that there's really abhorrent pornography, the question (is) what you do about it... Now, if I was to bump into Clive, I'd be wanting to have a glass of wine with him." Hamilton described feeling much the same.[49]

I agree

If there are two words that rank among the most powerful and critically important when seeking commonality, they would be "I agree."

As persuasive communication strategist Dave Lakhani describes it, "If you hope to persuade effectively, you must first examine the beliefs people hold true that are congruent to your position." The key then is to try and help the other person reframe their beliefs in a way that includes your perspective and get them to reaffirm their beliefs. This need not be as hard as it sounds.[50]

In the practice of classical rhetoric, this is called a "Commonplace"—a viewpoint that people with different perspectives hold in common. These can be shared values or rules of thumb on which everyone agrees. The power of establishing a commonplace is that it can disable the tribal impulses of our Instinctive Minds and provide a starting point for constructive engagement or dialogue.[51]

This dynamic was the focus of an experiment conducted by a team of psychologists in the UK. The researchers enlisted a group of devoted Manchester United fans and asked them to take part in a short writing task. Half of the participants were instructed to write a few paragraphs about what they loved about Manchester United, while the other half were asked to write about what they shared in common with soccer fans the world over.

After the groups had completed their writing exercise, an emergency was staged involving a passing runner tripping and falling. Significantly, the runner was wearing a shirt boasting the name of Manchester United's biggest rival. The researchers watched to see how the participants would respond as the jogger lay on the ground, clutching his ankle and screaming in pain.

Alarmingly, a mere 30 percent of those that had just written an account of what they loved about Manchester United looked to help the jogger—compared with 70 percent of those who had written about what they shared in common with soccer fans broadly.[52]

Miscalculating the chasm

The assumption that someone who disagrees with you shares nothing in common with you exists in all kinds of domains. For instance, members of religious and ethnic groups are often prone to believe other people's perceptions of the world are more different than they actually are. Yale researcher Zoe Chance points to the fact that "People miscalculate how much members of the opposing side disagree with them on many hot-button issues like gun control, racism, and religion. And the more vehement our own views are, the more extreme we imagine views on the other side to be."[53]

To this point, recent research by the American National Election Study found that almost 40 percent of Republicans agreed that "having an increasing number of people of many different races, ethnic groups, and nationalities in the United States makes this country a better place to live." Further still, 66.2 percent believed that background checks for gun purchases should be mandatory. In his interpretation of this data, Duke University's Chris Bail suggests that while polarization is a real issue, "it is fair to say that most Americans are not as extreme as one might think after spending an hour or two on social media."[54]

If we are to find a commonplace that allows goodwill and consensus to grow, we'd do well to focus on *values*. This is because at a values level, we will tend to share a lot in common—even with our most bitter adversaries. To this point, a September 2020 study by Harvard's Carr Center for Human Rights revealed that eight in ten Americans believe that "without our freedoms America is nothing." Of those studied, 93 percent say the right to privacy is important, and 92 percent agree that the right to a quality education is critical and that racial equality matters. Even in our hyper-polarized age, seven in ten Americans unknowingly had more in common with one another than not.[55]

Social psychologists Juliana Schroeder and Nick Epley suggest that simply hearing people's voices rather than relying on written communication is a key way to overcome this miscalculation of the chasm between us. They point to research showing that when we hear someone's voice rather than just reading their words, we find them more competent, thoughtful, and intelligent. When someone disagrees with us, we can't discount their opinion as easily while hearing their voice; it reminds us that they're thinking, feeling, fellow human beings.[56]

Make the middle ground your reference point

Once a commonplace has been established, the key is to frame your argument in a way that makes it seem consistent with what is already accepted by both sides. If an idea doesn't feel entirely foreign or uncomfortably new, it is more likely to be considered rather than rejected at the outset.

This was the very strategy used to successfully change public perceptions and views around the issue of same-sex marriage. While the push for legal change could have been framed as the Gay Marriage Movement or the LGBT Marriage Act, calling it "Marriage Equality" was a masterstroke according to branding strategists, Dan Gregory and Kieran Flanigan. "No matter what side of the line you stood on before the idea of 'marriage equality' was proposed, you definitely knew what marriage was and you hopefully had a good understanding of how important equality is," they observed. "By using some of the language and iconography of the civil rights movements of the 1960s and 1970s, activists linked the idea of marriage equality to racial equality. In other words, they conveyed the idea that this was not something new, but a continuation of a debate that had already been concluded in the affirmative."[57]

Familiarity breeds congeniality

As the marriage equality example demonstrates, fostering agreement and commonality can be as simple as using generally accepted concepts, words, names, and terms when proposing something new. If these familiar elements are perceived as good, correct, and virtuous, your new ideas will likely be perceived through that same lens.

Dave Lakhani offers valuable insights into what this can look like in practice. "In order to persuade effectively, you must identify what is familiar to the person or group that you hope to move. What shared experiences are readily available as middle ground? By understanding what is familiar you can join them in the middle ground of shared experience or desire."[58]

In much this way, Martin Luther King Jr. turned the tide of public opinion in the American South through appeals to shared values. As Jonathan Haidt and Greg Lukianoff observe in their book *The Coddling of the American Mind,* "Dr. King's genius was that he appealed to the shared morals and identities of Americans by using the unifying languages of religion and patriotism. He spoke often of the need for love and forgiveness, hearkening back to the words of Jesus and echoing ancient wisdom from many cultures." But it was King's referencing of America's "civil religion" rooted in the words of the Founding Fathers that was his masterstroke. "When the architects of our republic wrote the magnificent words of the Constitution and the Declaration of Independence," he proclaimed on the steps of the Lincoln Memorial, "they were signing a promissory note."[59]

Leveraging likeness

The good news is that fostering commonality need not be complicated or even ideological. There's a reason that birds of a feather flock together and that *like attracts like.* We gravitate toward the familiar—especially when what's familiar is a character trait or element of personal identity. And this begins young—even infants have been shown to smile more at adults whose facial expressions match their own.

Decades of research shows that when our gestures and body movements begin to match those of another, we actually begin to feel the same emotions as that person and a powerful form of affinity develops.

The reason synchronous behavior tends to build trust is that it activates the social bonding hormone oxytocin. Paul Zak explores this principle in his book *The Moral Molecule,* arguing that synchronicity causes people to develop a bond that is hard to explain but easy to perceive and incredibly powerful.[60]

To examine how this quirk of human psychology could be used to drive positive change, one group of Canadian researchers set out to see if synchronicity could reduce racial prejudice.

As part of their experiment, the researchers had a group of white individuals watch seven short videos of black people doing the simple action of picking up a glass of water, taking a sip, and then placing the glass back on the table. A portion of the groups merely observed the video clips while others were instructed to precisely mimic the actions of the people in the clips. Following the experiment, participants were quizzed using a rigorous diagnostic technique designed to measure prejudice.

The results were significant. While those who had merely observed the videos showed typical levels of racial prejudice, this was completely absent amongst those who had synchronized their actions with the actors in the videos. Of course, it would be naïve to suggest that simply synchronizing our actions with people in video clips will address a millennia of inherited and unconscious racism. But the findings of this study are significant in their own right.[61]

Academic research aside, we all know intuitively how powerful mimicry and synchronicity can be. Consider how contagious yawns are and that we tend to smile when we see others smiling. This influence is so powerful that people who live together for a long time do in fact begin to look alike due largely to the fact that they tend to imitate each other's facial expressions.

More than simply a functional dynamic, research indicates that growing to look alike over time is an important part of intimacy and that couples who start to look the same tend to be happier.[62]

Duke University's Tanya Chartrand is a social psychologist who specializes in the area of non-conscious influence and is famous for her research examining the role of physicality in building affinity.

In one of Chartrand's more noteworthy studies, she paired up unwitting research participants with a "confederate" (someone helping to facilitate the research by pretending to take part as a genuine participant). During a conversation exchange, the confederate was instructed to deliberately engage in a range of gestures and movements in a planned way. Some smiled excessively, some jiggled their foot, and others repeatedly touched their face throughout the conversation.

Chartrand and her team monitored the conversations closely and quickly found that many of the research subjects began to unconsciously copy the movements of their partner—20 percent copied the face touching and almost half mimicked the behavior of foot jiggling.

Curious to see how this imitation instinct shaped perceptions of the conversation, Chartrand reversed the process with a new set of subjects. This time, half of the confederates deliberately copied the movements of their counterpart while the other half did not. At the end of the conversation, the subjects were quizzed about their conversation partner and those who had been speaking with a confederate who unconsciously mimicked them rated their counterpart as significantly more likable.[63]

According to Columbia Business School's Adam Galinsky, this "chameleon effect" is not to be underestimated as a tool of influence and affinity. As Galinsky explains, this goes to our very roots as a species. Our inherently tribal instincts cause us to gravitate towards those who look and act like us. Historically, these subtle belonging cues allowed us to know who was from our group and was therefore both trustworthy and safe. However, as society has become more interconnected, diverse, and complex, our brains have struggled to identify the familiarity cues that indicate trustworthiness. And so, we rely on unconscious signals of being "in sync with other people" by seeking out matches in behavioral patterns.

Galinsky concludes that "Synching our mannerisms and vocal patterns to someone else so that we both understand and can be understood is fundamental to attunement."[64]

It goes without saying that using imitation to build affinity can quickly backfire if it isn't done sensitively and with discernment. Imitation is deeply linked to trust, so any hint that these approaches are being used to manipulate will be perceived, rightly, as a betrayal of that trust. Irreparable damage will be done, and affinity will be lost in an instant. When physicality is used well and in good faith, however, it is a powerful way to build rapport, trust, and the permission to persuade.

If the idea of matching someone's gestures or behavior feels a bit too unnatural, the good news is that evoking affinity can be as simple as finding points of likeness with the person you are seeking to engage with.

Research over recent years indicates just how strangely powerful this can be:[65]

- People who learn that they have a birthday, birthplace, or first name in common come to like each other more, which leads to heightened cooperativeness and helpfulness toward each other. Stanford University's Gregory Walton found that when college students believed they shared a birthday with a classmate, they were more motivated to complete group work with that student than in cases where there wasn't this point of commonality.[66]
- Potential customers are more willing to enroll in an exercise program if told they have the same date of birth as the personal trainer who'll be providing the service. Interestingly, it was also found that when subjects in a research study jogged on the spot and thus increased their heart rate, if someone watching was told they shared a birthdate with the jogger, the onlooker's heart rates also increased.[67]
- Young women are twice as likely to accept a friend request from a man who contacts them on Facebook if he claims to have the same birthday.[68]
- Small-business loans to citizens of developing nations brokered through a microfinance website are significantly more likely to be offered by loan providers to recipients whose names share their initials.[69]

- Individuals prefer people and products with names that share letters of the alphabet with their own names.[70]

Having conducted numerous studies examining the power of trait-based commonality, Gregory Walton concludes, "It's easy for people to take on the goals, motivations, emotions, and even physical reactions of people they feel even minimally connected to."[71]

Interestingly, the significance of the connection and point of commonality scarcely seems to matter. In fact, research reveals that the more unusual the point of commonality, the more meaningful and impactful it becomes.

Uncommon commonality

Jerry Burger, a psychology professor at Santa Clara University, examined the degree to which this is the case. In one of his more famous experiments, Burger paired college students with research assistants who informed their new partner that they had been placed together because they shared similar fingerprint patterns. The trick was that some participants were told that the fingerprint characteristics they shared were common while others were told that the fingerprint was very rare. They then engaged in a fake survey about astrology.

At the conclusion of the study and as the participants were exiting the room, the research assistant masquerading as a participant asked their fingerprint buddy if they'd be willing to lend a hand in proofreading an English assignment and writing a one-page critique.

Some of the study participants had not been made aware of any common fingerprint patterns so they could act as a control group. Of this first cohort, 48 percent were willing to help when the request was made. However, for those who believed the request was coming from someone with whom they shared a relatively common fingerprint, the willingness rate went up to 55 percent. Significantly though, among those subjects who were led to believe that their shared fingerprint was very rare, 82 percent were more than happy to help.[72]

Although the lure of commonality seems largely hardwired into humans, national culture can influence how we perceive and value it. In individualistic societies, for instance, people will be more persuaded if something speaks to their personal identity and sense of self. However, in collectivist societies it is most powerful if you frame an idea in terms of its relevance to a person's family identity or community. The effect of this has been demonstrated in numerous studies of advertising campaigns in Asian contexts where traditionally Western appeals to personal identity fell flat, while those that connected with a consumer's social identity resonated strongly.[73]

■ ■ ■

Fostering a tangible sense of commonality is essential in order to build affinity with those we are looking to persuade. Whether by building on "commonplace" beliefs and language or leveraging likeness, focusing on points of agreement lays a powerful foundation for influence.

PERSUASION TOOL #6 PRO TIPS

1. The two most powerful words when it comes to building affinity are "I agree." Even if you can't identify with someone's opinion or worldview, there are undoubtedly values that you share. Identify shared values and frame your argument or perspective in the context of what both parties agree to be important.

2. Be careful not to miscalculate the chasm and imagine that divisions are greater than they really are. We often assume others hold more extreme or divergent views than is actually the case.

3. It's easier to identify with people when we hear or see them rather than simply relying on the written word. Always aim to make human interactions as three-dimensional as possible in order to avoid simplistic characterizations.

4. As much as possible, communicate your ideas using words, symbols, names, and terms that another party will understand and agree with.

5. It's always easier for people to listen to those with whom they feel a likeness. Make every effort to identify points of commonality no matter how obscure they may seem.

CLOSING REFLECTIONS
ON AFFINITY

It's hard to overstate just how important affinity is in the process of changing minds. As Abraham Lincoln famously said, "If you would win a man to your cause, first convince him that you are his sincere friend."[74]

Whether through congeniality, vulnerability, or commonality, building affinity and trust lays the essential foundation for influence. Speaking to his disciple Tzu-Kung in 492 BC, Confucius famously advised: "Abandon weapons first, then food, but never abandon trust. Trust is more important than life."[75]

CHAPTER 5
DIGNITY

During the autumn of 1502 in Florence, Italy, Michelangelo was in the final stages of creating a new sculpture when the city's mayor Piero Soderini entered his studio. A few months earlier, Soderini had begged Michelangelo to try and salvage an enormous block of marble that had been all but destroyed by an amateur sculptor. Michelangelo agreed and devised a plan of what to create.

Soderini loved Michelangelo's vision and felt invested in its outcome. Added to this, he fancied himself as something of an amateur sculptor. As he surveyed the almost completed work, Soderini wondered out loud if the statue's nose was too big. Michelangelo seemingly accepted the feedback and leaned over to the statue's giant face and pretended to lightly tap his chisel. Standing below, Soderini could see the dust falling from the statue's face—dust that Michelangelo had carefully dislodged with his finger.

After this charade had gone on for a minute or so, Michelangelo stood back and gestured to the face, saying "What do you think now?" Soderini replied with delight, saying, "I like it better now. You've made it come alive." Of course, the statue hadn't changed at all but both men got back on with their days pleased with the fact that they had achieved exactly what they hoped.[1]

Imagine if Michelangelo had dug in his heels and resisted the request? While the end result would have been no different, the relational dynamic between these two formidable men would likely have been significantly strained—perhaps irreparably so. Michelangelo may have felt vindicated in having held his ground but it's highly unlikely that Soderini would have been persuaded that the master sculptor really did know best.

Within this story lies an important principle when it comes to changing minds, and it's one we will explore in the chapter ahead.

The clout of a compliment

While we may have been told as children that "flattery will get you nowhere," nothing could be further from the truth. According to research from the Hong Kong University of Science and Technology, flattery has a profoundly persuasive effect on others. "Even when we realize we are being flattered, there is still an underlying positive impression that can be strong and long lasting," according to the researchers. This subconscious positive impression about the person we are interacting with has an enormous influence on our view of them and our Instinctive Mind's willingness to consider their perspective.[2]

In the words of Oscar Wilde, "Anyone who doesn't like flattery has never been flattered." Mark Twain agreed. "I can live for two months on a good compliment," he said.[3]

To this point, consider the hairdressing salon whose staff trialed intentionally stroking the egos of their clients to see what tangible impact it might have. When hairstylists complimented customers saying, "Any hairstyle would look good on you!" customer tips rose by 37 percent. Or consider the college students who were sent a pre-printed brochure from a clothing retail store that said, "We're contacting you because you're fashionable and stylish." The students who received the brochure reported strong positive feelings toward the store and were more likely to shop there—even though the flattery was largely meaningless.[4]

According to political psychologists Brendan Nyhan and Jason Reifler, starting with affirmation is the best way to avoid the Backfire Effect we discussed in chapter 2. Nyhan and Reifler suggest that when we're trying to persuade someone to consider a different point of view, the last thing we want to do is make them feel cornered or shamed. This is a surefire way to trigger a limbic response of resistance. Instead, preserving another person's dignity and helping them feel validated and accepted is far more effective.

In his book *The 48 Laws of Power*, Robert Greene speaks to this theme suggesting that accounting for other people's ego and dignity is essential when it comes to persuasion. "Since each man believes that he is right, and words will rarely convince him otherwise, the arguer's reasoning falls on deaf ears. When cornered, he only argues more, digging his own grave. Once he has made the other person feel insecure and inferior in his beliefs, the eloquence of Socrates could not save the situation."[5]

Centuries ago, King Solomon had prescribed this very same strategy: "Use patience and kindness when you want to persuade leaders and watch them change their minds right in front of you," he said. "For your gentle wisdom will quell the strongest resistance."[6]

As Ed Coper similarly suggests in his book *Facts and Other Lies*, "We must find ways to operate with respect, and not force people to admit they are stupid in order to admit they're wrong."[7]

Give people space to save face

Some of the most formative research examining this dynamic was first conducted by Stanford University social psychologist Leon Festinger back in 1954. At the time, Festinger became intrigued with the rise to prominence of a doomsday cult called the Oak Park Study Group. Members of this particular cult had predicted that a massive flood would occur on December 21 of that year and destroy all life on Earth. Devotees were taught that on the eve of the cataclysm, an alien being from the planet Clarion would come to rescue the true believers from the fate that awaited humankind the next day.

When December 21 came and went, with neither an alien visit nor a devastating global flood, Festinger assumed that the cult members would grudgingly accept that they had been wrong and abandon the cult in short order. Curiously though, the very opposite occurred. Faced with the embarrassment that their certainty had been misplaced, the cult members doubled down in their commitment to both the cult leader and their belief that the world's end was imminent. They merely changed the date and searched for an alternative explanation. In fact, many drew the conclusion that the world had in fact been saved *because* of their devotion and faithfulness and so continued to preach their message with greater vigor than ever.[8]

By this point, Festinger's fascination had seen him infiltrate the group with a series of colleagues under the guise that they were also true believers. In conversations with cult members, he observed a common pattern: people have a powerful psychological need to maintain consistent attitudes and behavior.[9]

In an attempt to make sense of this pattern, Festinger coined the term "cognitive dissonance," which he defined as the distressing mental state in which people "find themselves doing things that don't fit with what they know or having opinions that do not fit with other opinions they hold."[10]

In the case of the cult members, persuasion expert Nick Kolenda suggests that the desire to preserve dignity also resulted in a complete unwillingness to backtrack on public declarations they had made. Kolenda observes that, prior to December 21, "cult members displayed behavior consistent with a belief in the end of the world (i.e. many had quit their jobs, sold their possessions). On December 21, when cult members realized that the flying saucer didn't arrive as predicted, their belief was challenged. However, to accept the idea that the world wasn't ending would be profoundly inconsistent with their original behavior.

In order to overcome that dissonance and discomfort, they needed to do something. And because they couldn't alter their past behavior, they changed the one thing that they could change: their attitude. Upon discovering that the flying saucer didn't arrive, most cult members developed stronger beliefs about the end of the world so that they could justify their original behavior."[11]

As we saw in chapter 3, the more committed to a belief that someone is, especially when that commitment is made publicly, the harder it is to relinquish that belief. In the face of overwhelming contradictory evidence, people will rarely accept that their belief was mistaken or in error but will instead adopt a new perspective that fortifies their view.[12]

It is this same dynamic that makes it so difficult for conspiracy theorists to reconsider views they have espoused passionately and publicly. Psychologist and conspiracy belief researcher Karen Douglas describes how this process shaped the reaction of QAnon devotees in the aftermath of Donald Trump's election loss in November 2020. "When conspiracy theories have bold predictions that don't come true, such as QAnon's claim that Trump would win re-election, followers twist themselves in logical knots to cling to their core beliefs. These beliefs are important to people, and letting them go means letting go of something important that has determined the way they see the world for some time."[13]

As author and QAnon researcher Mike Rothschild explores in his book *The Storm Is Upon Us, Donald Trump's election loss may have been confronting for many conspiracy believers, but they quickly regrouped.* "This type of failure was something that most of them never allowed to penetrate their minds, so to see it happening—and then be rendered powerless to stop it—is truly jarring." In an effort to make sense of the unthinkable, Rothschild points out that many QAnon followers simply did a paradigm pivot and began claiming that it was actually Biden, and not Trump, that had been their savior all along.[14]

Fringe QAnon belief aside, it speaks volumes that as of late 2022, a full 70 percent of Republicans still did not consider Joe Biden the legitimate winner of the 2020 U.S. election despite all reliable evidence indicating that this was the case.[15] Even a public endorsement of the election result from key Republican leaders wasn't enough to sway many right-leaning voters who found it near-impossible to abandon their ideological convictions.

The simple fact is that ego preservation often prevents our Instinctive Minds from arriving at constructive and reasonable conclusions.

Work with ego, not against it

The importance of dignity in the process of changing minds becomes clear when you consider the unconscious reasons why people tend to commit to any given action or idea.

While horse betting for most of us is an inherently illogical exercise in probability, research by a group of Canadian psychologists unearthed an interesting aspect of punter behavior that makes even less rational sense. What these researchers discovered was that as soon as an individual has made a bet on a horse, confidence that their horse will win immediately increases. Of course, the very act of placing a bet doesn't alter the weather, the track conditions, or the actual likelihood of a particular horse winning—all that has changed is the punter's perceptions of probability.

In looking at why this is the case, the researchers suggest that this is about cognitive dissonance—much like the case of the cult members. As humans, we want our beliefs to be consistent with decisions we have already made. In the case of horse betting, our actions influence our beliefs. As Robert Cialdini reflects, "Thirty seconds before putting down their money, (a horse better) had been tentative and uncertain; thirty seconds after the deed, they were significantly more optimistic and self-assured. The act of making a final decision—in this case, of buying a ticket—had been the critical factor. They simply convinced themselves that they had made the right choice and, no doubt, felt better about it all."[16]

Choice Supportive Bias

Behavioral economists refer to this as Choice Supportive Bias—a human tendency to overweigh the positive aspects of a decision we have made simply because we have made it. Al Ramadan in the book *Play Bigger* suggests that this bias means "once you've committed to a product or service, you're likely to feel certain that it is the best even if something slightly better comes along."[17]

We see this same dynamic play out on a much larger scale too. Oli and Rom Brafman suggest that Choice Supportive Bias was at play in President Johnson's decision to redouble his commitment to the war in Vietnam in the mid-1960s. Despite the fact that the war was spiraling dangerously out of control, and everyone could see it, President Johnson's resolve was more than a case of denial or sheer bloody mindedness. Rather, it was a function of the same dynamic at play with punters on race day. Once a commitment or decision has been made by our Instinctive Minds, we feel compelled to look for evidence that helps us feel certain that our choice was the right one. Daniel Kahneman and Amos Tversky suggest that when this happens, "the option of hanging on will therefore be relatively attractive, even if the chances of success are small and the cost of delaying failure is high."[18]

Wouldn't it be nice?

Famed economist John Maynard Keynes once rebuffed a critic who challenged his shifting positions over time. "When the facts change, I change my mind—what do you do, sir?" he'd said.

In much the same vein, the eighteenth-century poet Alexander Pope suggested "A man should never be ashamed to own he has been in the wrong, which is but saying that he is wiser today than he was yesterday."[19]

While this sort of "reasonableness" is nice in theory, the reality is that we generally struggle to allow ourselves (or others) to rethink previous assumptions without seeing it as an act of weakness.

Even when a counterpart sees the sense in our argument or perspective, the most rock-solid logic will have little effect if they feel ego-bound to maintain their position. The other party may agree with us deep down, but they'll never admit it if they feel unable to change their mind without losing face.

It was the iconic poet Robert Frost who said, "I am not a teacher but an awakener." In the pursuit of persuasion, we are all awakeners. As in the literal sense, we would do well to wake people gently and carefully. Be too brash or forceful, and those we're waking will likely lash out.

As such, we must be very careful when asking people to adopt a new idea or course of action that we allow them to preserve their dignity while shifting their view. In the pages ahead we'll look at three tools for doing just this.

PERSUASION TOOL #7
LESSEN THE LOSS

Fear is the number one enemy of openness. In fact, when someone seems stubborn, dismissive, or unwilling to listen, more often than not it is fear and insecurity at play. In much the same way that a horse's first instinct when you or I walk behind it is to kick, so it is with humans. We lash out at the first hint of a threat.

Bearing this in mind, a key step to persuading another person is to account for their fears. If we push people when they don't feel safe, they'll double down in resistance. It's equally counterproductive to make others feel backed into a corner by "catching them out" in an argument or interaction. While you may win a point in the moment, you'll rarely win them to your view. Threatened people don't change—they attack, they retreat, or they dig in their heels.

The reason for this is that whenever we are challenged to reconsider an idea or opinion, there is something we need to give up and it is this loss that we resist at all costs.

One of the most profound insights from Andrew O'Keeffe's research into human instincts is that, contrary to conventional wisdom, we are not actually afraid of change. It is not change but loss that we fear most.[20] This has enormous implications for the process of persuasion. As American writer and political activist Upton Sinclair observed, "It is difficult to get a man to understand something when his salary depends upon his not understanding it."[21]

Interestingly, our instinct to fear or avoid loss is something that trumps even our desire for gain—something commonly known as Loss Aversion.

Loss Aversion describes the tendency of our Instinctive Minds to perceive the pain of loss as much greater than the joy of gaining something of equivalent value. The result of this is that we tend to overestimate the value of something we could lose (or have lost) and make decisions accordingly.

American economist Richard Thaler offers a good example of Loss Aversion in his book *Misbehaving*. He tells the story of a man named Stan who mowed his lawn every weekend and hated doing so because it gave him unbearable hay fever. When Thaler asked Stan why he didn't just hire a teenager to mow his lawn, he said he didn't want to fork out the $10. When he asked Stan whether he would mow his neighbor's lawn for $20, he replied "No, of course not." As Richard Thaler points out, this makes no logical or economic sense but is a case in point of the human compulsion to avoid loss more earnestly than the motivation to achieve gain.[22]

Interestingly, this primal impulse is not unique to humans. Animals in the wild will also fight harder to prevent losses than to achieve gains. Consider the fact that animals defending their territory will invariably prevail over a challenger or aggressor. And this is more than simply a home-ground advantage. It's the instinct to stop at nothing to maintain what is already ours. As one leading biologist observes "when a territory holder is challenged by a rival, the owner almost always wins the contest—usually in a matter of seconds."[23]

In order to ensure people feel safe enough to think and rethink, we must work to address the three most important loss-related fears:

a. Loss of Pride
b. Loss of Power
c. Loss of Certainty

a. LOSS OF PRIDE

It's a universal desire to feel respected and respectable. As such, any appeal to change our minds that could result in humiliation or embarrassment will be perceived as too threatening to consider.

One of the most helpful techniques I have ever come across for safeguarding people's pride in the process of persuasion is one called "feel/felt/found." This approach is a powerful way to allow someone to come to a point of realization at their own pace, and in their own way. It is especially valuable when dealing with someone who has an objection to your viewpoint and is resistant or confrontational.

Feel

The first step is to acknowledge how the other person feels about an idea or issue. Even though you may be presenting a view or idea that is dramatically different from how your counterpart currently sees things, it's important to start by affirming their existing perspective. This creates safety and neutralizes the limbic reflex of defensiveness. It lets the other party know you accept and respect them—and that they are not alone.

Some phrases that characterize this validation could include:

- I understand how you feel...
- I can see how you'd think that...
- I can only imagine...
- That perspective must make perfect sense considering...

Importantly, empathy or identification must not be merely an intellectual exercise of imagining another person's perspective. Try to truly get into the other person's shoes and feel what they feel if you want to become powerfully persuasive.

Felt

The second step is to adopt a position of personal or referred empathy. The key is to reveal that you have shared the other person's view or felt the same way at some stage—or that you know others who have.

This was one of the techniques St. Paul famously used when giving his defense to King Agrippa in Caesarea. The Biblical account in Acts Chapter 26 sees Paul offering his reasons for converting to Christianity and imploring the king to consider doing the same—an audacious move if ever there was one.

As he began delivering his case, Paul said, "I, too, at one point believed..."

This very sentence was more than merely biographical—it was designed to be deliberately disarming. Paul was validating the very worldview he once held—and one that had previously seen him arrest and persecute Christians. So effective was Paul's rhetorical prowess that at the end of his delivery, King Agrippa responded, "In such a short time, you are nearly persuading me to become a Christian."[24]

Some phrases that can help acknowledge that you or others you know have shared the view of someone you're looking to persuade could be:

- That's quite a common perspective...
- Many people I work with have felt the same way...
- I can certainly relate to that point of view...[25]

Hostage negotiators have long understood the critical role of this process in defusing tense situations. In fact, the first three steps of the FBI's famed five-step *Behavioral Change Stairway Model* are dedicated to getting into the other person's shoes. The FBI training emphasizes the importance of establishing rapport, actively listening, and communicating empathy before negotiators make any attempts to influence the behavior or beliefs of the person they're negotiating with.

The principle underpinning this approach is that until another party senses that they have been heard and understood, there is no point trying to drive a resolution.[26]

Found

The final step is to highlight the factors that shifted your view or the opinions of someone you know.[27] Pointing to the changed views of others can be powerful because it creates social proof while avoiding a combative or adversarial tone.

Some phrases that explain a change in yours or another's view could be:

- What we've found over years of doing this is...
- It turns out that...
- When my friend looked closer, they found that...

The bishop brings the big guns

In a superb example of the feel/felt/found approach being used to overcome deeply entrenched views, consider an open letter penned by Bishop TD Jakes and featured in *The Wall Street Journal* in February 2021. In an effort to address

COVID vaccine hesitancy among black Americans, Jakes sought to validate common attitudes, empathize with these perspectives, and then point people to a different view.

Below are excerpts from Jakes' letter, which I have broken up to show how each element models the feel/felt/found approach:

FEEL

"Like many African-Americans, I had a great deal of trepidation about the Covid-19 vaccine. But last week my wife and I completed our course of vaccinations. My experience as a pastor and leader in the black community led me to believe it was the right thing to do..."

FELT

"Unfounded rumors about an attempt to use the vaccine to wipe out the black community have gained currency among my fellow African-Americans. I understand the general mistrust, but the painful truth is that blacks need the vaccine more than anyone. The Centers for Disease Control and Prevention says we are nearly three times as likely as whites to die from Covid.

As a minister, I have witnessed these deaths personally. I have buried many friends and church members. At the peak of the pandemic, I regularly received reports of two or three deaths each day. I have struggled to console and counsel their survivors, most of whom couldn't be in the same room with their loved ones as they took their last breaths.

FOUND

As a father, grandfather, pastor and community leader, I grasped the importance of understanding the vaccine. That meant getting the facts early on from the most qualified scientists and doctors. I received invaluable advice from my long-time physician, a black woman and member of my church who has herself received the vaccine.

Eventually, it came down to common sense. I am a 63-year-old black man, a little overweight and with an underlying health condition. The vaccine has been proven to diminish chances of people like me getting the virus. To date, the vaccine's side effects have been minimal or nonexistent.

I don't consider myself an advocate for taking the vaccine. That is a personal decision. But you shouldn't make a critically important personal decision with no information—or poor information.

Here's my unsolicited counsel: Do your own research. Pray. Consult multiple credible sources, from your personal physician to federal agencies like the CDC. Your earnest quest for the truth could save your life—and your loved ones."[28]

Given his standing and trusted reputation in the black community, TD Jakes's letter packed a significant persuasive punch. But it was more than his reputation that counted. It was the way he shared his own fears, concerns, and reservations—coupled with what he found when did his own research—that gave his words significant weight.

While the feel/felt/found approach isn't foolproof, it's a powerful way to avoid confrontation. It accounts for your counterpart's self-pride and allows them to save face all while giving them permission to revise previously held views or opinions.

More importantly, it releases the other person to change their mind not because they lost a debate but as a result of them considering a different perspective.

b. LOSS OF POWER

Over five centuries ago, Nicolo Machiavelli wrote that "there is nothing more difficult to carry out, nor more doubtful of success, nor more dangerous to handle, than to initiate a new order of things; for the reformer has enemies in all those who profit by the old order."

Historians suggest that it was this very dynamic that explained why Mikhail Gorbachev's attempts to transform Russia consistently failed. Decades after Gorbachev stepped down from power, the former USSR is still a totalitarian state run by a strongman. The reason for this is that Gorbachev's efforts to persuade Russia to become a fundamentally different nation were stymied by the aristocratic class who felt threatened by his vision for change. It was not the general populace who resisted change but rather those in power.

In his book *The Structure of Scientific Revolutions,* Thomas Kuhn observes how this fear of losing power by the "old guard" has a significant effect on stunting scientific development. Rather than being a measured and reason-bound process, the evolution of scientific thought tends to be a bumpy, messy process. Put simply, those who hold the keys to the intellectual kingdom hold on to old theories far too long, even when obvious and reliable new evidence emerges.[29]

Nobel Prize-winning physicist Max Planck rather cynically agrees. According to Planck, "A new scientific truth does not triumph by convincing its opponents and making them see the light, but rather because its opponents eventually die, and a new generation grows up that is familiar with it." Or as Gabriel Weinberg and Lauren McCann put it, "Science progresses one funeral at a time."[30]

Even if we convince people that our opinion or idea is sensible or advantageous, if accepting it comes at the cost of that person's power, they are unlikely to change their opinion or behavior readily.

In his profound and ground-breaking book, *The 48 Laws of Power,* Robert Greene suggests a series of ways we can make allowances for this natural tendency. "A simple gesture like using an old title, or keeping the same number for a group, will tie you to the past and support you with the authority of history,"[31] he observes. "Too much innovation is traumatic and will lead to revolt. If you are new to a position of power, or an outsider trying to build a power base, make a show of respecting the old way of doing things. If change is necessary, make it feel like a gentle improvement on the past."[32]

To this point, I've often marveled at the genius of eighteenth-century inventor, James Watt, in using "horsepower" to describe the capability of mechanical engines. Recognizing that new steam turbines could be seen as a threatening or confronting technology, Watt used terminology that would have made sense to people at the time and thus allayed their concerns.

Another valuable technique for addressing the fear of losing power is to help a counterpart feel that they have "won" in the process of accepting a different view. This may mean allowing them to adopt the appearance that it was their own idea. Or it could mean making concessions (real or perceived) so that the other party can accept a new position without feeling they have given up ground.

The bottom line is that it's vital that we allow people to change their perspective without feeling powerless.[33]

c. LOSS OF CERTAINTY

There's a reason why humans are referred to as creatures of habit. We tend to gravitate toward the safe, the predictable, and the established.

While this is harmless when it comes to our favorite holiday destinations, restaurants and ways of driving to work, our preference for precedent becomes dangerous when it causes our Instinctive Minds to reject new ideas and perspectives simply because they're new.

Even the most adaptable and adventurous among us still tends to feel apprehensive about uncertainty—even if only unconsciously. Behavioral psychologists have spent years examining this dynamic and looking at why our Instinctive Minds tend to favor the familiar. Sometimes this causes us to reject things that could benefit us greatly.[34] As we saw in chapter 2, asking people to consider even the most advantageous idea is a big ask indeed if this challenges someone's established ideology.

Businesses know well that the seduction of the status quo can be a very powerful force indeed. Once we have formed a habit of purchasing a certain brand or product, tempting us to consider an alternative can be very difficult. It's also why banks, for instance, spend so much time wooing young children with bank accounts, money boxes, and loyalty programs. The data is clear that many of us will stick for life with the bank where we open our very first account.

Cass Sunstein observes that our habitual nature influences not just the products we buy but the way we use them: "The current settings on almost anything we own—from phones to televisions to web browsers—are probably still mostly set to the factory defaults. And if you have played around with those settings, you probably did it just once, and then left it as is," he suggests.[35]

When we are attempting to persuade others to consider a new idea or approach, we need to realize that there is often a sense of certainty and security wrapped up in the status quo. We'd do well not to ignore this reality.

Fostering an appetite for organs

In a potent example of the importance of allaying the fear of uncertainty, consider the challenge facing U.S. government officials in January 1943. Having entered World War II just over a year earlier, officials were tasked with persuading the national population to change what they ate. This was more than merely adopting new cuisines as it went to the core of America's gastronomic identity.

The change? To free up resources for troops on the battlefront by eating a lot less meat on the home front. Initial efforts by former President Herbert Hoover had centered on likening meat to munitions. "Meats and fats are just as much munitions in this war as are tanks and airplanes," he'd urged. Beyond supplying feed for their own forces, America was being called on to help supply provisions for Allied forces whose farmland and food supplies had been ravaged by warfare.

While Americans were accustomed to rations of cheese and butter, having to cut down on red meat was another thing entirely. Meat was seen to be an essential part of a "proper meal"—especially among the working class.

To take the place of traditional red meat like steak, roasts, and chops, the plan was to convince Americans to consider consuming inferior cuts of meat that the soldiers themselves wouldn't consume. From hearts to liver, tongue, and other organ meats, advertising campaigns, posters, and pamphlets implored Americans to consider their consumption a matter of patriotism. "Americans! Share the meat as a wartime necessity" and "Do with less so they'll have enough," they implored. Public information campaigns also touted the low cost and high nutritional value of organ meat. And yet, these efforts largely failed to persuade the American populace.

As Jonah Berger suggests in *The Catalyst*, "It wasn't that the public didn't care about the boys overseas. Or that they didn't understand that organ meats could be nutritious. They both cared and understood; they just didn't shift their behavior. Blame inertia or squeamishness. Consumption of liver, tongue, and sweetbreads barely budged."

This was baffling to even the brightest minds of the era. After all, up until this point, the assumption was that all that was required to persuade people to embrace change was to use education and emotion. The prevailing belief was that if the facts were communicated clearly and correctly, the public would become interested, impressed, and persuaded by them. If this could be tied to a core value such as patriotism, change was a sure bet. Or so it was assumed. And yet the uptake in organ meat stalled.

In response, the Department of Defense engaged a psychologist named Kurt Lewin to craft a new strategy. Rather than trying to coax people into change by dialing up the education and emotion in campaigns, Lewin believed that a different approach was needed. According to Lewin, the key question was "why weren't people eating organ meat in the first place?" There must have been something that was stopping them. This was where any persuasion campaign must start.

After conducting scores of consumer surveys, Lewin found that among the key barriers to embracing organ meat was the uncertainty people had about it. These new foods were simply too unfamiliar to embrace. Jonah Berger observes "Housewives didn't know what brains tasted like or how to prepare kidneys, and without that familiarity they weren't going to risk cooking it for their families."[36]

Put simply, the general public was afraid. They were afraid of something they didn't understand and this led to a fear of embarrassment. In turn, this was merely compounded by the widely held belief that organ meats were something that "other people" ate. Organ meat was seen as the food that only poor or rural families consumed. "A middle-class woman in 1940 would sooner starve than despoil her table with tongue or tripe," suggested Charles Duhigg in *The Power of Habit*.[37] What became clear was that the battle for organ meat acceptance was more about ego than education or emotion.

These insights caused a dramatic change in strategy for government officials. Instead of appealing to patriotism or a sense of sacrifice, the focus became on reducing uncertainty and recasting organ meats as a food fit for middle-class tables. In order to reduce uncertainty, recipe cards and cooking tips became widely available everywhere organ meat was sold.

Rather than organizing lectures in local communities to espouse the economic and nutritional benefits of organ meat, Lewin started organizing small group discussion forums where "housewives like yourself" could share their experiences in adapting to wartime food rations. These allowed people to see that they were not alone and that neighbors they admired were embracing the change. Following these discussion forums, Lewin surveyed attendees to see if they were willing to serve organ meat before the next meeting—and almost a third of women said they now would.[38]

Beyond practically reducing uncertainty, Lewin also advised that deliberate attempts be made to make new foods feel familiar. This was a strategy that had been successfully employed on the front line a few months earlier. In early 1943 when fresh cabbage was first served to soldiers, it was thoroughly rejected. It was simply too unfamiliar and exotic. As a result, army cooks began chopping and boiling the cabbage until it resembled every other vegetable on the soldier's plates and the soldiers began eating cabbage without complaint. The same tactic worked with housewives at home too. The focus was on teaching wives and mothers how to make intestines, stomachs, livers, and kidneys look, taste, and smell as similar to familiar foods as possible.[39] Steak and kidney pies and liver meat loafs quickly became the norm.

The effectiveness of these combined efforts was staggering. In no time, kidney became a dinnertime staple and liver even started to be seen as something of a delicacy.[40] By the time the war ended, offal consumption had risen by 33 percent and by 1955 it was up 50 percent.[41] It's worth noting that even well after the need for change was removed, the shift in a nation's eating habits was so profound that it persists to this day. And much of the success of this campaign can be attributed to addressing the uncertainty-driven fears that would otherwise have prevented the change from occurring.

We've been taught since the youngest age that "when in doubt, don't"—and most of us live our lives by this maxim. Part of this is about a natural fear of the unknown, but often it also results from the desire to avoid uncertainty that may result in us feeling disorientated or out of our depth. When asking people to consider a change of mindset or behavior, the more we can address this fear of losing certainty, the more successful we are likely to be.

■ ■ ■

Whether we are looking to persuade the thinking of others or are considering the roadblocks to reconsidering our own viewpoint, being keenly aware of the role that fear plays is essential. When change could mean a loss of pride, power, or certainty, maintaining the status quo will have an immense appeal.

Allowing for these fears and lessening the perceived loss associated with change is an essential precursor to persuasion.

PERSUASION TOOL #7 PRO TIPS

1. Fear is the number one enemy of open-mindedness. But contrary to conventional wisdom, it is not change that we fear, but loss. Always take into account how what you are suggesting or proposing may be perceived as a loss in the eyes of your counterpart.

2. While it can be helpful to focus on how change will benefit someone else, remember that our Instinctive Minds are more motivated to avoid loss than they are to achieve gains. So be careful to minimize any perceived losses while at the same time overemphasizing possible gains in order to tip the scales in your favor.

3. Our natural sense of ego and pride means we will resist anything or anyone that threatens to humiliate us. When looking to persuade someone, try using the feel/felt/found approach in order to help people maintain their dignity in the process of changing their mind.

4. Even if people are convinced that our opinion or idea is sensible or beneficial, they'll struggle to truly embrace it if this comes at the cost of their power or status. As such, try making anything new feel like a gentle improvement on the past and give a nod to tradition through the preservation of titles, language, and symbols.

5. Always try letting people feel like an idea was their own or that they have won in the process of change. Sometimes this may mean you need to make concessions or compromises that you'd otherwise rather not.

6. Remember that humans are known as creatures of habit for a reason. We love predictability and certainty so make every effort to show how a change will not mean stepping into the abyss. If new ideas or possibilities feel safe and secure, they're more likely to be considered seriously.

BECOME A MASTER ASKER

According to former Apple engineer Mike Bell, getting Steve Jobs to see the benefits of developing streaming technology for video and audio was a tough ask indeed.

Bell had been listening to music on his Mac computer but was getting frustrated that every time he changed rooms, he had to lug his computer with him. After considering various solutions to this problem, he began work designing a new "box" that would stream audio to different devices in an Apple user's home. The first hurdle was to get Steve Jobs on board with the idea.

Jobs's ego and intransigence was legendary and when Bell first floated his plan, it was met with a dismissive reaction. "Who the f--- would ever want to stream video?" Jobs fired back. Bell knew that the secret was to put Jobs in the driver's seat and so he used a different approach when suggesting the idea again a few weeks later.

This time, he casually mentioned that it was unlikely that even the most committed Apple user would have a Mac in every room of their house. He began asking questions about how Apple could improve the interconnectivity and user experience with music and video content. Bell's goal was to draw out Jobs's equally legendary creativity and the approach worked.

Jobs's tone quickly changed by the end of the meeting, and he ended up instructing everyone in the design team to get behind Bell's idea for a media streaming box—a project that ended up becoming Apple TV.[42]

Questions are the answer

Whether you're looking to persuade a hard-headed CEO or a hot-tempered toddler, asking effective questions is an important part of the persuasion process. The reason for this is that questions help another person come to a point of realization without feeling that their will has been crossed or their dignity undermined. As we saw in the previous pages, one of our Instinctive Mind's prerequisites for considering change is that it doesn't impinge on our pride and ego.

Kevin Hogan and James Speakman describe this dynamic well in their book *Covert Persuasion*. "We all like to decide for ourselves," they suggest. "We like to come to our own conclusions about the situations in our lives. We like to be in control. We do not like to be told what to do. Therefore, the best way to bring the other person to the predetermined outcome that you're looking for is to ask questions that involve the other person."[43] As author Nancy Willard suggests, "Sometimes questions are more important than answers."[44]

According to negotiation experts Neil Rackham and John Carlisle, the success of any negotiation is directly related to how many questions are asked. In one study, they monitored hundreds of negotiators in action to figure out the difference between average and master negotiators. The frequency of questions used became immediately apparent as a deciding factor. Their key finding was that skilled negotiators ask more than twice as many questions as their less skilled counterparts.[45] These questions were also a key element of the planned "dance steps" expert negotiators entered an engagement with, as explored in chapter 4.

Four reasons questions are key

There are four main reasons questions are so vital and effective in the process of changing minds:

1. Questions allow the other person to listen to themselves

A good question always elicits a response. The reality is that people are more likely to believe what they tell themselves than what you tell them. Asking counterparts a question that causes them to arrive at an answer which bolsters your case can make all the difference—even if they only answer the question in their head.

The legendary 1980 presidential debate between Ronald Reagan and Jimmy Carter stands as one of the most effective examples of this principle. Unseating an incumbent is always a tall order and Reagan knew that Carter's handling of the economy was a point of weakness. However, rather than quoting spiraling unemployment and inflation figures, Reagan posed a question that turned the tide in his favor in the blink of an eye.

During a live televised debate, he simply asked viewers, "Are you better off today than you were four years ago?" Being on live television, this was an entirely rhetorical question. But the answer voters gave in their minds influenced their thinking in profound and permanent ways. This is often regarded as the moment when the 1980 election was decided.[46]

The other benefit of asking good questions is that they prompt people to rethink their assumptions. Reflecting on the power of this process, Adam Grant in his book *Think Again* says, "We're swift to recognize when other people need to think again. We question the judgment of experts whenever we seek out a second opinion on a medical diagnosis. Unfortunately, when it comes to our own knowledge and opinions, we often favor feeling right over being right. We need to develop the habit of forming our own second opinions."[47]

Asking good questions can become a catalyst for doing just this.

2. Questions clarify points of resistance or misunderstanding

By asking questions that allow people to share their concerns and objections, the guesswork on our part gets eliminated. Better yet, a well-asked question gives you the chance to double check that your perceptions are accurate. This can be as simple as sharing how you're seeing a situation or issue and asking the other person if they are on the same page.

Questions can also be a powerful way to address objections that result from deeply unconscious expectations. For instance, if someone complains that your product costs too much, that their tax rates are too high, or that the project will take too long, simply ask what price, tax rate, or project duration would seem reasonable or appropriate.

When the other individual begins to pin down what their expectations actually are, there is often a moment of realization where they recognize that their preconceptions were not realistic. Or perhaps they come to realize that they didn't have any firm expectations at all and that what has been proposed is indeed reasonable.

3. Questions activate aspiration and expectation

Asking questions can be a great way to overcome an instinctive resistance to external influence. In one study conducted by communication scientists San Bolkan and Peter Andersen, individuals were approached at random in shopping centers by clipboard-toting researchers. When passers-by were asked if they could spare a few minutes to answer some questions for a survey, a predictably minuscule number said yes. However, by simply asking one question before requesting assistance with the survey, the percentage of people willing to stop and give up a few minutes of their time jumped to 77.3 percent. That question? "Do you consider yourself a helpful person?"

Pre-empting a request by asking questions that activate a positive expectation is highly effective. For instance, if you want to get someone on board or on your side with an idea, start by saying something along the lines of "You probably know a lot more about this than I do—how would you approach this situation?" By genuinely asking for input or advice, we make the other person an expert and set the positive expectation bar high. This is a powerful technique because it's amazing how readily people will live up to the expectations set by or for them, as we saw in chapter 3.

Naturally, this technique must be sincere otherwise it will be perceived, rightly, as an exercise in manipulation. But the power of approaches like this is that paying a compliment can in turn pay significant dividends in terms of another person's willingness to engage wholeheartedly.[48]

4. Questions invite commitment rather than compliance

While directly stating what you want from another person tends to trigger resistance, questions are a highly effective way of guiding people's choices. They allow the other person to make a decision based on a range of options you have intentionally established.

This approach is especially effective in parent-child dynamics, which are so often fraught with the potential for conflict. For instance, rather than dictating the time you want your teenager to be home, asking "What time do you think you'll be home tonight?" or even something more pointed like "Can we expect you back in time for dinner?" is far more likely to result in the outcome you're hoping for. Furthermore, because the time was offered by the child rather than specified by the parent, they are far more likely to stick to it.

Another powerful commitment technique is to use "choice questions" that move another party to a point of action or resolution. For instance, if options have been discussed and ideas fleshed out, sometimes a question is the best way to land the conversation. For instance, you might want to ask whether a potential customer would like to purchase using a credit card or whether they'd like you to invoice them later? Or you could ask whether they would like to pick up their order or have it delivered? Or you might ask if an investor would prefer to make a cash investment in the business or take an equity share instead?

Obviously choice questions need to be used with integrity as they can easily become coercive. However, when used in good faith, they are a powerful technique for gaining commitment.[49]

'Will I?', not 'I will'

Beyond their effectiveness when communicating with others, we can also use commitment-inducing questions to persuade *ourselves* too. Research by Ibrahim Senay of the University of Illinois indicates that simply changing the beginning of a statement from "I will..." to a question starting with "Will I..." radically changes our likelihood to follow through.

Senay explored the effect of this on people's commitment to physical exercise. What he found is that research participants who made the statement "I will exercise three times a week" were far less likely to follow through than those who asked themselves the question "Will I exercise three times a week?"

This may seem counterintuitive as the statement seems like a stronger indication of intent than the question. However, Senay found that by asking themselves the question, the internal reply of "yes" meant that research participants were more likely to commit to the activity when push came to shove.[50]

Motivational Interviewing

While there are scores of techniques for asking effective questions, the most reliable one from a persuasion standpoint is an approach known as "Motivational Interviewing."

First developed in the early 1980s by two clinical psychologists Stephen Rollnick and William R. Miller, Motivational Interviewing arose out of research examining what actually worked in persuading drug addicts to change their behavior.

Having trawled through decades of data regarding various approaches to treating addiction, Miller's findings were both controversial and confronting. His discovery offended most of his colleagues who had spent years building their careers and credibility based on various drug addiction therapies that were revealed to be ineffective.

What Miller found was that the only meaningful distinction between therapeutic practices that persuaded addicts to change—and those that didn't—was whether the focus was on negative consequences or positive benefits. He found evidence that the common practice of confronting addicts with their demons and their loved ones via an intervention actually *increased* addictive behavior and tended to see people dig in their heels.[51]

Armed with these insights, Miller set out to find a way to persuade addicts to change that got lasting results. After much trial and error, he found that the key was to start with helping patients reach their own conclusions about the aspirations and values that were most important to them. And the best way to do this was to ask open and non-directive questions. Rather than trying to control behavior or impose an agenda, the key was to replace judgment with empathy and lectures with questions.[52]

The Motivational Interviewing technique has been the focus of more than a thousand controlled trials and has been shown to result in meaningful behavior change. It has seen rates of unsafe sex drop, people's nutrition habits improve, and has been used to effectively address voting prejudice and climate change skepticism. On balance, it is one of the most statistically reliable approaches to emerge in behavioral science with success indicators in three out of every four studies.[53]

Why is the approach so effective?

Where Motivational Interviewing departs from other persuasion techniques is that it taps into the implicit motivation of another person rather than trying to change them through promises of reward or threats of punishment. The central premise is that we can rarely induce someone else to change through coercion so would be better off helping them find their own motivation to do so.[54]

Be mindful of your motivation in Motivational Interviewing

Adam Grant suggests that the way you approach the use of this technique makes all the difference. "Motivational Interviewing starts with an attitude of humility and curiosity. We don't know what might motivate someone else to change, but we're genuinely eager to find out. Our role is to hold up a mirror so they can see themselves more clearly, and then empower them to examine their beliefs and behaviors." As Grant describes, Motivational Interviewing is about "asking open-ended questions, engaging in reflective listening, and affirming the person's desire and ability to change."[55] Michael Pantalon of the Yale School of Medicine has spent decades examining how to use Motivational Interviewing to persuade others and has devised a method for what he calls "instant influence."

At the core of Pantalon's approach is a deliberate sequence of very specific questions. "For the purposes of moving others, all questions are not created equal," according to Pantalon. And he's got the data to prove it. As a psychologist and researcher, Michael Pantalon has demonstrated through repeated scientific studies that his approach can unlock even the most obstinate or mindstuck individuals in seven minutes or less.[56]

This is achieved by asking two vitally important questions:

1. "On a scale of 1 to 10, how ready are you to _____? (exercise, stop smoking, do your homework, tidy your room, file your quarterly reports, call your pending client list, turn up to work on time, etc)." 1 out of 10 is "not at all ready" and 10 out of 10 is "totally ready."

This of course isn't the only wording or question format you could use. Other alternatives could include:

On a scale of 1 to 10...

- how likely are you to change your mind regarding X?
- how willing are you to consider doing X?
- how happy would you feel about X?

Once the person has given an answer between 1 and 10, you then ask the second question.

2. "Why didn't you choose a lower number?"

It is this follow-up question that is the key to Michael Pantalon's approach. The reason it is so important is that if you simply asked someone a binary yes/no question as to whether they're likely to do something, they're likely to say no if there is even the faintest hint of doubt or resistance.

However, by asking why the number they gave in the first answer wasn't lower, you shift the other individual's focus to the latent reasons or motivation they already have for taking action or being persuaded—no matter how slight that motivation is. In other words, you are encouraging the other person to articulate some of the reasons why they want to behave or think differently. According to Pantalon, this allows people to clarify their own personal, positive, and intrinsic motivation rather than feeling they are being coerced or forced to do something.[57]

Importantly, the actual number an individual gives to the initial question doesn't actually matter all that much. A low number doesn't automatically mean they are unlikely to take action, and vice versa. The key point of the process is that people are encouraged to think of their own reasons for doing something. Once they are engaged in thinking positively and proactively, then and only then can persuasion take place.[58]

Going deeper

Once you've ascertained why someone didn't pick a lower number, the next step is to explore why they might be motivated to change. It's about activating their imagination, visualizing a different scenario or situation, and considering why a change could be positive and beneficial.[59]

Some questions that are helpful in doing this are:

- What might the benefit be of X?
- Might there be a reason you would X?

- If you were to theoretically consider doing X, what do you think that'd feel like?
- Imagine you've already (made the X change being suggested), how do you think you'd benefit from that?
- Imagine we could magically make this situation different with no effort or cost—what would the benefits be?
- If you had all the time/money you needed, why might you consider doing X?[60]

The key in all of this is to tap into unconscious motivation by using questions that are open rather than closed. As their name suggests, open questions are ones that lead to reflection, expression, and discussion. The best way to ensure a question is open is to begin it with words like *What, Why, When, Describe, Where, How* or *Tell.* Closed questions in comparison tend to lead to a yes or no answer and shut down conversation and consideration. Closed questions are useful for confirming or testing information but not influencing another person's perspective. The words to avoid because they lead to closed questions are *Are, Will, Can, Would, If, Did.*[61]

The mighty power of might

A word of caution: while "why" questions can be effective in fostering open reflection, not all why questions will have the same impact. For instance, why questions that focus on the negatives should be avoided. Some examples are:

- Why don't you...?
- Why haven't you...?
- Why wouldn't you...?
- Why can't you...?
- Why shouldn't you...?
- Why couldn't you...?
- Why aren't you...?

As an alternative, try using "why" questions that emphasize the word "might" and thus point people toward a positive outcome. These include:

- Why might you...?
- Why might it be good for you to...?
- Why might it work for you to...?
- Why might it benefit you...?
- Why might you want to...?
- Why might you decide to...?
- Why might you even think about...?[62]

The importance of emphasizing the benefits in this process is key. Decades of research has shown that people are more likely to change if they focus on the upside of changing, rather than the downside of not changing. Consider one study which found that focusing on the benefits of not smoking (such as feeling healthier, improved taste, approval of family, or clothes not smelling, etc.) was three times more likely to persuade people to quit than if the persuasive efforts focused on the negatives (such as cancer, smelly clothes, or social alienation, etc.).[63]

Don't be discouraged by defiance

Interestingly, one of the counterintuitive signs that Motivational Interviewing is working is when resistance to your ideas or suggestion increases. This often indicates that change is being considered. When this happens, it's important not to push the other person if they express concerns or even anger. Instead, it's vital to allow the process to play itself out. In the same way, silence can be a good sign that reflection and consideration is occurring. Don't rush to fill the void. Persuasion is often a result of what is not said as much as what is.

By the same token, if someone starts to offer excuses for why a change isn't possible or fair, this can also be a good sign. It may well mean that the other person is seriously entertaining the idea of change. Michael Pantelon suggests the best response when excuses are presented is to not engage with them head-on but rather use further questions to point toward benefits and possibilities. He suggests asking questions like "But why would you do it, if that reason not to didn't exist?" or "If you could wave a magic wand and make that problem disappear, then why would you do it?"[64]

The most important underlying principle of Motivational Interviewing is that individuals already have the drive necessary to change, no matter how small it may be. As such, it's always better to focus on the motivation that exists rather than getting tripped up by the points of resistance or the reasons not to change. This insight dates back to research by social psychologist, Leon Festinger, who in 1957 found that the process of hearing ourselves describe what we'd like to do, even if we don't feel we can do it, unlocks a desire to change.[65]

People who feel listened to are more likely to listen

Naturally, it scarcely matters how well we ask questions of others if we are unable or unwilling to listen to the answers they give. Unless we have a desire to listen, then our questions become little more than a tool for exerting power or control.

Effective listening is more than simply not talking—it's about showing a genuine interest in another person and their views. Stephen Covey recommended listening with the intent to *understand* rather than *reply*, and this remains a timeless truth.

The key point here is that we need to lead with curiosity rather than conviction when engaging with people who we are looking to persuade. By all means we can be confident in our position and ideas, but we must always adopt a posture of openness.

This will often mean resisting the urge to jump in and "correct" the other person or state our point of view too quickly. Instead, we'd do well to keep asking questions. To keep drawing the other person out. To help them hear themselves and their views and allow this to bring the clarity needed. After all, people mean what they say but don't always say what they mean.

As journalist Kate Murphy suggests, the key to listening well is to ask "truly curious questions that don't have the hidden agenda of fixing, saving, advising, convincing, or correcting." More importantly, Murphy describes listening as the process of "facilitating the clear expression of another person's thoughts."[66] What a beautiful way to put it.

In a practical sense, maintaining an open listening posture can be aided by us responding to people with words like "how interesting," "that's fascinating," and "how incredible." These are wonderfully neutral terms that make sure another person feels heard without requiring us to feel obligated to agree with them or affirm their view. As Australian academic Mark Stephens suggests, "Listening does not constitute affirmation, and understanding does not constitute endorsement."[67] And sometimes it's the silence of genuinely listening that will have the biggest impact. Something powerful happens when we allow for space and silence. Nineteenth-century humorist Josh Billings suggests that "Silence is one of the hardest arguments to refute."[68] In a similar vein, America's thirtieth president Calvin Coolidge observed that "No man ever listened his way out of a job."

Speak like you're right, listen like you're wrong

While listening with an open mind can be a great way to develop deep understanding or bring clarity, there is another important benefit: you may discover things you didn't previously know. The Dalai Lama observed that "When you talk, you are only repeating what you already know. But if you listen, you may learn something new." In a similar vein, actress Elizabeth Bibesco once quipped "We learn nothing by being right."

In our efforts to persuade others, it's vital to remain open to the possibility that it may be *us* that needs to change. Perhaps there is a different perspective or new body of evidence we have not considered before.

Actor Alan Alda put it best when he said, "Real listening is a willingness to let the other person change you." I like that. In fact, even if we persuade another person to substantially change their view, there's a good chance we will leave the same interaction with our own perspective tempered or enriched. As organizational psychologist Adam Grant recommends, "Argue like you're right and listen like you're wrong."

Beyond the benefit of allowing the best ideas to win, genuinely listening makes an allowance for the dignity of the other person. If they feel that they have landed a few points and nudged your thinking even a little, they will be more open to taking your perspective on board. People who feel listened to are more likely to listen.

■ ■ ■

In order to preserve the dignity of others in the process of persuasion, questions are the answer. Asking, rather than telling, is always going to be the most effective way to influence the perspectives of others.

Voltaire once wrote that we ought to "Judge a man by his questions, rather than his answers."[69] In the same way, the quality of our arguments, our attempts to persuade, and our ability to influence will be best judged by the quality of our questions rather than the quality of our answers.

PERSUASION TOOL #8 PRO TIPS

1. Remember that sometimes the best answer to a question is one you never hear. Don't underestimate the power of asking people questions they may answer only to themselves. After all, people are more likely to believe what they tell themselves than what they are told.

2. Before making a suggestion or request, try asking questions that activate a positive expectation. If people are in a frame of mind where they are expecting the best, they are more likely to be open-minded too.

3. Rather than trying to coerce or convince people, use the question-asking technique of Motivational Interviewing to tap into their existing reasons to change.

4. Always opt for open rather than closed questions by beginning with words like *What, Why, When, Describe, Where* rather than *Are, Will, Can, Would, If, Did.*

5. When asking 'why' questions, never overlook the power of including the word "might" in order to point people toward a positive outcome

6. People who feel listened to are more likely to listen. Remember that effective listening is more than simply not talking—it's about showing a genuine interest in another person and their views.

7. When it comes to communication and engagement, silence is golden. Leave more space and silence then you might otherwise feel comfortable with as this is where deep consideration often occurs.

Civic engagement expert Peter Block put it well when he observed that the "yes" of another person means nothing if they don't have the ability to say "no." "There can be no commitment if there is no choice," says Block.[70]

In the same vein, the authors of the *New York Times* bestselling book *Influencers* put it well when they suggest that autonomy and choice are critical for activating human motivation. This is because "Compulsion first replaces and then erases motivation. You can never hope to engage people's commitment if they don't have permission to say no. One of the deepest human drives stems from the desire to retain our will." They continue, "The history of civilization frequently demonstrates that we would rather lose our lives than surrender our freedom. It almost doesn't matter how small the encroachment on our agency; we've been known to go to war over it."[71]

The choice is yours

In a potent example of how people respond when their autonomy is encroached upon, consider the events that unfolded when mandatory COVID-19 vaccination requirements for construction workers were introduced in the Australian state of Victoria.

Shortly following this being announced in October 2021, violent protests erupted on cue. Given that research indicated more than a third of workers in the sector were unsure about or unwilling to be vaccinated, this policy was always going to be "combustible," as social commentator Waleed Aly observed. "It is a very grave thing to tell someone who genuinely fears taking a vaccine that they will lose their livelihood, even if those fears are hugely misguided. You can't mandate those fears away," said Ali.[72]

The contrast with the strategy pursued in the neighboring state of New

South Wales is an informative example of why preserving autonomy matters. Rather than issue a vaccination mandate for construction workers, the NSW government restricted worksites to 50 percent capacity if unvaccinated workers were on site. This effectively turned the decision to get vaccinated, or not, into one that had implications for a construction worker's friends and colleagues. If they refused to have the jab, there would be less work to go around. The result was that construction sector vaccination rates in NSW soared.[73]

Autonomy has a unique way of bringing out our best sides. When we feel in charge of an outcome, we are willing to strive, to adapt, and to exhibit self-control. This is something healthcare professionals have known for decades. For instance, if a patient is given control over the dose administration of IV painkillers, they'll actually use far less of the drug than if the painkillers are provided by a nurse. Give someone agency and autonomy and they will invariably "step up to the plate." However, remove their control and they'll fight you at every point—even to their own willful detriment.[74]

Choice makes us feel in control

Bearing this tendency in mind, the importance of preserving autonomy by providing options is vital. When our options become limited, we feel that our freedom is under assault.

Put simply: **options = autonomy**, and **choice = control.**

Sheena Iyengar underscored this principle in her 2010 book *The Art of Choosing*. Iyengar highlights numerous studies with rats, monkeys, and pigeons that indicate that when given the choice between a direct or single-option path to rewards (food) and paths that had multiple options or branches to choose from, the instinctive preference was always for the multiple-branch path.

Iyengar suggests that it's much the same for humans. In one experiment conducted at a casino, players had the choice of a table with one roulette wheel and another with two. Almost without exception, people opted for the two-wheel table even though the wheels were identical and there was no real benefit in doing so.

Even when it is a perception rather than a reality, "we equate having choices with having control," says Iyengar. "Our instincts tell us that controlling the environment means an increase in the probability of survival. We need to feel that we're in control and that we have options. Interestingly, people won't necessarily choose the fastest way to get something done but instead will opt for the path that gives them the greatest sense of control."[75]

Yale researcher Zoe Chance recommends that simply requesting someone's permission before asking them a question can be a powerful way to foster a sense of autonomy. Furthermore, giving another party the freedom to choose whether they want to meet, jump on a phone call, or even just correspond via email can make all the difference. "This might seem a little odd," Chance acknowledges. "Of course, you're not granting them freedom of choice; they've got that already. You're just affirming the fundamental truth that they are already free."[76]

This is not to say that we give other individuals complete free-range. In fact, an abundance of options often has the effect of overwhelming and paralyzing people. Instead, preserving autonomy and dignity in the process of persuasion is about steering people's choices by offering a menu of options. Iyengar suggests the ideal number of choices is three or four at most.[77]

University of Pennsylvania Professor Jonah Berger explores this theme in his book *The Catalyst*. According to Berger, effective persuasion is about guiding the choices and decisions of another individual, and he uses the context of parenting to illustrate. "Let them choose how they get where you are hoping they'll go," Berger recommends. "You need to go to the doctor to get a shot; do you want it in the right or left arm? You need to get ready for bed; do you want to take a bath now or after you brush your teeth? Guided choices like these let children retain a sense of freedom and control while helping parents reach their desired outcomes. Smart bosses often do the same thing."[78]

If done well, this approach is incredibly effective. After all, if we try to convince someone to do something, they will immediately look for reasons why what you're suggesting is unfair, unreasonable, or a bad idea. However, when people are presented with a range of options that they can choose from, the tone of the interaction immediately shifts. "Rather than thinking about what is wrong with whatever was suggested, they think about which one is better," says Berger. "And because they've been participating, they're much more likely to go along with one of them in the end."[79]

As a curious aside, research indicates that one of the most persuasive options we can give someone is the choice to "do nothing."

Giving people an "out" almost guarantees they'll opt in

Beyond offering choice, the way we frame an appeal or request is also critical. One of the most effective techniques for doing this is to use these fifteen words after making a request: *"If you can't do it, I'll completely understand."* Then after a brief pause, you continue: *"If you can, I'd really appreciate it."*[80]

Of course, there are plenty of variations to this approach that use slightly more or fewer words than fifteen, but the principle remains the same. The reason this works is that it positions the request as one that preserves autonomy. The other person has the power to choose. It also highlights what the most helpful and generous choice could be (i.e., to commit or agree), which is a choice the other individual is more likely to make if they feel in control.

In this regard, Yale's Michael Pantalon offers a collection of phrases that will help affirm someone's autonomy and power to choose:

- Please don't feel obligated.
- It is your choice, not mine.
- It's completely your decision.
- You're free to do whatever you want.
- I can't make this choice for you—it's up to you.
- What you decide at this point is up to you.
- Right now, I'm not interested in my reasons but in your reasons.
- Even though others will have their own reactions, you're the only one who can make this decision.
- Only you can decide what you want to do. Of course, your choice will have consequences. But it's still your choice to make.
- I think it's a good idea, but that's just me.
- If it were completely up to me, here's what I'd like to see happen. But it's not up to me. This is your call.[81]

Indicative of how powerful an affirmation of autonomy like this can be, a review of forty-two psychology studies incorporating 22,000 people revealed that this approach doubled the chance of someone saying yes to a request or suggestion. Whether the invitation was to donate to a charity, participate in a survey, or adopt a new viewpoint, the research indicates that people feel most willing and able to change when they feel powerful and in control.[82]

As with anything, it's important that reinforcing autonomy is approached sincerely. If there is even the faintest hint of technique or strategy, people will start to dig their heels in and resist any attempts at changing their minds. This is one of the reasons why ideas we overhear being shared between other people have been demonstrated to be especially effective in influencing our own views.[83]

Throw away your sticks

An important element of encouraging autonomy has to do with the tone of what you are communicating. As we saw in the opening pages of Part II, although using negative emotions like fear, anger, and disgust are effective in getting people's attention, the impact can be short-lived or counterproductive.

Validating this point, a 2008 analysis examining various approaches to public influence over thirty years revealed that messages that were framed positively were significantly more persuasive and impactful in the long term.[84] The researchers behind this analysis, Daniel J. O'Keefe and Jakob D. Jensen, found that this is because negative or loss-framed messages can feel like we're being bullied or coerced.[85] This has enormous implications for many of the pressing issues of persuasion facing society currently—especially when it comes to climate change.

While many sustainability and conservation campaigns focus on the negative impacts of failing to act (disaster, destruction, economic cost), neuroscience research indicates that these approaches simply don't get results. In fact, rather than inspiring or motivating people to change, they often arouse resentment and resistance. In fact, the only time when negatively framed or fear-inducing messages will work is when the person you're looking to persuade is already anxious. In every other instance, a positive frame that focuses on benefits will always be much more effective in driving sustained change.[86]

Speaking to this theme, Australian behavioral scientist Sarah A. Glenister suggests, "Messages that focus on health, preparedness, ethics, and opportunity are less likely to trigger negative emotional responses. Reframe your message so that the information you provide will induce hope, not dread. This isn't sugar-coating, but reframing."[87]

While giving options, offering people an "out" and accentuating the positives are powerful ways to preserve autonomy. Another effective way to allow for a person's dignity in the process of persuasion is through co-creation.

Involvement drives commitment

If you've ever held on to a piece of IKEA furniture for longer than you really should have or needed to, you're not alone. In fact, Harvard business professor, Michael Norton, says this behavior is so common that he has devised a term to describe it: "The IKEA Effect." At the core of this psychological phenomenon is the fact that we tend to place a disproportionate value on things that we have had a hand in creating.

In an effort to examine how this dynamic functions, Norton recruited a group of individuals and offered to pay them $5 to take part in a research study. The first half of the group were told that the experiment required them to construct a plain black "Kassett" IKEA storage box. The other half were given an assembled storage box and were simply asked to inspect it for any faults.

At the end of the experiment, Norton asked participants in both groups two questions:

1. How much would you be prepared to pay for the storage box?
2. How much do you like the box on a scale of 1 (don't like it) to 7 (love it)?

The results spoke volumes. Those who had constructed the IKEA storage box themselves placed a higher value on it than those who had merely inspected the completed product ($0.78 vs $0.48). They also reported a much greater liking for it (3.8 rating versus 2.5).[88]

Buy-in makes a big difference

Robert Cialdini examined the dynamics of co-creation in his 2016 book *Pre-suasion*. He states that "If managers had been led to believe they'd had a large role in the development of the end product, they viewed it 50 percent more favorably." So, the principle is simple—if you want to get your leader on board with your idea, help him or her feel like they have been a key part of its development.

And the simplest way to do this? Ask for advice. As Cialdini observes, asking for the advice of our superiors helps them feel as though they are intrinsically involved in the idea or project and its success.[89]

This is an approach that can also work wonders if you're looking to get people on board with a cause or initiative. Rather than asking others to sign up to membership or commit to ongoing financial support, start out by asking for help in more simple and short-term ways. For instance, you might ask someone to sit in on a board meeting in order to offer their feedback and advice. Or you could request they join a volunteer committee for a defined period of time or assist with a small and specific project. More often than not, the very process of helping and contributing in even the smallest ways tends to result in people adopting a cause as their own.

The same principle applies to getting a customer onboard. "Companies struggle to get consumers to feel bonded with their brands," says Cialdini. The key is not to simply point out new features and benefits of a product or to even ask the customer for their opinion. Instead, "consumer input must be framed as advice to the company, not as opinions about or expectations for the company." Cialdini suggests that the very process of asking for advice causes people to link their identity to the individual or group they are giving advice to. It has the effect of making your problem someone else's problem.

This principle can have powerful implications for the fundraising and charity sector. When looking to get people on side, one of the most underused and effective tactics is to give potential donors ownership.

My colleague Adam Ferrier discovered the power of this in research he conducted with Australia's Deakin University on behalf of global aid charity Save the Children. The aim was to experiment with a number of different appeal tactics for attracting donations.

For the research, subjects were divided into four groups. The first group received a traditional charity appeal including facts and statistics highlighting the plight of the world's poorest children. The second group was exposed to an emotive message designed to inspire donations through exposure to images of smiling and happy kids along with a moving music track. The third group was asked to create an advertising campaign for the charity while the fourth group acted as a control and were simply asked to do unrelated puzzles.

When each of the four groups were asked to donate to the cause, the average donations were:

- Group 1—$2.39
- Group 2—$3.69
- Group 3—$4.03
- Group 4—$2.58

Looking at this data, the first significant and perhaps surprising revelation was that being exposed to a traditional charity appeal actually yielded poorer results than no appeal at all. As we have seen previously, this is likely because the facts and statistics activated people's Inquiring Mind and got in the way of their emotional engagement.

The more important finding, however, was that by engaging people as partners or co-creators in the cause, they became more willing to personally contribute. The very act of co-creation fostered a sense of ownership and fed people's healthy sense of pride.[90] And better yet, they felt they had a high degree of control over not just the process but the outcome—an autonomy-affirming masterstroke if ever there was one.

■ ■ ■

Agency and autonomy are essential to preserving dignity. Even if what is being asked of us is something we want to do, or is in our own interest, we will naturally resist being told to do it. Our tendency is to dig in our heels if we don't feel in control of our own destiny. Whether through offering people choice, giving them an out, appealing to hope and aspiration, or involving them through co-creation, the more autonomy we can give others, the more open-minded they will be.

PERSUASION TOOL #9 PRO TIPS

1. There is no commitment without choice. Someone's yes means nothing if they didn't have the option to say no. Always make sure the other person feels empowered before you implore them to consider changing.

2. Remember that options = autonomy, and choice = control. One way to ensure people feel they have choices and options is to seek their permission at the beginning of any engagement or communication.

3. One of the most persuasive options we can give anyone is the choice to "do nothing." Giving people an "out" almost guarantees they'll opt in. Let others know they mustn't in any way feel obligated to act on your ideas or suggestions.

4. After making a request, try using these fifteen words: *"If you can't do it, I'll completely understand."* Then after a brief pause, continue by saying: *"If you can, I'd really appreciate it."* Naturally, if you say this, you need to mean it.

5. Negatively-framed messages can make people feel like they are being bullied or coerced. As such, it's smart to communicate your perspective or argument in a way that induces hope, not dread.

6. People feel committed to something they helped create. Involve others in the process of change by asking for their advice, input or contribution, and they'll feel like they were in the driver's seat.

CLOSING REFLECTIONS
ON DIGNITY

Aesop's famed fable *The North Wind and the Sun* teaches us a valuable lesson when it comes to changing minds.

If you recall, the sun and the wind were arguing one day about which of them was the most powerful. In order to settle the dispute, each challenged the other to try and make a passing traveler remove his coat. The North Wind blew with all his might, but the traveler only wrapped his coat tighter. The sun however, merely shone gently on the passing traveler until he willingly took off his coat.

The moral to the story? Coercion rarely works as well as self-driven motivation.

Coaxing others to change is never effective in the long term. The secret to meaningful persuasion lies in getting an individual to commit to changing for reasons that make sense to them. Savvy persuaders always recognize that the key to changing people is to ensure that they feel like they're in control.

By its very nature, our dignity is concerned with self. As such, any attempts to persuade others must start and end with the person we are looking to persuade. It is not about the strength of our ideas, the clarity of our conviction, or the reliability of our facts. Instead, what counts is that the other person feels safe, seen, and heard.

As political strategist Frank Luntz describes, the critical task in persuasion is "to look at the world from your listener's point of view. What matters isn't what you say, it's what people hear."[91] And people are more likely to be able to hear what we say if we take their dignity into account by allaying their fears, asking sensitive and strategic questions, and allowing for autonomy.

CHAPTER 6
CONFORMITY

In 1895, a Frenchman named Gustave Le Bon released a book that would fundamentally redefine our understanding of human nature. Simply titled *The Crowd*, Le Bon's book was a ground-breaking examination of how the collective thinking of a crowd differs from the thinking of the individuals that make it up.

More than simply highlighting how crowds function, Le Bon's work was critical in revealing why they behave the way they do. "Perfectly reasonable individuals become something else when gathered together," observed Le Bon. Further still, when an individual gets swept up in a crowd, their thinking "descends several rungs in the ladder" and the crowd takes on a mind that is unwieldy. He described the crowd mind as impulsive, irritable, and incapable of logic or sound reason. Crowds as a collective are emotionally driven, reactive, and prone to destructive impulses—something akin to a collective Instinctive Mind.[1]

Research by English social psychologist Wilfred Trotter built on Le Bon's work with Trotter coining the term "herd instinct" to describe the dynamic that occurs when groups of individuals develop a shared identity.[2]

Monkey see, monkey do

While crowd dynamics have an impact on our beliefs, opinions, and perceptions, they also influence us in more mundane and bizarre ways. One study by researchers at Cornell is a case in point.

The setup for the study involved a woman who had just walked into an optometrist's waiting room. The unsuspecting patient took a seat, picked up a magazine, and began flipping through the pages. Although she didn't know it, this woman had just walked into an experiment and the other individuals in the room were actors.

Out of nowhere, there was an audible beeping sound. Everyone in the room immediately stood to their feet for a moment and then resumed their places sitting down. This happened once more, and again, until after the third beep and standing up cycle, the bemused woman joined her compatriots in standing to her feet when the alert sounded. In the coming minutes, each of the other waiting "patients" were called in to their appointments. All the while, the beeping and standing routine continued.

Eventually, the woman was left alone in the waiting room and, amazingly, continued to stand each time the beep occurred. Gradually, new patients entered the waiting room—genuine patients and not actors—and they in turn slowly began complying with the standing routine every time the beep sounded. When one of the new entrants inquired as to why they were standing up, the woman responded, "everyone else was doing it so I thought I was supposed to."[3]

The brain science of belonging

While the compulsion to conform has been studied anecdotally for decades, it's only recently that brain scans have revealed how it functions in practice. This has seen psychologists revising some long-held assumptions.

As we explored in chapter 1, it's been long understood that the amygdala is directly involved in identifying threats and danger. However, we now know that this powerful element of our Instinctive Mind also plays an important role in the development of social connections.

When we receive "social cues" of belonging and acceptance, our amygdala fires up in a very different way than it does when we sense physical danger or threat. According to New York University social neuroscientist Jay Van Bavel, "The moment you're part of a group, the amygdala tunes in to who's in that group and starts intensely tracking them." Van Bavel suggests this immediately begins to change our behavior. "(These people) were strangers before, but they're on your team now, and that changes the whole dynamic. It's such a powerful switch—it's a big top-down change, a total reconfiguration of the entire motivational and decision-making system."[4] The tribal impulses of our Instinctive Mind are strong indeed.

As Daniel Coyle describes in his book *The Culture Code*, our brains are wired to seek out and preserve a sense of belonging at all costs. When we sense we are accepted, our brains draw the conclusion "We are close, we are safe, we share a future."[5]

Speaking to this same theme, psychologist Albert Bandura suggests that when faced with decisions about what to do and how to think in any given situation, the compulsion to conform causes us unconsciously to ask ourselves questions like: *How will I look if I undertake this behavior? What are the social norms around this behavior?*

Furthermore, Bandura suggests that social pressure is one of the most powerful motivators of human behavior—more so even than intrinsic motivation or external incentives.

The reasons we reuse

If you're anything like me and spend a good amount of any given month or year in a hotel room, you'd be familiar with the signs and laminated cards placed conspicuously in hotel bathrooms. Some of these describe the hotel's commitment to the environment and implore you to partner with them in reducing water and soap consumption. Others are perhaps a little more mercenary—offering a discount at the restaurant or a free drink at the bar for guests who hang up their towels to use again.

I've often wondered how effective these various strategies and approaches are. How many people actually reuse their towels—and which conservation messaging works best? A few years ago, I discovered that I am not the only one to be curious about this. In fact, a considerable amount of research has been done over the past decade examining which approaches work, and which ones don't. The findings of these studies are incredibly significant for our understanding of the role of conformity in persuading mindstuck people.

While the wording of a hotel conservation sign matters, it does so in ways that might surprise you. For instance, one team of researchers examined two different conservation approaches:

a. *Help save the environment—please reuse your towel.*

b. *Join your fellow guests in helping to save the environment—please reuse your towel. 75% of our guests do.*

As you might have guessed, people were more likely to comply with the second request than the first—37 percent and 44 percent respectively. When examining why this was the case, it became immediately apparent that the instinct to conform was at play. We are wired to make decisions based on what other people seem to be doing—especially if we deem those other people to be similar to us. This is often a deeply unconscious process and one we'd never imagine ourselves unthinkingly falling prey to. We all like to think we're individuals, after all.[6]

Intrigued by this dynamic and wondering how far its influence extended, the researchers then took it one step further. They tested a third variant:

c. *Join your fellow guests in helping to save the environment—please reuse your towel. 75% of the guests who stayed in this room do.*

When the message was personalized to people who stayed in the very same room as the guest reading the card, amazingly the compliance rate jumped to 49 percent.[7] It's nothing short of extraordinary that 33 percent more guests were persuaded to change their behavior if the request was both socialized (other people are doing it) and personalized (other people like *you* are doing it).

And herein lies an important point. While our tribal instincts can sometimes manifest in negative ways, they can also be a catalyst for positive change too. In the coming pages, we'll explore three tools for doing just this.

PERSUASION TOOL #10
DEFER TO THE POWER OF "THEY"

When I first moved to Sydney from regional Australia after graduating university, I remember just how steep the learning curve was. From working out the best way to commute to work on the traffic-crammed roads, to getting my head around the rivalries in different regions of the city, it was all a big adjustment. But one of the things I needed to figure out was which news network to watch in the evening. In my hometown, we had local stations with familiar faces sitting behind the news desk. In Sydney, the channels and faces were different.

One day sitting in choked traffic on Sydney's M4 motorway, I looked up and saw a massive billboard stretched across the six-lane road simply saying, "Thanks for making the switch to Channel 7 Nightly News." And that was all. No data on viewership increases. No attempt to back up the claim that people were in fact making the switch. Just the bold statement.

When I arrived home that evening and reached for the remote control to turn on the news, you can probably guess which channel I tuned into: Channel 7. After all, everyone else in my new home city seemed to be doing so, and I figured I should too. Amazingly, all these years on, it is still my go-to news broadcast in the evening. That was one highly effective billboard!

The subtle power of social proof

When it comes to using conformity to persuade people, the first and most important key is to create social proof. The perception that the mythical "they" are buying a certain product, supporting a certain political party, or watching a certain news channel is extraordinarily powerful. Of course, "they" tends to be little more than a perceived critical mass of people who we deem to be much like we are.

Sometimes we are influenced by the choices of others because we assume "they" have information we don't. This is especially true when we are unsure or unclear of what to do or think. This is why we will always gravitate toward a crowded café or restaurant if we're visiting an unfamiliar town or suburb. If it's busy, there's probably a reason for that. If lots of other people like it, we probably will too, we assume.[8]

It's for this reason that product manufacturers will advertise a chocolate or beer or mattress as the "world's favorite" or "#1 consumer choice" and why Colgate repeatedly tells us that "nine out of ten dentists" recommend their toothpaste.[9] If we're told that everyone else is already acting in a certain way, we invariably follow suit. It's no wonder that McDonald's spent many years boasting "Billion and Billions Served" on their billboards.[10]

This can be a powerful persuasive force when trying to change people's attitudes and actions. For instance, we are more likely to leave tips at a restaurant if a tip jar seems full—and more likely to give larger denomination tips if that tip jar is jammed with notes rather than coins.[11] Similarly, research shows that when restaurants add the label "most popular" to a few of their dishes, demand for these dishes immediately increases by 13-20 percent.[12]

Politicians know this all too well. It's a powerful tool indeed to create the sense that everyone else is on board with a certain agenda or political party. These sorts of tactics often become self-fulfilling prophecies.[13] This is one of the reasons political candidates are careful to position their most ardent and passionate supporters directly behind them and in sight at political rallies. The smiles, nods, and applause of these supporters has more of an influence on viewers than most of us realize.

The power of this dynamic has not gone unnoticed as a business opportunity too. One company called Crowds on Demand, for instance, provides "devotees for hire" for campaign rallies, protests, and corporate marketing events. According to the company's website, the illusion of support they can create works wonders: "A foreign government used Crowds on Demand to help generate a positive reception for its newly elected leader during the UN General Assembly... The crowds that we deployed drew in more supporters creating a strong presence for this leader at the UN and an improved perception of him by the American public," the company boasts.[14]

Why everyone started using designated drivers

In a compelling example of the power of social proof to drive positive change, consider the origins of the "designated driver" concept. We are so accustomed these days to this idea that it'd be easy to assume that it has always simply been "a thing." Yet the very term and notion of designated driver is a relatively recent invention.

Having seen the concept work in Scandinavian countries, Harvard public health professor Jay Winsten decided to set a goal in the late 1980s of making designated drivers a social norm in America too. Recognizing the principle in advertising that repeated exposure to an idea or concept was the key to shifting public perception, Winsten teamed up writers and producers of over 160 television programs that were airing in prime time. Winsten's request was for these programs to subtly weave references to the "designated driver" concept into plot lines on hit shows at the time ranging from *Cheers* to *the Cosby Show* and *L.A Law*.

According to Grant Tinker who was the vice president of NBC at the time, "Jay's crusade was one that we could do something about fairly easily, unlike a lot of other worthwhile causes." Whether it was designated driver posters on the wall of the *Cheers* bar, or Harry Hamlin's character asking a bartender to call his designated driver in an episode of *L.A Law*, gradually the message that this was "something everyone is doing" began to sink in.

Within three years, the success of the campaign became very clear. By late 1991, nine out of ten American adults were familiar with the concept and ter-minology of "designated driver" and their behavior was beginning to change. Thirty-seven percent of people said they had been a designated driver at some point themselves, and 54 percent had relied on one to get home after a big night out.

More importantly, lives were being saved. Between 1988 and 1992, the number of alcohol-related road deaths had declined by 28 percent.[15]

What's everyone looking at?

Numerous studies over the years have examined the degree to which our behavior and choices can be influenced by what everyone else seems to be doing. One notable experiment conducted in the late 1960s involved planting a random individual on a busy New York sidewalk staring up at the sky for sixty seconds. When it was just the sole sky gazer, passers-by barely noticed his existence. However, when the researchers placed a group of five people on the same busy sidewalk looking heavenwards, the number of people who stopped to look up quadrupled.[16]

When the researchers increased the group of sky gazers to fifteen people, a full 45 percent of pedestrians stopped in curiosity to look up. By increasing the numbers of the experiment further, the researchers unconsciously convinced a full 80 percent of passers-by to stop and look up.[17]

Tax officials in Minnesota discovered a similar principle when trying to persuade residents to lodge returns and pay their tax on time. To see what would work best in motivating compliance amounts taxpayers, four different messages were given:

1. Please pay your taxes—they contribute to important local services including education, policing, and fire protection.
2. Failure to pay taxes will result in significant fines and other consequences.
3. If you need help or are confused about certain tax requirements, please reach out for help.
4. Ninety percent of your fellow Minnesotans already complied, in full, with their obligations under the tax law.

As you can probably guess, the data was unequivocal. The fourth approach resulted in significantly higher rates of tax compliance than the other three messages combined.[18]

Focus on what you want to foster

Illustrating the power of highlighting the positive choices of others, consider the experience of New York's Metropolitan Transportation Authority a few years ago. Facing rising costs from fare evasion, the MTA examined options for addressing the problem.

The traditional approach of threatening fare evaders with hefty fines or prosecution wasn't working. Despite flooding the network with hundreds of enforcement officers and police, fare evasion on buses barely budged (merely dropping from 24 percent to 22 percent), while it actually rose from 3.9 percent to 4.7 percent among subway users. With fare evasion losses exceeding $300 million per year, a new approach was required—and fast.

New York MTA officials looked abroad to see what other cities had found successful. In examining strategies for addressing evasion in cities like Melbourne and Dublin, it appeared the emphasis of the MTA's punitive campaigns was part of the problem.

Steve Martin, a visiting professor of behavioral science at Columbia Business School, had worked on programs to address the issue in numerous cities worldwide. Martin suggested that the key was to emphasize the good choices a majority were making—rather than focus on those that were breaking the law. "Ninety-five percent of people in New York are honest, and the MTA is missing a massive trend by not leveraging that," he said. According to Martin, whatever you emphasize in communication creates social proof and therefore drives more of that very result. By focusing ad campaigns on people not paying fares, the public had started to believe that fare evasion was more widespread than was actually the case. Because of this, evasion increased due to the notion that "If everyone else is doing it, it's probably OK for me to do it as well."

When Australian transport officials had taken on board Martin's suggestion to emphasize positive social proof, fare evasion in the city of Melbourne dropped from 9.5 percent to 7.5 percent.

Graham Currie, a professor of public transport at Monash University in Melbourne, suggests it's important to understand the psychology of fare evaders when looking to change their behavior. Repeat-offending fare evasion generally isn't a crime of poverty, according to Currie's research. Instead, fare evaders are from every part of society and are motivated by a love of risk-taking or an ideological opposition to paying for transportation. Either way, the best way to persuade fare evaders is to leave them in little doubt that "people like them" pay their fares. A positive approach is far more likely to change behavior and attitudes than a punitive one.[19]

What this means is that if you were trying to stop theft, problem drinking, graffiti, or any other undesirable public behavior, you'd be better placed to emphasize the good choices that a majority make rather than identifying and emphasizing the behavior you're looking to stop. Examining this principle in his book *Methods of Persuasion*, Nick Kolenda offers the example of discouraging alcohol abuse on college campuses. Rather than posting signs saying "Recent polls suggest that an alarming number of students on this campus abuse alcohol. Please drink safely," a far more effective sign would read "Recent polls suggest that most students on this campus use caution when drinking. Please continue to drink safely."[20]

The magnetic middle

While social proof can be a powerful tool for persuading people to cease undesirable behavior, it is equally effective in influencing individuals to make positive choices from the outset.

Consider the study conducted by social psychologist Wes Schultz of California State University. Schultz and his team set out to examine ways to persuade homeowners in California to reduce their power consumption. At the outset of the study, the research team conducted meter readings at the beginning and end of a week for 300 participating homes in order to get a baseline of household energy consumption. At the conclusion of the week, each home received a "score card" giving them a rating for how their energy consumption compared with the neighborhood average.

This score card information alone motivated households that had been consuming more energy than average to reduce their consumption by 5.7 percent. Significantly and surprisingly, however, households that had been consuming less energy than average actually *increased* their consumption by 8.6 percent on average—another example of how counterproductive negative social proof can be.

The researchers described these initial results as evidence of what is often referred to as the "magnetic middle." This term describes the tendency for humans to adjust their behavior automatically and unconsciously to move toward the mean once they are aware of what the average is.

Keen to explore other ways to influence people to change their behavior— ideally without the unintended negative side effects—the research team decided to experiment with using emojis as a rating system. For households that used more energy than average, adding a "frowny face" to their score card resulted in a similar decrease in energy consumption from when numbers alone were used. However, for the households that were consuming less power than average, the addition of a "smiley face" to their scorecard caused their low energy use to remain the same.

This is significant. Whereas the affirming scorecard alone had seen low energy use households increase their consumption enormously, the inclusion of a smiley face neutralized this tendency.[21]

This dynamic is vital for leaders looking to use social proof to acknowledge positive behavior. As Goldstein, Martin, and Cialdini observe in their bestselling book *Yes: 60 Secrets from the Science of Persuasion*, rather than simply identifying that an individual or group is performing better than average, adding a clear sense of appreciation or gratitude for this behavior can make all the difference. As we saw in chapter 5, dignity and pride are powerful motivating factors for change. We all want to feel appreciated and will work hard to win the approval of our tribe.

Insights from an infomercial

Years ago, I released a book named *Memento* that took me way out of my comfort zone. Unlike my previous nonfiction business books, *Memento* was for a completely new market and required an entirely different approach. It was a gift-book journal featuring a series of questions designed to prompt parents to write down their life stories as a keepsake for their children. Ten months after signing a big publishing deal with Chronicle Books in San Francisco, my family and I packed up and headed to the U.S. for a PR tour leading up to the book's release.

While the media flurry took the predictable form of radio and print interviews, one appearance that popped into my PR calendar intrigued me. It was to record an infomercial on the Home Shopping Network. When the day of filming arrived, I caught a plane to Fort Lauderdale in Florida. At the airport, I was met by a driver who whisked me straight to the studios for hair and makeup. Little did I know how fascinating the experience would be.

To be honest, I have never paid much attention to infomercials and have always found them to be a bit ludicrous. I could never take seriously the toned and tanned models promising that you, too, could look like them if you just purchased the Ab Roller 4000 for five easy installments of $29.95 + postage. I had no doubt the infomercial strategy worked, but it always just seemed like such an odd and unsophisticated way to sell products.

And yet as I found myself on set watching the hosts craft the pitch for my book and record and then re-record the call to action with the in-ear coaching of the producer, I gained a newfound appreciation for the world of infomercials.

And when the phone lines opened, the sales flurry was unbelievable. Contrary to my prejudiced assumptions, the home shopping sector is in fact highly sophisticated and strategic.

Colleen Szot is legendary in the industry for her ability to write scripts for on-air campaigns that always hit the mark. One of her noteworthy contributions was the NordicTrack exercise machine campaign that broke a two-decade-old Home Shopping Network record. According to Szot, her success came down to seven simple words.

Instead of adopting the standard call to action "Operators are waiting, please call now," Szot changed the script to be "If operators are busy, please call again." At face value, this may seem like an insignificant difference and one that could even backfire. After all, wouldn't alluding to the fact that customers may face delays or inconvenience be a disincentive to them calling to order in the first place?

On the contrary, this wording created social proof. It indicated that everyone else was buying a product and that you'd be crazy not to do the same. But more than simply tapping into the tribal impulses we explored in chapter 2, this approach activated another powerful dynamic—that of scarcity.[22]

Scarcity sells

I remember seeing this principle in action when driving out of the airport precinct a few years ago in Auckland, New Zealand. As I was about to pull onto the freeway, I glanced up to see a billboard for a newly released Lexus SUV. Rather than touting the features, benefits, and selling points of the sleek new vehicle, the billboard simply stated, "You don't see them everywhere, and that's just the way we like it." With the sense of elitism and scarcity that this tagline evoked, there was nothing else that needed to be said.

We all know how this dynamic works in daily life. For instance, if you find yourself at the liquor store looking to buy a bottle of wine but don't recognize any of the labels on offer, you will invariably go for the wine that only has two bottles left on the shelf rather than the one with fifteen bottles piled up.[23] This dynamic speaks to the fact that we are motivated to not just do what others seem to be doing, but also to act fast, so we don't miss out.

■ ■ ■

Despite our assertions that we are individual thinkers and free agents, our Instinctive Minds tend to look to others when making decisions and arriving at judgments. As advertising strategist Mark Earls writes in his book *Herd: How to Change Mass Behavior by Harnessing our True Nature*, "We use other people's brains to navigate the world."[24]

It's powerful indeed to leverage the impact of social proof when guiding people's thinking and actions. Because we are impulsively wired to avoid missing out or being left out, once we know what "they" are doing, the decision regarding what "we" will do or think becomes a remarkably clear one.

PERSUASION TOOL #10 PRO TIPS

1. A clear sense of what others are thinking or doing has a powerful influence on us as individuals. As such, it helps to emphasize data and evidence that shows others are in support of your cause or argument—especially if it's clear that they are a "silent majority."

2. In the same way that demand for certain dishes increases if restaurants label them as being "most popular," always couch your ideas and messages as well-liked or widely accepted.

3. When using social proof to support your position, always make sure you focus on what you want to foster. Emphasize the positive choices that others are making rather than focusing on the behavior you're looking to stop.

4. Humans are not only naturally conformist, but we are also competitive. By using benchmarks, you can help people get a clear sense of where they sit relative to others. Rather than relying solely on numeric benchmarks, try using symbols, graphical indicators, or emojis.

5. Humans are powerfully influenced by FOMO—the Fear of Missing Out. Use scarcity and urgency to shape people's perceptions and decisions.

PERSUASION TOOL #11
HARNESS THE HERD INSTINCT

As we discussed at the beginning of this chapter, one of the most significant discoveries in psychology over the last century is how much our behavior differs when we are in a group as opposed to on our own.

Intuitively, we all know this to be true. After all, who hasn't gotten swept up in the exuberance of the crowd at a sports match or let their inhibitions slip on a packed dance floor with friends? However, it is not only our actions that change in group settings. What we believe and how we think are influenced by group dynamics too. But this is due to more than the conscious influence of social proof as we have seen in the previous pages. Something powerful happens when the dynamic of unconscious social pressure and the herd instinct also comes into play.

To this point, a recent study invited participants to specify what they thought the most important problem facing society was. There were five alternatives offered: economic recession, educational facilities, subversive activities, mental health, and crime and corruption. When surveyed individually, just 12 percent of people said "subversive activities" were the number one challenge. However, when people were informed that this had been the most common answer given among other individuals, 48 percent of respondents went with the perceived consensus vote.[25]

The prevalence of this, and the mechanism by which it happens, has been the focus of numerous studies. Perhaps the first and most earnest of these was conducted in the mid-1950s by one of the pioneers of social psychology, Solomon Asch.

In one of Asch's more famous experiments, he and his research team at Swarthmore College in Pennsylvania recruited groups of four individuals and sat them at a long table. The individuals were shown two cards: the first card featured a single straight vertical line and the second had three vertical lines printed on it—one of which was the same length as the line on the first card. The participants were then asked which of the three lines was the same length as the line on the first card.

This was not an exercise in optical illusion. The correct answer was clear to anyone with even relatively poor eyesight. The trick was that all but one of the participants sitting at the table were actors—a fact that the remaining fourth individual was not aware of. The actors were instructed to confidently give the incorrect answer to examine the influence this had on the only genuine participant.

Each time the experiment was conducted, the fourth participant conformed with the group belief 70 percent of the time and gave the wrong answer—even though it contradicted what they could plainly see with their own eyes.[26] (It's worth mentioning that the individuals in Asch's experiments were complete strangers so there was no relational or emotional reason to conform.)[27]

Crowd-sourced conviction

Even as you read these findings, you might be wondering how this could be the case. You might imagine yourself in Asch's research lab and suppose that when it came time for you to share which line on card B matched the line on card A, you'd not be swayed by group consensus. Based on decades of research, however, the odds are you probably would. Not because you're weak-willed or particularly impressionable, but because you are human. Richard Thaler and Cass Sunstein suggest in their book *Nudge*, "It is almost as if people can be nudged into identifying a picture of a dog as a cat as long as other people before them have done so."[28]

As one behavioral researcher puts it, Asch's experiment "demonstrated our willingness to go along with the crowd, even when we know the crowd is wrong. This curious quirk of human psychology can help explain everything from fads and fashion to street riots and membership of the Nazi party in 1930s Germany."[29]

Asch himself summed up the human bent toward conformity warning "we have found the tendency to conformity in our society is so strong that reasonably intelligent and well-meaning young people are willing to call white, black."[30]

Extrapolating the implications of Asch's experiment to the modern online world, we are all sitting in a much bigger "room" surrounded by a much bigger group of people influencing our views. Whether in mainstream media coverage or on social media, we can easily begin to think that the viewpoints that appear to be held by the majority must be correct. The online environment replicates Asch's experiment at scale and has become fertile ground for groupthink and conformist behavior to take root.

In a fascinating and significant twist, Asch did discover that the slightest glimmer of dissent within a group has enormous power to "break the spell" of conformity. In a series of follow-up experiments to the ones above, he asked one of the actors to actually give the correct answer. Just this single lone voice gave the genuine participant permission to break ranks and hold fast to what they knew to be true.[31]

The latent fear of being left behind

One of the reasons we so readily defer to the collective when making decisions is that we instinctively fear being left behind or stranded. If we sense that others are making certain choices or heading in a particular direction, we'll generally follow. Part of this is likely a hangover from our nomadic past as humans.[32]

This compulsion helps explain why we voluntarily comply with social norms. By mimicking and copying the behavior and customs of others, we help ensure the acceptance of our tribe. Breaking social norms or dissenting is dangerous as it can see us expelled from the group—or, at the very least, shamed and embarrassed.[33]

Reflecting on how this dynamic plays out in practice, Tim Urban in his book *What's Our Problem* suggests "Those who challenge the sacred ideas (of a tribe) are seen not just as wrong but as bad people. As such, violators are slapped with the social fines of status reduction or reputation damage, the social jail time of ostracism, and even the social death penalty of permanent excommunication."[34]

This dynamic was a key factor in China's one-child policy being so effective over so many years. While government laws were a strong deterrent to parents having more than one child, it was social factors that played an even bigger role. In speaking with colleagues and clients in China over the years, they shared that the people most likely to flout the law and have multiple children were the rural poor. Chinese culture being as it is, proud urban dwellers would do almost anything to avoid being associated with "unsophisticated" agricultural peasants. So, when having more than one child became a source of social pride or shame, government enforcement of the rules was scarcely necessary.

The compound effect of conformity

One of the most significant and persuasive features of the herd instinct is the way that momentum operates in a collective setting. Once an idea seems to have taken hold in a group, its popularity and acceptance increases exponentially.

Furthermore, majority beliefs can quickly become unanimous. For instance, research indicates that once a belief is held by 75 percent of the members of a group, a further 15 percent will be automatically influenced to adopt the same belief without any process of critical evaluation. This means that there's no need to persuade 100 percent of people about an idea or perspective—a 75 percent majority is more than enough.

Importantly, the reverse is also true, if momentum begins working against your message or view, as soon as less than 75 percent of the group are on board, the compulsion to conform starts working against you.[35] This can mean that when a point of view, idea, or news story gains enough traction with enough people, it begins to take on a life of its own. Even if facts or details arise that contradict the established narrative or view, if the momentum is strong enough, new evidence is unlikely to get a fair hearing or make any impact at all.

Reflecting on this, Mark Roeder writes in his book *The Big Mo*, "This is why so many news stories, particularly the big ones, seem to have a predetermined air about them. Rarely are we surprised by a sudden turn of events. Once a storyline becomes established in the public mind, even if it is false, it becomes difficult to dislodge. Politicians know that if they can create enough momentum for their cause, keep feeding it, and stay 'on message,' it will soon become a self-perpetuating force that is difficult for their opponents to stop."[36] Once the herd has latched onto an idea and started moving in a certain direction, very little can stand in its way.

Timing is everything

This herd-like nature of large-scale change offers insights into how public opinion can shift—and often quite quickly. As a result, there is something to be said for working with existing momentum around an issue. In other words, rather than trying to create a wave, help people jump onto one that's already in motion.

Any surfer knows that riding a wave is all about timing—and it's much the same with the waves of change. Timing really is everything in determining whether new ideas or behaviors gain widespread traction or not.

The ancient rhetoricians of Athens called this "Kairos," or the art of seizing the perfect instant for persuasion. In his book *Thank You for Arguing,* Jay Heinrichs suggests that Kairos is all about recognizing when an individual or group is most likely to be open to your perspective and then making the most of this "persuasive moment."[37] Heinrichs maintains that one of the modern masters of Kairos was Martin Luther King Jr. When he was imprisoned, King knew instinctively that a large proportion of white Americans were ready to consider a black man in prison as a martyr—something they may not have done just a few years earlier.[38]

Beyond identifying when the herd may be on the move and capitalizing on that momentum, meaningful persuasion is also about tapping into people's inherent sense of responsibility to the collective.

Living up to our responsibilities

The word "Switzerland" likely conjures up images of lush green pastures, majestic snow-laden peaks, clear running streams, and quaint log cabins. What probably doesn't come to mind is nuclear waste. But perhaps it should.

Decades ago, the Swiss made a decisive move toward nuclear power and now 40 percent of the country runs on it. All of that electricity generation may have worked beautifully for the environment, but it has created a lot of waste over the years. In 1993, the Swiss government began searching in earnest for a solution to their waste problem. In the end, they identified two towns that made logical sense as waste depositories. The biggest hurdle, however, was to first persuade the local residents to get on board with the plan.

Unsure of how the townspeople would react, Swiss officials engaged researchers from the University of Zurich to survey residents. The researchers gathered a sample group of locals together in a Town Hall meeting and asked them outright: "Suppose that the National Cooperative for the Storage of Radioactive Waste (NAGRA), after completing exploratory drilling, proposed to build the repository for low- and mid-level radioactive waste in your hometown. How likely would you be to accept the proposal?"

Understandably, many residents felt nervous about the idea but, nevertheless, more than half of them (50.8 percent) supported the plan. The researchers supposed that this was likely a function of national pride and a commitment to the common good—the notion that the towns would have to "take one for the team." For government officials, this was an incredibly positive sign but the challenge remained of how to win over the remaining 49.2 percent of residents.

In an attempt to discover what might garner additional support, the researchers gathered a different group of residents together and shared the same proposal. However, the key difference was that residents were informed that they would be paid 5,000 Swiss francs per person each year as compensation for their town being a waste repository.

On a purely economic basis alone, this approach seemed a sure bet in winning over a greater proportion of the residents than in the first group—or so the researchers presumed. It was baffling then, when votes were cast, to discover that just 24.5 percent of people were in favor—roughly half of the number who were willing to accept it with no compensation. Curiously, when the researchers doubled the financial incentive, the acceptance rates didn't budge at all. Counterintuitively, the financial compensation was seen as a disincentive.[39]

This flies in the face of common sense and common practice. Most of us operate under the assumption that if we want to motivate someone into doing something unpleasant, the best approach is to offer them some form of compensation. However, a growing body of research suggests that incentives are not only less motivating than social responsibility but that they can even be counterproductive.

Incentives and Altruism: We must choose

According to researchers at the US National Institutes of Health (NIH), this is a function of the different parts of the brain that incentives and social responsibility stimulate.

Brain function scans conducted by the NIH have found that traditional rewards like cash payments stimulate a brain region called the Nucleus Accumbens. This part of our brains is often referred to as the pleasure center and is responsible for the release of the powerful reward hormone dopamine. In effect, being offered a cash incentive creates feelings of contentment, exuberance, and ecstasy—a process not unlike what occurs when someone takes a dose of cocaine.

In contrast, when asked to help, contribute, or to feel generally responsible to and for others, it is the Posterior Superior Temporal Sulcus that lights up. This is the part of the brain that is responsible for social interactions and powerfully influences the way we form human connections, relationships, and perceptions of others. It is highly sensitive to altruism and the social cues of being connected to our tribe.[40]

Here's the trick. Unlike other parts of our brain that can function simultaneously (such as the parts that control speech and movement) the "social" and "reward" parts of our brain cannot both function at the same time. One or the other takes over control of our thinking and decision-making.

Reflecting on the implications of these findings in the Swiss nuclear waste experience, organizational culture expert Ori Brafman suggests: "In the first half of the study when no money was offered, the altruism center took charge, as people weighed the danger of having a nuclear dump nearby against the opportunity to help their country. The moment money was introduced, on the other hand, the entire situation was processed differently. The pleasure center took over, and in people's minds the choice came down to the dangers of the dump on one side and making a 'quick franc' on the other. But the 5,000-franc stipend was much too low to excite the pleasure center."[41]

Brafman goes on to liken the two parts of our brain to two engines that cannot operate simultaneously. In any situation, we will inevitably approach a decision from either an altruistic or self-interested perspective.

Wired to be helpful

Exploring the implications of this dynamic, Dan Ariely in his bestselling book *Predictably Irrational* offers a powerful example of how counterproductive it can be to confuse altruism with self-interest motivators. Ariely points to a day care center that was trying to address the issue of parents arriving late to pick up their children. In an effort to motivate punctuality, the day care center instigated a fine for late pickups only to find that this resulted in *more* parents turning up late. In fact, the number almost doubled.[42]

In examining why this was the case, Ariely suggests that before the fine was implemented, there was an unconscious social pressure for parents to arrive on time. They knew that failing to do so would mean their child's teacher would have to stay back, so being late was something parents felt guilty about. Running late might still happen from time to time due to prevailing circumstances, but altruism and empathy meant that parents tried to be on time whenever they could.

However, once the fine was imposed, the decision to be on time or not became an economic one. Whether or not parents arrived late became a cost-benefit analysis. The parents were in effect paying for their lateness and so if the cost of the fine was lower than the benefit of being able to squeeze more into their afternoon, lateness seemed like a reasonable choice—and more people made that very choice.

A few weeks later, the day care center realized their mistake and decided to remove the fine. As Ariely writes, this is where the story got interesting. "Now the center was back to the social norm. Would the parents also return to the social norm? Would their guilt return as well? Not at all. Once the fine was removed, the behavior of the parents didn't change. They continued to pick up their kids late. In fact, when the fine was removed, there was a slight increase in the number of tardy pickups (after all, both the social norms and the fine had been removed)."[43] Reflecting on the implications of this, Ariely suggests that once altruistic motivators are replaced by self-interest, it's hard to go back.[44]

Looking at a very different application of this principle, a few years ago two Swedish researchers set out to examine the impact of reward-based incentives on people's willingness to donate blood. The duo visited a blood donation center in Gothenburg and enlisted a group of women who were interested in donating.

Having agreed to be part of the study, these women were broken into three groups. The first cohort were thanked for considering the option of being blood donors but told they wouldn't be financially compensated for doing so. Those in the second group were offered a cash payment of 50 Swedish kronor (about

$7 USD) for making a blood donation, while the third group were informed that the 50 Swedish kronor payment could be contributed to a children's cancer charity if they chose to donate their blood.

As you could probably guess by this point, 52 percent of women in the first group agreed to go ahead and become blood donors. In contrast, only 30 percent of those in the second group did the same. Significantly, the highest donation rate was amongst those in the third group where 53 percent agreed to give their blood. As Dan Pink suggests in his book *Drive*, the financial incentive offered "tainted an altruistic act and 'crowded out' the intrinsic desire to do something good."[45]

The bottom line is this: When herd-related social norms become confused with economic motivators, things get messy very quickly.

Obligated by honor

Importantly, our sense of responsibility to the collective is not only driven by altruism but also our sense of honor.

This was something researchers at the Pentagon discovered a number of years ago when trying to persuade service members and their families to be inoculated with the MILVAX immunization for smallpox. The Pentagon feared that rogue states or terrorists may use the disease as a biological weapon and so it was believed that the MILVAX injection was a matter of national security.

Despite the logic of the request, service members were resisting it strongly. This was not because of some sort of anti-vaccination sentiment but rather because the injection resulted in a permanent scar just above the tricep. For many of the male soldiers, the resistance was that this was prime tattoo territory, while many servicewomen worried what they'd look like when wearing sleeveless dresses. Although those in charge could have simply ordered the vaccinations to occur, they decided to investigate ways to persuade soldiers to accept it willingly.

They turned to persuasion expert Jay Heinrichs to explore the approach that would work best. After extensive interviews and research, Heinrichs advised that the best strategy would be to not shy away from the issue of scarring but rather turn the scar into a symbol of honor. During one focus group, the attendees acknowledged that military scars are generally seen as symbols of strength, courage, and sacrifice. They are noble wounds and, almost literally, "badges of honor" as one serviceman described it in the discussion.

This epiphany led to a social media campaign where service members were encouraged to post videos of themselves flexing their arms and displaying their scars while saying who their scar was for. Some said their scar was for "For my country." Others said it was for their kids, or their dog, and the list went on. Almost overnight, the general feeling in the US military regarding the MILVAX immunization changed. No longer was the scar something that was a symbol of loss or cost but rather a symbol of honor and pride.[46]

The eyes have it

While altruism and honor are powerful motivators of human behavior, our herd instincts are not merely about doing socially acceptable things but also being seen to be doing so. Amazingly, even if our behavior is not being watched by our peers, the subtle hint that we are being watched will persuade us to do the socially responsible thing. Indicative of this, multiple studies have found that the mere presence of eyes motivates us to behave differently—even if they are nothing more than in a photo.

Researchers discovered this when looking to persuade university students to stop littering in a college cafeteria. In two separate experiments, the research team placed a picture of some flowers on the cafeteria wall and then replaced this image with a poster that featured eyes. When this second poster was displayed, the mere presence of an image with eyes halved littering rates immediately. Interestingly, subsequent experiments examined the impact of the "eyes image" and found that its effectiveness increased if there were more people in the cafeteria.[47]

To examine whether this same dynamic occurred when trying to coax people to *do* something (rather than stop doing some, as in the case of littering), three researchers named Bateson, Nettle & Roberts placed similar images on the wall next to an honesty box where people paid for their coffee and tea at an office kitchen at Newcastle University in the UK. When comparing the impact of the flowers image as opposed to the eyes image, the presence of eyes on the wall near the honesty box resulted in contributions that were three times larger. This was tested numerous times over many weeks to ensure that other causal factors could be reliably ruled out.[48]

These findings correlate with a study conducted by researchers at the University of Virginia who displayed a set of eyes above a donation box at a children's museum. In this instance, the presence of the eyes increased visitor donations by a staggering 80 percent—something the researchers dubbed "the watching eyes effect." Reflecting on why this works so effectively, University of Virginia psychology professor Amrisha Vaish suggests that it is all about our sense of responsibility to the herd. Put simply, we are wired to be helpful, generous, and honorable and also be perceived by others to be so.

Beyond appealing to people's sense of social responsibility, another powerful tool for harnessing the herd instinct when inspiring change is that of synchronicity.

Groups that act alike, think alike

There is something uniquely persuasive about acting in unison with others. Numerous studies have shown that by synchronizing our actions or behavior in a group setting, we begin to see ourselves as being more similar to those we are in unison with. More significantly, we begin to evaluate the individuals in our synchronous group more positively too.

To this point, there is abundant evidence that music and singing are uniquely powerful agents of influence. Persuasion expert Robert Cialdini suggests that there is a good reason that music is an ever-present feature of human civilization from the beginning of recorded history. With its unique combination of rhythm, meter, intensity and tone, music "possesses rare synchronizing power."

As evidence of this, consider one particular study in Germany featuring four-year-old children. One group of the children were instructed to walk around in circles with a partner while stepping in time with the music and singing. The second group of children walked around the circle in pairs but without any accompanying music.

After a period of time, the children were asked to do something specifically helpful for their partner. This helpfulness would require the child to sacrifice playtime—no small ask for self-absorbed four-year-olds. Interestingly, students who had been in the group that walked around to the sound of music were three times more likely to help their partner than those that walked in silence.

Reflecting on the significance of this study's findings, Cialdini observes that "the children's personal sacrifice didn't arise from any rational weighting of the reasons for and against providing assistance. The help wasn't rooted in rationality at all. It was spontaneous, intuitive, and based on an emotional sense of connection that naturally accompanies shared musical engagement."[49] The synchronicity that comes through music seems to somehow activate our Instinctive Mind and is therefore immensely powerful from a persuasion perspective.

This can make us dangerously gullible and prone to poor thinking when under the influence of music—especially when it synchronizes our behavior with the herd. Speaking to this theme, Voltaire once famously suggested "Anything too stupid to be spoken is sung." The old advertising industry adage puts it in a similar way: "If you can't make your case to an audience with facts, sing it to them."[50]

In an effort to understand the persuasive power of synchronous behavior in adults, Scott Wiltermuth and Chip Heath conducted a series of experiments involving people engaging in various synchronous activities. Some people walked in step while others engaged in activities as diverse as dance, yoga clapping, and group singing.

The most striking finding of Wiltermuth and Heath's research was the connection between synchronicity and cooperation. The findings were unequivocal: people who engaged in synchronous behavior were always more cooperative afterwards than those who merely gathered in a group setting as a collection of individuals. Significantly, they found that this was the case even when people didn't have a particular affinity for others in the group. And it doesn't need to involve singing, marching, or clapping in time, even laughing together as a group seems to do the trick.[51]

■ ■ ■

The herd instinct is powerful indeed in shaping our behaviors, attitudes, and opinions. We are wired to comply with those around us and this can be an effective way to shift the thinking of individuals and groups if it is harnessed well. Better yet, our compulsion toward social approval means appeals to responsibility, honor, and altruism can motivate change in ways that self-interest simply cannot.

PERSUASION TOOL #11 PRO TIPS

1. When it comes to changing individuals or groups, do everything you can to get momentum working on your side. The good news is that you don't need to get everyone across the line with a new idea or perspective. If you can win over 75 percent, the herd instinct will take care of the rest.

2. Timing is everything when it comes to making the most of group dynamics. Read the room and choose your moment carefully. Even better, identify where there is already movement in a helpful direction and jump on that wave.

3. The herd instinct means people will do things for the collective that they won't do for themselves. While traditional incentives can motivate change, it can be smarter to appeal to people's sense of altruism and obligation to their tribe. But remember, social and reward parts of the brain don't work well in tandem. Beware the trap of appealing to altruism and self-interest at the same time as this will invariably backfire.

4. The desire to be and be perceived as honorable can be powerful indeed. Try framing any change agenda in terms of a responsibility to the collective good and the values it prioritizes.

5. Groups that act alike think alike. By encouraging people to engage in synchronous actions and experiences, they are more likely to feel connected to and influenced by the herd. This can be as simple as having people moving, clapping, or laughing in unison.

PERSUASION TOOL #12
RELY ON RECIPROCITY

The notion that one good turn deserves another is drilled into us from a young age—but it need not be. Whether or not we're told that we ought to reciprocate the kindness or efforts of another, this is something we appear to do instinctively as humans. According to research by sociologist Alvin Gouldner, there isn't an observed human society where reciprocity doesn't govern social norms.

Archaeologist Richard Leakey agrees, observing that human society would not have developed without the dynamic of mutual obligation. "We are human because our ancestors learned to share their food and their skills in an honored network of obligation," he says.[52]

The underlying principle is that a vacuum is created when somebody does something for us—and nature abhors a vacuum. When we are indebted to someone, we are immediately compelled to balance the ledger and invariably go even further than the point of balance. We often aim to repay more than we received in the first place.

Whether the social debt is a smile, a compliment, a favor, or a gift, the law of reciprocity means we feel obligated to repay it even if what we have received was unsolicited or uninvited.[53] As the famed Japanese saying suggests, "Nothing is more costly than something given free of charge."[54]

The social compulsion to reciprocate can be used to powerfully guide people's decisions and behavior. However, it's a persuasion tool that must be wielded with care lest it become a means of manipulation. If used with sensitivity and integrity, reciprocity and generosity can be enormously effective in shifting stubborn people.

When incentives work

In reflecting on the power of reciprocity, Robert Cialdini puts it simply: "People say yes to those they owe." We see this dynamic in play constantly in everyday interactions. For instance, 42 percent of shoppers at a candy store were found to be more likely to make a purchase if they'd received a small chocolate as a gift upon entry.

Further still, Cialdini cites research that offers a revealing twist in the hotel towel reuse experiments described at the beginning of this chapter. Upon entering their room, some unknowing participants in a study encountered a card asking them to reuse their towels in order to help the environment. However, the card went on to explain that the hotel had already made a financial contribution to a sustainability-focused charity in the name of its guests. Other guests received cards that informed the guest that a charitable donation would be made after checkout if the guest opted to reuse their towels. Tellingly, the before-the-act donation approach proved to be 47 percent more effective than the after-the-act one.[55]

Despite the effectiveness of tactics like this, Cialdini cautions that invoking the law of reciprocity does pose risks. "Certain recipients might resent being given something they didn't invite, while others might not judge (the incentive) as beneficial to them."[56]

A recipe for reciprocity

In examining the nature of a gift's perceived value, behavioral scientist David Strohmetz set out to investigate whether giving restaurant guests a piece of chocolate would influence the amount they tipped their food server.

In the first of a series of experiments, servers were instructed to give diners a single piece of candy for each person at the table when presenting the bill. In comparison to not giving a piece of chocolate at all, this gesture saw a fairly small increase of 3.3 percent in the amount tipped. In the second experiment, the servers gave each diner two chocolates and the tips rose by 14.1 percent.

At face value, this increase makes sense practically and economically. After all, the more someone gives us, the more we are likely to reciprocate in kind. However, this is where Strohmetz's research took a curious turn. In the third experiment, after offering each of the diners a piece of chocolate from her basket, the server turned to walk away then stopped. She turned around and walked back to the table and offered a second piece of chocolate to each diner—almost as if it were an afterthought or spontaneous gesture. This simple "performance" saw tips rise by an enormous 21.3 percent. Similar increases were demonstrated time and time again with different groups of restaurant guests.

Reflecting on the findings of his research, Strohmetz suggests there are three factors that influence how persuasive and effective reciprocity will be. Gifts and gestures must be:

- Significant
- Unexpected
- Personalized

In considering these three elements in the case of handing out chocolate to restaurant customers, the giving of two pieces rather than one was both unexpected and significant because giving a single piece is seen as fairly common practice. It's worth noting too that "significant" doesn't have to mean "big." After all, a single extra piece of chocolate wasn't an enormous financial outlay for the restaurant but the perceived value of the gift was far greater. The jump in tips from 3.3 percent to 14.1 percent attested to that perception of value.

However, it was the third element of personalization that seems to be the magic ingredient. It was the way the gift was given rather than the value of the gift itself that counted. By turning around and then walking back to the table to deliver the second piece of chocolate as an afterthought, the message to the third set of diners was that this wasn't something that every table was going to receive. The gesture was something special and was the result of the food server showing a special liking for that particular table—an affinity that was reciprocated in the tip offered by the diners.

Naturally, an approach like this needs to be authentic at some level. Simply using this tactic with every table would quickly be seen as insincere and would backfire. However, the findings of Strohmetz's work are significant. In order to unlock the power of reciprocity in changing or motivating behavior, make sure a gesture, favor, or gift is one that will be seen as significant, unexpected, and personalized to those receiving it. This can take a bit of thought, creativity, and research but it's well worth the effort.[57]

Favors must be fresh

While decades of research validates the importance of gestures and gifts that are significant, unexpected, and personalized, I'd suggest there is a fourth reciprocity factor that should be added to the list: timeliness.

According to experiments by Professor Francis Flynn of Stanford's Graduate School of Business, the value perception of gifts and favors changes over time. According to Flynn's research, immediately after a favor is performed, the person receiving it places significantly more value on the gesture than the favor-doer. As time passes, however, this reverses. Essentially the favor-doer begins to overestimate the value of their generosity while the receiver gradually places less and less value on the favor.

Flynn suggests that there are numerous reasons this dynamic occurs—most notably that over time our perceptions and memories tend to get distorted. Many of us like to think of ourselves in the best possible light and so remember a kind gesture we've made as more grand and noble than it was. By the same token, a receiver likely begins to underestimate how much they appreciated or needed the help or gift at the time.

The implications of Flynn's research are important. For starters, if you are aiming for someone to reciprocate in response to something you have done for them, try moving them to action as quickly as possible or prime them for reciprocation in the future by saying something like "I'm sure you'd do the same thing for me if the situation was ever reversed." Naturally this needs to be done sensitively lest it appear that your favor was nothing more than a manipulative attempt to earn credit in the relational bank.[58]

Making someone feel special

While the previous pages have explored the role of gifts and favors in motivating reciprocity, it's worth highlighting one approach that costs absolutely nothing at all: disclosure.

By bringing someone into your confidence, sharing a secret or disclosing privileged information, you establish a powerful sense of obligation. Everyone wants to be in the know and privy to details that make them feel special. The more personal these details are, the better. This is a common tool in the "good cop" routine of negotiation. By saying to another party "Off the record, I think you should know..." or, "I shouldn't be telling you this, but..." you create an instant bond that makes the listener feel important and will motivate them to view you positively and perhaps even reciprocate and share something significant themselves.[59]

Again, disclosure is a powerful tool of reciprocity, but it must be used with sensitivity and integrity. There are few things that will stop persuasive efforts dead in their tracks quicker than when people feel they are being played.

In his book *Brainfluence*, Roger Dooley outlines a series of ideas for enlisting the trust and reciprocal confidence of another party including:

- Making a loan or trial product available with very few restrictions.
- Establishing credit without lengthy forms and an onerous screening process.
- Sharing confidential information without making the customer sign a nondisclosure agreement.[60]

As Dooley observes, using approaches like this to build trust has a powerful ability to spark social obligation because "a customer who thinks you trust him or her will be far more likely to reciprocate."[61]

Behavioral psychologist, Susan Weinschenk, agrees: "If people trust you, then they'll be more likely to do what you want them to do." In order to foster the sort of trust that leads to reciprocity, Weinschenk offers her own list of tips and ideas:

- Ask them to do an important task that you usually do yourself and don't check up on them.
- Give someone the keys to your apartment and ask them to check on your pets or water your plants while you're away on holidays.
- Let someone borrow your car or some other valuable object.
- Ask them to make a presentation at an important meeting.

The power of approaches like these, according to Weinschenk, is that they trigger the release of the social bonding hormone oxytocin. As we have already seen, this powerful hormone is an essential ingredient in trust, affinity, and thus reciprocity.[62]

While the power of activating reciprocity through offering gifts, benefits, and privileges is relatively well understood, the principles of mutual obligation also work in ways you might not expect.

Favors that win favor

When running for his second term as clerk of the Pennsylvania Assembly, one of Benjamin Franklin's sharpest critics delivered a scathing speech attacking him and his character—even though the two had never actually met. Despite being upset about the speech, Franklin reacted in a surprising way. Instead of responding in-kind with a stinging rebuke, he wrote his opponent a letter asking if he could borrow a rare book. Upon receiving the letter, his adversary was surprised by the request but was more than willing to agree to it. A short while later, Franklin returned the book with a thank you note.

When the two men eventually did cross paths in person, they had a conversation that Franklin described in his biography as "incredibly civil" and eventually the two men became lifelong friends. Franklin knew that if you want to get someone on your side or feel favorably toward you, simply ask them for a favor. The positive feelings associated with helping another person often convert into positive feelings toward that person.[63]

A century after Franklin's book borrowing experiment, two researchers named Jon Jecker and David Landy set out to see if the great man had been right in his assumptions that the favor itself was the factor that shifted the relational dynamic. As part of their experiment, participants won a sum of money from the researchers as part of a contest. Upon being advised of their win, the participants were then approached and asked if they'd consider returning the cash they'd won because the researcher had funded their prize personally and was now running low on money. The overwhelming majority willingly agreed to the request. The remainder of the winners were not approached after their prize money was paid.

When anonymously surveyed after the fact, the participants were asked what their feelings toward the researcher were. The results were a revealing validation of Franklin's approach. Those who had been asked to return the prize money rated the researcher far more favorably than those who had not received the repayment request.

This dynamic works in almost every conceivable context. Researchers at Georgetown University's School of Business in Washington, D.C., have found that invoking the law of reciprocity is one of the most powerful tactics for successful negotiations. By making early concessions with an accompanying request for a favor, a successful outcome or deal is far more likely to result.

To explore this principle, the Georgetown researchers conducted an experiment where they teamed up a series of suppliers and buyers. Half of the suppliers participating in the research were instructed to offer a price discount immediately followed by a request that the buyer write a review or make a referral to a colleague. In comparison, the remaining suppliers were told to offer the discount and not follow up with the request for a favor. While 40 percent of buyers agreed to the deal when offered the price discount alone, amazingly 62 percent agreed when the price concession came with the request of a favor.[64]

As award-winning advertising executive Adam Ferrier observes, this has powerful implications for leaders and businesses. "If you can get others to invest something of themselves into you, they will like you more." In a counterintuitive reframe of JFK's famous speech, Ferrier's advice is to "stop asking what you can do for your consumer, and instead ask what my consumer do for me?" At the same time, Ferrier warns consumers of the power this technique can wield. "If you are a consumer, be careful about doing favors for brands—it will just make you like them more."[65]

■ ■ ■

Mutual obligation has an amazing capacity for motivating humans. By giving to or sharing things with others in ways that are significant, unexpected, personalized, and timely, we can use reciprocity to pave the way to real change. In reflecting on the extraordinary success of the TED movement, TED CEO Chris Anderson, points to the simple power of being generous. When Anderson was asked for one piece of advice to give leaders and business owners, he suggested to always err on the side of generosity. "Try and figure out what the most radical thing you could give away to others might be–even if there's no guarantee you'll get anything back." According to Anderson, this posture and paradigm attracts people to you and your vision in ways that few other things can.

While reciprocity is a powerful tool for persuasion that needs to be used with care, it can make all the difference in overcoming obstinance and influencing others.

PERSUASION TOOL #12 PRO TIPS

1. One good turn really does deserve another and we tend to feel a natural sense of indebtedness when we have received something from others. While we must never manipulate people by giving gifts that create a sense of artificial obligation, we can cultivate a sense of willingness by making concessions or offering meaningful benefits before we make a request of any form.

2. In order to activate reciprocity, make sure what you are giving or offering others is significant, unexpected, and personalized. This means getting to know the other individual and what really matters to them.

3. Remember that good deeds don't age well. Favors are seen as most impactful and influential when they are fresh in the mind of the recipient.

4. Make people feel special by bringing them into your confidence, communicating your trust in them, or extending meaningful privileges to them.

5. Asking others for help or a favor is one of the best ways to have them view you more favorably. The act of helping others builds trust and makes people feel invested and involved.

CLOSING REFLECTIONS ON CONFORMITY

The social factors involved in changing minds are hard to overstate. We are compelled to cooperate, conform, and contribute, and this has a uniquely effective way of unlocking stubborn minds.

Whether by deferring to the power of "they," harnessing the herd instinct, or leveraging reciprocity, there is great power in using social influences to change people's behavior and beliefs. Better yet, this dynamic works just as well whether you're looking to inspire change in a group or an individual.

CHAPTER 7
EMPATHY

I n Victorian England, to be poor and destitute was a dreadful thing indeed. More than the constant pang of hunger and the fear for personal safety, there was a strong undercurrent of shame attached to those who found themselves down-and-out—the "underclass" as they were sometimes called.

This was especially true of orphans who were not viewed with enormous sympathy but were instead seen as a threat or social problem to be dealt with—and often ruthlessly.

Into this social environment stepped an emerging novelist named Charles Dickens. Dickens was no stranger to hardship and trauma. As a child, his father had been imprisoned for failing to repay debts and Dickens found himself working in a shoe-blacking factory at the age of twelve.

While Dickens was not the first novelist to address the social ills of his era, he became "one of the most important social commentators" of the nineteenth century, according to English literature expert Dr. Andrzej Diniejko. Diniejko observed, "Dickens succeeded in making Victorian public opinion more aware of the conditions of the poor. He depicted persuasively the disorder, squalor, blight, decay, and the human misery of a modern industrial city."[1]

This was perhaps most obvious in his book *Oliver Twist*, which had a profound and lasting impact on the way society viewed poverty and the plight of orphans. By recasting the underclass as vulnerable victims of social injustice, public sentiment shifted dramatically. People developed a newfound compassion that sparked an outpouring of benevolence and generosity.

Of course, Dickens's persuasive success was not merely a function of good writing. Instead, the power of his work was that it enabled and even forced the public to confront realities and complexities they had previously avoided. But above all else, it forced them to empathize with people whose lives they scarcely understood. This was the power of pathos at work.

A window into another's world

As Dickens shows us, entertainment—from books to songs, artwork, movies, and television—can play a key role in changing minds. Whether fictitious or not, these enable us to see the world through someone else's eyes and awaken us to a different view of the world. As French novelist Marcel Proust suggested, "The real voyage of discovery consists not in seeking new landscapes, but in having new eyes."

Consider how the UK's roll out of the COVID-19 vaccine was influenced by the 2011 Steven Soderbergh film *Contagion*. Throughout the pandemic, this close-to-home blockbuster rocketed up the streaming charts as millions searched for hints about how bad the COVID-19 outbreak could get. According to Warner Bros, the movie jumped from its 270th most-watched film in December 2019 to second highest in March 2020.

Among the fans who tuned into *Contagion* during 2020 was Britain's health secretary at the time, Matt Hancock. Of all the vivid and confronting themes in the movie, Hancock was most impacted by its depiction of social disintegration as people fought over scarce vaccine supplies. In one scene, an abducted doctor is handed over in exchange for 100 doses of the lifesaving jab. In another, vials are in such hot demand that recipients must be determined by a lottery based on birth dates.

Hancock was so moved by this depiction that he immediately directed health bureaucrats to secure 100 million doses of the Oxford-AstraZeneca vaccine despite the formal advice to buy 30 million. In hindsight, this decision was a critical element in the UK's successful vaccination program.[2]

There have been many powerful examples in recent decades of the persuasive impact of entertainment. Consider just a few:

- The iconic hit TV series *MASH* shifted public sentiment on the Korean War.
- The movie *Philadelphia* changed people's views on the gay community and the scourge of AIDS.
- *Blood Diamond* raised awareness about exploitation and the dark underbelly of the diamond industry.
- Al Gore's *An Inconvenient Truth* radically changed public awareness and sentiment about climate change.

It's hard to overstate the significance of this final example. While awareness and concern about human-induced climate change had been growing since the mid-2000s, the issue had failed to gain meaningful momentum. Even when the Intergovernmental Panel on Climate Change (IPCC) published its 2007 report that showed a high likelihood that global temperatures were set to rise by up to 6 percent by 2100 and that 18-35 percent of animal and plant species would be extinct by 2050, the report remained a scientific document that was filed away.

But it was Al Gore's documentary and the inconvenient truths it highlighted that really got people's attention. As the film began to play in cinemas around the world, the conversation started to shift. While the movie-length documentary communicated largely the same facts and research contained in the IPCC report, Al Gore's methods were entirely different. The film's producers evocatively depicted the true cost of climate change on people and animals in a way that was hard to ignore. It made a scientific issue a powerfully emotional one.[3] In contrast with Gore's sequel, which suffered from a lack of ethos or credibility as we explored at the beginning of Part II, *An Inconvenient Truth* has gone down in history as a true game changer.

What's clear is that empathy is a key ingredient in any attempt to change minds. We must empathize deeply with the perspectives and context of those we are looking to influence so we can frame our appeal in a way that is both relevant and compelling. As Vincent Van Gogh said, "You have to first experience what you want to express."[4]

Similarly reflecting on the importance of empathy in the process of change, Kotter and Cohen in their book *The Heart of Change* suggest that successfully shifting the beliefs and behavior of others is never a result of the ANALYZE-THINK-CHANGE sequence. Instead, they observed that enduring impact is always a result of SEE-FEEL-CHANGE.

Empathy isn't easy

The unique power of empathy is that it has an ability to reapply the light and shade, the color, the texture, and the nuance that 2-D thinking can remove. Humans are complex, three-dimensional beings and keeping this truth front of mind allows us to engage open-mindedly and wholeheartedly with those who may appear very different from us.

To this end, I love the often-quoted sentiment from Abraham Lincoln: "I don't like that man very much. I'm going to have to get to know him better."[5]

The trick is that we tend to find it hard to get ourselves into the metaphorical shoes of those we're looking to influence. This was demonstrated in a recent study by Professor Matthew Feinberg from the University of Toronto and Stanford University sociologist Robb Willer.

Feinberg and Willer enlisted a group of participants to construct arguments that would win over people whose views about contentious social issues were very different to their own. For instance, conservative participants were asked to construct an argument that English should be designated the national language of the U.S.—but to do so in a way that would appeal to liberals. For their part, liberals had to argue in favor of same sex marriage in a way that would resonate with conservative values.

Feinberg and Willer assumed this should not be an enormously difficult challenge. After all, liberals could frame same-sex marriage as something that appealed to conservative values of loyalty and nationalism—that gay Americans "deserve to stand alongside us." By the same token, conservatives could easily have framed a uniform national language as an issue of equity and a key step in removing discrimination.

And yet neither side seemed able to genuinely put themselves in the shoes of their ideological opponents. Either they lacked the capacity to see the world from an opposing perspective, or lacked the will to do so. In the end, only 8 percent of conservatives were able to construct an argument that appealed to liberals, and it was much the same for liberals seeking to do the reverse. Had they been aware of the Moral Foundations framework we discussed in chapter 3, perhaps participants in the study would have found this easier to do.

Reflecting on the findings of this study in his book *The Soulful Art of Persuasion*, Jason Harris observed that "What these political partisans lacked was the ability to see hot button topics through the eyes of those who disagreed with them. They lacked empathy. And as a result, they were hopeless persuaders."[6]

Wharton School psychologist Adam Grant acknowledges that while the common advice of placing ourselves in someone else's shoes is valuable, doing so really is easier said than done. Over twenty experiments examining this have found that attempting to see something from an opponent's point of view actually left people feeling greater enmity for their counterparts. In explaining why this was the case, Grant argued that "we're terrible mind readers" when it comes to imagining the interests and intentions of those different from us.

Part of the solution to this, according to Grant, is intimacy and familiarity.

To really empathize with another person and their views, we need to genuinely know them. Unless we can accept that the views of others are as complex as our own, we have little hope of being able to empathize with them deeply. To this point, polls reveal that most Democrats wildly underestimate the number of Republicans who share their concern about racism and sexism, while Republicans for their part have little awareness of how many Democrats oppose open borders and are proud patriots.[7]

Developing empathy in and not just empathy for

Leo Tolstoy in *War and Peace* quoted the French proverb *Tout comprendre, c'est tout pardonner*, or roughly translated, *to understand all is to forgive all*. And it's true. There is a certain sense of grace that we extend to people and situations once we get a more complete picture. This is one of the most powerful elements of empathy—it opens us up to the nuance our Instinctive Minds often find hard to identify.

As we explored in chapter 2, one of the biggest barriers to meaningful dialogue and engagement is the 2-D trap where other people are oversimplified to the point of being deified or demonized. It is much easier to dismiss, dislike, or feel disgust toward someone you don't personally know. Simplistic judgments, however, rarely stand the test of intimacy.

Writing in the *New York Times*, sociologist Christopher Bail speaks to this very theme. "Social psychologists have long argued that positive, intimate contact between members of rival groups across an extended period can produce compromise."[8] When we get to know another individual up close or see things from their perspective, our judgments and arrogant assertions rarely seem to make sense. As writer and peace activist Gene Knudsen Hoffman was fond of saying "An enemy is one whose story we have not heard."[9]

Research in a variety of contexts points to the fact that merely listening to others share their views has a moderating effect on strong opinions. For instance, numerous studies across government and private sector organizations have found that placing people in "listening circles" where every person has the chance to share their perspective or views, results in the attitudes of individual group members becoming more complex and less extreme.[10]

Social commentator Dr. Natasha Moore suggests that this has important implications for how we engage in arguments and ideological exchanges. Developing empathy for those we don't agree with or understand "won't necessarily lead us to agree with them," says Moore, "but it will almost certainly help us to judge them less harshly, and to hold our own opinions more humbly and less aggressively."

To Moore's point, empathy is beneficial in that it not only adds nuance to another person, idea, or circumstance, but it also smooths off some of the hard edges of our own view on reality. In addition, empathy generally leads to a posture of openness—it compels us to try and understand rather than rush to judgment. This sort of deep understanding "will make it impossible for us to write off vast swathes of our countrymen and women as blind and bigoted. It will encourage open debate instead of angry calls to silence opposing views."[11]

But more than making us open and curious, empathy ensures that our ideas and messages are relevant.

Identifying with, before influencing

Attempting to change someone's view without trying to understand the ideological lens through which they view the world is akin to a conversation between someone speaking Spanish and another speaking German. The exchange will be fruitless and frustrating for both parties. Both sides could be forgiven for thinking the other was crazy or unintelligible. As such, before you can even try and get your message across to another person or have them see things from your perspective, you need to take theirs into account.

Legendary persuader Dr. Frank Luntz spoke of the importance of this in his book *Words that Work*. "You can have the best message in the world, but the person on the receiving end will always understand it through the prism of his or her own emotions, preconceptions, prejudices, and preexisting beliefs. It's not enough to be correct or reasonable or even brilliant. The key to successful communication is to take the imaginative leap of stuffing yourself right into your listener's shoes to know what they are thinking and feeling in the deepest recesses of their mind and heart. How that person perceives what you say is even more real, at least in a practical sense, than how you perceive yourself."[12]

In the pages ahead, we will explore three ways to use empathy to make an argument or point of view more salient, relevant, and impossible to ignore. Better yet, we will look at how empathy can counteract the sort of entrenched thinking that so often gets in the way of persuasion.

MAKE PRINCIPLES PERSONAL

On April 24, 2015, a turquoise vending machine was placed in the middle of a market square in Berlin. Would-be customers were tempted by a sign that said, "T-Shirts only 2 Euros."

It was an offer almost too good to refuse. Some customers wondered if a price like this might mean there was a catch—and indeed there was. After paying their Euros but before their order was processed, customers would be required to watch a short video showing the conditions of sweatshop workers whose exploitation had made the cheap clothing possible.

It turned out that this initiative was an experiment to coincide with the second anniversary of the devastating Rana Plaza garment factory collapse in Bangladesh that killed 1,133 sweatshop workers. Researchers wondered whether the video would trigger the recent memories of the disaster and influence people to change their purchasing decision. And it most certainly did.

Out of the 150 people who stopped to buy a cheap t-shirt, 90 percent decided to not proceed with their order after watching the video and instead opted to donate their 2 euros to a charity designed to address exploitation in fashion supply chains.[13]

It's significant that each of those 90 percent of people who stopped to buy a cheap item of clothing likely knew full-well that a shirt this cheap couldn't have been sourced equitably. So, what changed their mind? Well suddenly sweatshop workers were more than a vague group of people working in a foreign land. Instead, the video left German shoppers keenly aware that these are real people with real stories facing real misery. When a human face was put to the issue, it was hard to ignore.

When issues have an identity

A legendary campaign launched in the 1980s by the Violence Against Women Coalition employed a similar tactic to draw attention to the issue of women's safety and domestic violence. By its nature, this is an insidious problem that occurs almost exclusively behind closed doors. It's easy to turn a blind eye or just imagine it isn't happening in our street, our neighborhood, or our city.

The campaign featured bold black text against a white background that proclaimed "One in four women will be raped in her lifetime. Will it be your mother, your sister, your daughter, or your wife?"

My friend, marketing strategist Dan Gregory, reports that it was this campaign that both inspired him as to the power of effective advertising and shifted his worldview as a man. "What (made) this such an extraordinary piece of communication, one that has haunted me for twenty years, is not that it makes the case for women's safety, but that it makes women's safety a man's issue... it makes women's safety my issue."[14]

The power of personalizing an issue was also evident in the case of former white supremacist Derek Black who had a dramatic about-face as chronicled in the book *Rising Out of Hatred* by Pulitzer Prize-winning writer Eli Saslow. From a young age, Black had been primed for white supremacy belief by his father, Don, who founded white nationalist website Stormfront and has done prison time for plotting to overthrow the Caribbean island of Dominica in order to establish a white ethno-state there. Derek's godfather, the former Ku Klux Klan grand wizard and Louisiana state representative David Duke, also exerted significant influence. Even as a young child, Derek was pegged as a future leader of the white nationalist movement and had created a kids' section of the Stormfront website for the purposes of recruiting the "white children of the globe."

However, when Derek Black became a student at New College in Florida, he was suddenly exposed to people who challenged the view of the world he'd grown up with. One fellow student, an observant Jew named Matthew, invited Derek to Shabbat dinners that routinely included the attendance of a number of Orthodox Jews and immigrants. But it was a woman named Allison who Derek met through these gatherings that impacted him most.

As a romantic relationship with Allison began to blossom, Derek was forced to reconsider the views he had been raised with. Allison pushed back on Derek's far-right attitudes and gradually his position began to soften. "For years Derek had been hearing about the abstract evils of racism, which he had always dismissed as empty rhetoric from his enemies on the liberal left," Saslow writes. But Allison "made Derek begin to wonder if in fact he had been wrong."

The clincher was when the issues became personal. One afternoon while Derek and Allison were discussing calls by white nationalists to deport minorities and immigrants, Allison confronted Derek with the fact that this would threaten the lives of the very friends he had met through Matthew at the Shabbat dinners. When the "great deportation" came, Allison asked whether Derek himself would be willing to break into the homes of his friends and force them out? And if he wasn't willing to be actively involved, could Derek stand by and watch as his father and other Stormfront members did it for him?

When Derek confronted his father with this same question, the response was a defining moment. Don Black admitted that the strategy white nationalists advocated for would see "immigrants, Jews, and blacks forced to leave." It was that simple.

Derek had a decision to make. Now that the agenda he'd believed in for so many years translated into a real cost for real people he knew and loved, he could no longer hide beyond hate-filled slogans and rhetoric. In the end, Derek made the significant decision to walk away from the ideology that had defined his family and childhood. "I'm done. I don't believe in it, and I'm not going to be involved," he told Allison.[15]

Look at the one

This power of humanizing and personalizing an idea is something that persuasive leaders ranging from Stalin to Mother Teresa well understood.

Mother Teresa once said, "If I look at the mass, I will never act. If I look at the one, I will."[16] In more sinister terms, Stalin was famous for saying, "One death is a tragedy; a million is a statistic."[17]

Paul Slovic, who specializes in decision research at the University of Oregon, has explored this very theme and the impact it has on how people respond when presented with a request to donate to charity. In one of Slovic's studies, a group of participants was shown the image of a single starving child in the poor African nation of Mali while a second group was shown a photo featuring two destitute children. The research subjects were told the names of each child in the two photos and then the request for a charitable contribution was made.

When the results were collated, those who had been shown the photo of two children donated a full 15 percent less than those who had been shown the photo of a single child. To examine just how pervasive this dynamic was, a follow-up study showed potential donors an image of eight starving children and the rate of donation was just half of what was given when only one child was shown.

As Slovic concluded, "This tendency may be hardwired. We are drawn to stories about one person in crisis, but mass starvation or rampant disease barely engages us."[18]

The bigger the issue, the less we care

This same finding was revealed in 2004 research at Carnegie Mellon University. Researchers offered participants $5 each to complete a survey on technology usage. The survey was not relevant to the research but was designed to ensure that participants were armed with five $1 bills.

Accompanying their cash payment, each participant was handed an envelope featuring a request for a donation to Save the Children. The first request letter featured a range of statistics about the plight of the world's poorest children, such as:

- Food shortages in Malawi are affecting more than 3 million children.
- In Zambia, severe rainfall deficits have resulted in a 42 percent drop in maize production in the past four years, meaning 3 million Zambians face hunger.
- Four million Angolans—one-third of the population—have been forced to flee their homes.
- More than 11 million people in Ethiopia need immediate food assistance.

The second group received an appeal letter featuring the story of a seven-year-old girl living in Mali named Rokia. The appeal described that Rokia "is desperately poor and faces the threat of severe hunger or even starvation. Her life will be changed for the better as a result of your financial gift. With your support, and the support of other caring sponsors, Save the Children will work with Rokia's family and other members of the community to help feed and educate her and provide basic medical care and hygiene education."

After the participants were handed their appeal letter, they faced the decision of whether to donate some or all of their five $1 bills. These donations could be placed into the envelope, sealed, and returned to the researcher.

When the donation results were collated, the variations were significant. The average donation of those who had read the general large-scale appeal donated $1.14. In comparison, those who had learned about Rokia's plight contributed an average of $2.38—more than double.

Next, the Carnegie Mellon researchers gave a third group of research participants an appeal card featuring both Rokia's story and the statistics to see what the difference in their giving would be. The results were significant—those in this third group gave almost a dollar less on average ($1.43) than those who had received the Rokia appeal alone.

In making sense of their findings, the research team put the difference in donation rates down to what they called the "drop in the bucket effect." They concluded that those who had received the statistics were overwhelmed by the enormity of the challenge and felt that their small donation would be meaningless. In other words, learning about the breadth and gravity of Africa's poor children actually made people *less* charitable than if they were giving in order to help one individual.[19]

Added to this, the researchers suggest that "thinking about statistics shifts people into a more analytical frame of mind. When people think analytically, they're less likely to think emotionally—and the researchers believed it was people's emotional response to Rokia's plight that led them to act." As we explored in chapter 1, this dynamic speaks to what happens when our Inquiring Mind gets activated by statistics, evidence or "logos." When we start out by engaging with issues deliberatively and analytically, this effectively prevents us from engaging with them emotionally.

When it comes to fostering empathy, the key message is that we'd do well to keep the scope as narrow as possible. The principle that both Mother Teresa and Stalin understood well is that the potency of a message drops away quickly when the scope grows. Put simply, the bigger the issue, the less we care. Or as Christopher Graves suggests, "Human empathy does not scale well. We can care very deeply about one, single stranger, but that empathy wanes rapidly as the group of victims grows. Once it becomes a large number, we cease caring."[20]

The pain is real

Recent years have seen numerous approaches used to engage the broader public with the pressing issue of climate change. While there is still debate as to which appeals are most effective, perhaps scientists would do well to use sex to sell the message.

Announcing the release of new research linking climate change to frequency of intercourse, one particularly arresting headline proclaimed: *Stop climate change; get laid more.* While this tabloid-style claim may seem more sensational than scientific, new evidence indicates that we're far less likely to have sex in hot weather. In addition, warm weather makes conception far less likely with semen quality and ovulation being impacted.

In arriving at this conclusion, a group of researchers examined almost a century of data and found clear evidence of the link between temperature spikes and reduced fertility. In fact, even a slight increase in the number of days above 27 degrees Celsius (80 degrees Fahrenheit) in any month results in a clear drop in birth rates eight to ten months later.

While it may be an overreach to claim that reversing climate change will single-handedly result in more frequent and fruitful sex, it is approaches like this that make the issue very personal that could well get cut-through where other campaigns have failed.[21]

The call of the wild

In a more serious example of the power of making principles personal, consider David Attenborough's moving plea in the 2020 documentary *A Life on our Planet.* In the closing moments of this movie, which he described as his "Witness Statement" and a summary of his life's work, Attenborough says, "This is not about saving our planet but about saving ourselves." In these prescient words, David Attenborough makes the issue of conservation more than a political or philosophical one—it is deeply personal for every living being.

This technique of personalizing and humanizing the issue of climate change was in fact employed throughout the entire documentary. Highlighting the importance of deep empathy in moving people to action, Attenborough reflected on the radical shift in public awareness and concern for whale conservation in the early 1970s. When whale calls were first captured by underwater microphones at the time, animal welfare activists took the unexpected step of including the recordings in their testimony before the U.S. Congress. In calling for greater protections for whales, the activists played the recordings and then simply said "Having heard their songs, I believe you can imagine what their screams would be."[22]

It was moments like this that made the issue of whale hunting more than just an economic or cultural one. This was more than simply a debate about the harvest of oil and meat. In the eyes of legislators and the public, whales became complex and beautiful animals with a personality. Their wholesale slaughter thus became harder to justify or ignore.

A similar project in Cambridge, Massachusetts, is allowing people to listen to the sound of trees courtesy of sensors attached to leaves. These sensors measure micro-voltage changes across leaf surfaces caused by moisture movement. By associating different notes to the electrical signals in different leaves, each tree creates "a unique and ever-changing song." The project is a partnership between artist, Skooby Laposky, and the Cambridge Department of Public Works Urban Forestry, and it is designed to increase awareness of the city's disappearing canopy.

"Most people probably love trees and [still] don't consider them all the time," Laposky says. "In cities, the trees are there, but unless they're providing shade or you're picking apples from them, I feel like people don't necessarily consider trees and their importance." By showing the distinctly different songs produced by different types of trees in different types of weather or seasons, Laposky hopes that this exercise in "humanizing the issue" will cause people to become more aware of and personally engaged with the natural environment.[23]

The person behind the persona

This power of humanizing an idea or issue was highlighted poignantly by the legendary American advertising executive Rosser Reeves in the early 1950s. On a sunny April afternoon, Reeves and a colleague were on the way back to their Madison Avenue offices after having lunch in Central Park. As they walked along the busy streets, they encountered a beggar sitting on the sidewalk with a cardboard sign that read "I am blind."

As Reeves recalls, he was dismayed to see that the man's donation cup only had a few coins in it. Turning to his colleague, Reeves said "I bet I can dramatically increase the amount of money that guy is raising simply by adding four words to his sign."

When his skeptical but curious companion accepted the bet, Reeves went over to the blind man. After introducing himself as someone who knew a few things about advertising, he asked the beggar if he could alter his sign a little to attract more donations. The blind man eagerly agreed.

Reeves took out a marker, added just four words, and then re-joined his companion to stand across the street and watch what would happen. The difference was immediate. People began dropping coins and then notes into the blind man's donation cup to the point where it was soon overflowing.

The four words Reeves added? "It is spring time..." When passers-by saw the sign, they were prompted not to simply observe yet another beggar in the street but to imagine the plight of a man who was not able to see a beautiful spring day.[24]

Seeing the individual not the issue

The persuasive power of personalizing and humanizing issues is hard to overstate. Consider the New Zealand road safety campaign that sought to address the rates of death and injury in cyclists on the country's roads. Between 2008-2012, an average of 121 cyclists were seriously injured in accidents involving cars—nine of whom died. In 75 percent of cases, it was found that the car driver was responsible for the crash.

Nevertheless, research over many years indicated that the majority of drivers saw cyclists as the problem. There was a widely held view that bike riders were a nuisance and, unconsciously, motorists felt that their aggressive driving or disregard for cyclists was justified.

The challenge, then, was to shift the public's perception and attitude toward bike users. Authorities realized they needed to recast bike users as people rather than a faceless nuisance on the road.

The public awareness campaign was simple but brilliant. It used images of bike riders accompanied by labels such as "daughter," "brother," or "aunt."[25] All of a sudden, cyclists became three-dimensional people that drivers identified with rather than a mere nuisance to be tolerated on the roads. The incidence of aggressive behavior toward bike riders changed quickly.

Research indicates that in addition to making issues more real, helping others identify with individual people in a group can be a powerful way to break down the barriers of prejudice. However, this engagement needs to be done face-to face.

In a meta-analysis of 500 studies involving 250,000 participants, face-to-face interaction with people from the "other side" reduced prejudice in an impressive 94 percent of cases. As Wharton School psychologist Adam Grant observes: "Sometimes letting go of stereotypes means realizing that many members of a hated group aren't so terrible after all. And that's more likely to happen when we actually come face-to-face with them."[26]

Power of touch

While humanizing others can be an intellectual process, there is also a deeply physical dimension to it. Psychologists have long been aware of the persuasive power of touch. Subconsciously, touch makes us feel appreciated and liked, and can make others significantly more receptive to our ideas.

In one study exploring this, librarians experimented with doing two different things when returning library cards to students who were borrowing books. The first group had their card simply handed back to them, while for the second group, librarians made light physical contact with the student by placing a hand over their palm. Unaware of the experiment, students were surveyed upon leaving the library and asked to rate the library's services. Those who had received a touch by the librarian gave a significantly higher rating than those in the non-touch group.

Similar research has found that waiters who warmly and appropriately touch customers on the arm when asking if they were enjoying their meal received higher guest evaluations and larger tips than those who did not. And retail-sector research has found that customers who make physical contact with a salesperson buy more and evaluate the store more favorably than in those instances where there is no physical touch.

In one such study exploring this dynamic, Syracuse professor Jacob Hornik found that bookstore customers shopped for longer and spent more if they received a friendly touch on the arm from the sales assistant than if they didn't. The data indicated that touch resulted in an average shopping time in store of 22.11 minutes (versus 13.56 minutes) and an average spend of $15.03 (versus $12.23).[27]

In findings that are significant for the process of persuasion, one study found that when a request was made to sign a petition, 81 percent of people agreed to help when they were touched by the canvasser warmly on the upper arm—as opposed to 55 percent when no physical contact was made.[28]

Interestingly, one study found that when flight attendants touch passengers on the shoulder or forearm during a flight, the passengers reported not just a greater liking for the attendant and the airline, but also reported higher perceived safety during the flight.[29] What's clear is that the human touch can literally make all the difference in how people perceive us or our ideas.

■ ■ ■

As we have seen in previous pages, when an issue or argument remains abstract, vague, or nebulous, it is easy to ignore. However, when the same idea is personalized and humanized, we are forced to engage much more thoughtfully. This not only changes the behavior of others but also their perspective.

PERSUASION TOOL #13 PRO TIPS

1. Wherever possible, try and put a real human face to an argument or idea. It's harder to ignore an issue when it is attached to a real, three-dimensional identity.

2. Remember, human empathy doesn't scale well. When making a principle personal, keep the scope narrow. Tell one person's story or highlight one person's perspective. As Mother Theresa suggested, "If I look at the mass, I will never act. If I look at the one, I will."

3. Be careful when using statistics or numbers in communicating an issue. This will tend to engage people's Inquiring Mind and can make consideration deliberative and dispassionate. If you are going to use numbers, make it clear these numbers relate to real people and their stories.

4. Even non-human issues can be humanized if we engage the senses. Allow others to viscerally feel, hear, or see what it is you're trying to get them to understand.

5. The human touch can literally make all the difference in how people perceive us or our ideas. Physical contact when used appropriately can go a long way to breaking down barriers and building affinity.

PERSUASION TOOL #14
HARNESS THE HYPOTHETICAL

The use of hypotheticals to promote deep consideration has a long and storied history—most notably through the "devil's advocate" practice developed by the Catholic Church in the sixteenth-century.

Designed as an error-correcting and bias-avoiding technique, the original devil's advocates were individuals appointed as part of the vetting process for sainthood. Before someone was canonized a saint, the devil's advocate was tasked with adopting a hypothetical and skeptical view—critically assessing all evidence compiled during the investigation of the nominated saint, and then laying out every reasonable argument for why canonization should be denied.[30]

But the use of hypotheticals has countless modern applications too. For instance, it could take the form of asking another person questions that compel them to ponder whether there is a different explanation for what they believe or are seeing, reading, and thinking. This can be as simple as asking "Could it be possible that there's more to the story?"

The power of asking effective hypothetical questions is that they can encourage someone to consider an alternative view without sparking defensiveness or reactance.[31] This can be especially valuable in the context of conflict or deep disagreement. When emotions and tempers are running high, it can be hard for an individual to genuinely consider another perspective—much less be persuaded that it may be entirely valid.

In the *New York Times* bestselling book *Crucial Conversations*, the authors suggest that the first key to persuading others is to recognize and challenge the narratives that another party may be telling themselves.

The three most common story archetypes they identify are *victim stories*, *villain stories*, and *helpless stories*:

- **Victim stories** are the ones we tell ourselves where nothing is our fault.
- **Villain stories** center on the people or situations that are to blame.
- **Helpless stories** foster a belief that nothing can or will change.

It's hard to persuade or influence any individual stuck in one of these storylines. Hypothetical questions are powerful in "unlocking" people's narratives and thus shifting the conversation.

To shift the **victim narrative**, it's important to ask questions that allow the other individual to consider whether it's possible they played any role in creating a given situation. This is not about assigning blame but allowing a "victim" to see themselves as a capable actor.

To shift the **villain narrative**, the key is to ask questions that allow an appreciation for nuance and possible alternate explanations for a situation or individual's actions. The authors of *Crucial Conversations* suggest asking "Why would a reasonable, rational, and decent person do what this person is doing?"[32] The process of searching for plausible answers to this question humanizes the other party. Empathy often replaces judgment as we consider alternate explanations for the actions of other people.

To shift the **helpless narrative**, the first step is to ask questions that challenge another individual to clarify what they really want—for themselves, for others, and for the situation. The powerful question is: "What would you do right now if you really wanted these results?"[33]

As we saw in Chapter 5, good questions are an effective way of combating deeply held beliefs that might otherwise be beyond consideration. Rather than engaging in an argument or battle of logic, consider asking questions such as:

- "How likely is that view to be true?" The key here is to think in terms of *probability* rather than binary right/wrong or yes/no scenarios.
- "When and how did you form this view, and have you always held that view?" The reality is that most opinions are developed unconsciously and without deep reflection or even evidence. By encouraging people to consider the basis—or lack thereof—of an opinion, you can open them up to the idea of reconsidering it.

- "What evidence would you need to change your mind?" or "Is there anything that would convince you there might be more to the story?"[34] If the other person acknowledges that there is no evidence that would ever convince them to change their view, this response speaks volumes. It indicates they likely are not using their rational faculties and that their view is probably stuck in identity and ideology.

- "Could it be possible that...?" The key here is to ask the other individual to consider for a moment, even hypothetically, that what they believe could be an inaccurate or incomplete view of reality. Importantly, you're not asking them to change their view but just consider an alternate one for a moment.

- "What would it take...?" Yale researcher Zoe Chance describes this as the Magic Question because it frames a request in the least adversarial and awkward way. For instance, if you are seeking a pay rise or promotion, the magic question could be something like "What would it take for me to get to the next step in my career?" or "What would it take for me to be at the top of the salary band for this role?"[35]

A similar approach to use if you're looking to get a raise would be to ask your superior the question "What would I need to do to get a raise?" This changes the entire posture of the discussion. It sets the boss's mind to what the criteria for getting a raise might be while also establishing, indirectly, that a raise is on the cards if those criteria can be met.[36]

Beyond using questions to prompt hypothetical consideration, Australian psychotherapist, Jackie Furey, suggests that there are numerous exercises that can unlock people's perspectives. One of her favorites is a technique called The Two Chairs. Whether working with feuding married couples or sparring business partners, Furey suggests that the Two Chairs approach is a powerful way to encourage hypothetical reflection and empathy.

The Two Chairs technique starts with each party sitting, facing the other, and presenting the argument for their point of view in the most persuasive way possible. Then the individuals swap chairs. Now the exercise flips and the goal is for each person to argue on behalf of their counterpart's view. The rule is that the individual speaking must raise their hand every time they are about to make a point that would win the argument on their opponent's behalf. It's not necessary to actually disclose what the point was, just to raise one's hand.

As each party goes back and forth, arguing on behalf of their opponent's view, the raising of hands starts to become more frequent. "The tone changes very quickly," says Furey. "The two individuals almost always end up in laughter."

The reason this hypothetical technique works so well is that it frees each individual to acknowledge that a very different viewpoint is valid and worth considering.

Seek out the third story

Authors Douglas Stone, Bruce Patton, and Sheila Heen propose a different but equally effective technique for promoting hypothetical consideration called the Third Story. In their book *Difficult Conversations*, Stone, Patton, and Heen suggest that every story has not two sides, but three. While the first two sides are the perspectives of each party, the third story is the one that an impartial and objective observer would tell if they were summarizing the impasse.

By challenging individuals to consider what this "third story" might be, feuding parties are encouraged to consider which elements of the other person's perspective might be considered valid and reasonable if viewed by someone outside the situation.

While this process is one that quarreling parties may engage in grudgingly, it does have the effect of forcing them to see the situation for what it is—neither black nor white but complex and nuanced.[37]

The benefits of an MRI

Another great hypothetical tool proposed by Gabriel Weinberg and Lauren McCann in their book *Super Thinking* is called the Most Respectful Interpretation (MRI). This approach is all about challenging an individual to interpret the behavior, beliefs and choices of another party in the most generous way possible.[38] It's about giving people the benefit of the doubt and maintaining what is often referred to as a "Presumption of Positive Intent."

Something powerful occurs when we begin to shift the imagined motives of another party. Rather than casting them as our enemy, we begin to see them as three-dimensional people who are likely doing their best with the knowledge and skills they have.

The important thing about the MRI approach is that it doesn't require someone to abandon or discount their own point of view. Instead, it challenges an individual to consider whether there is more to the situation than what their Instinctive Mind may conclude. For instance, are there other ways of understanding or explaining the behavior of another person without resorting immediately to judgment?

To promote this line of thought, Weinberg and McCann suggest using something called Hanlon's Razor. Like the famed Occam's Razor, which suggests that *the simplest explanation is usually the right one*, Hanlon's Razor is named after author, Robert Hanlon, and warns to *never attribute to malice that which is adequately explained by carelessness.* On most occasions, the behavior and choices of others are not malicious but are the result of thoughtlessness or laziness.[39]

Whether you use the Two Chairs, Third Story, or the MRI approach, the power of each of these hypothetical techniques is that they counteract something commonly known as Fundamental Attribution Error.

Fundamental Attribution Error

One of the more interesting quirks of human nature is the way we use a very different yardstick to judge our own decisions and behavior compared with the one we use when evaluating others. While we tend to judge ourselves based on context or circumstances, we often judge the behavior and choices of others as an indication of character.

For instance, if we pull up in a "No Stopping" zone in front of our kid's school for pickup, we feel entirely justified because we sprained our ankle last week, which still makes walking difficult and, besides, it looks like it's going to rain shortly and yet again the umbrella wasn't put back in the car by whichever family member last used it. However, should another parent dare do the same, we immediately dismiss them as selfish and rude.

More than simply being a case of hypocrisy or double standards, experts suggest that Fundamental Attribution Error is all about knowledge—we know everything about our situation but lack the same insight into the situation of others.[40]

In order to make balanced and reasonable assessments, we'd do well to account for the tendency of our Instinctive Minds to make snap moral and character judgments about others without first trying to see things from their point of view.[41]

To this end, the perspective of Berkshire Hathaway vice chairman Charlie Munger is worth keeping in mind. "I never allow myself to have an opinion on anything when I don't know the other side's argument better than they do," says Munger.[42]

Empathize with thoughts not feelings

Herein lies a key point of departure from the classical notions of empathy. We tend to consider empathy as an exercise in understanding how another party feels. However, a more effective form of empathy when it comes to persuasion focuses on what someone *thinks*. While identifying with the emotions of another party is helpful, trying to empathize with their mental or cognitive perspective is actually more useful.

As Dan Pink suggests in his book *To Sell is Human*, "When it comes to moving others, it is more beneficial to get inside their heads than to have them inside one's own heart."[43]

■ ■ ■

Henry Ford famously once suggested that "If there is any one secret of success, it lies in the ability to appreciate the other person's point of view and see things from that person's angle as well as from your own."

While this may sound like a simple or obvious insight, it's amazing how failing to see an issue from a different perspective is the very thing that tends to get in the way of meaningful persuasion. Hypothetical questions and exercises can be a powerful way to leverage empathy as they help reveal many of the unconscious assumptions people may have that would otherwise distort their perceptions.

PERSUASION TOOL #14 PRO TIPS

1. Stubbornness is often a function of being wrapped up in a victim story, a villain story, or a helpless story. Try asking people hypothetical questions that allow them challenge these narratives and judgments they lead to.

2. When dealing with individuals who have deeply entrenched views, don't engage using logic or reason but instead try asking questions that begin with words like "Could it be possible that...?", "How likely is that view to be true?" or "What evidence would you need to change your mind?"

3. To help others see a different side of an issue or circumstance, encourage them to hypothetically consider what the "Third Story" or "Most Respectful Interpretation" of the matter at hand might be.

4. Be mindful of how prone we all are to Fundamental Attribution Error. Where possible, urge people to consider the degree to which they are judging themselves based on context while evaluating the behavior and choices of others as an indication of character.

5. While empathy is often considered an exercise in understanding how another person feels, it's just as important to deeply understand what and how others are thinking. Try and get inside another person's head rather than merely trying to identify with their emotional state.

PERSUASION TOOL #15
LET EXPERIENCE DO THE EXPLAINING

Having been an ambassador for Rotary International over the years, I've had the privilege of witnessing first-hand some of the most inspiring humanitarian initiatives around the globe.

My first encounter with the work of Rotary was when I presented at a regional Rotarians summit in the northern Australian city of Rockhampton. Before I spoke, a group of district leaders took to the podium to report on a mosquito net program that was currently being rolled out across Papua New Guinea. I was truly shocked to learn how many people are infected with malaria and other mosquito-borne diseases each day, and how devastating this is for local communities.

With this information still fresh in my mind, I watched with interest a few weeks later when Bill Gates addressed the issue of malaria prevention at a conference in Long Beach, California. Having outlined various ways that his foundation was looking to address the scourge of malaria, Gates went one step further than highlighting the numbers.

During his presentation, he casually walked over to a waist-high table on the platform. "Malaria is spread by mosquitoes," he proclaimed, "and I have brought some with me today." After picking up a jar on the table, Gates took off the lid and continued, "Here, I'll let them roam around—there is no reason only poor people should be infected." After a few moments of the visibly uncomfortable audience shuffling in their seats, Gates informed them that the mosquitoes were in fact malaria-free. But his point was made—and powerfully so.[44]

The truth is generally seen and rarely heard

Ideas become far more compelling when they are *demonstrated* as opposed to when they are *debated*. In the words of seventeenth-century Spanish writer and philosopher Baltasar Gracian, "The truth is generally seen, rarely heard."

Famed neuroscientist Mike Gazzaniga suggests that in order for an individual to change their mind, "a major intervention has to take place." According to Gazzaniga, shifting people's perspectives around deeply held political or religious views tends to be a function of something *felt* rather than something *learned*. "Without an intervening experience, people will never change their position," he suggests.[45]

When we see visceral proof of an idea or feel its reality, it is harder to ignore than if we merely hear arguments on its behalf. Robert Cialdini suggests that "Making (others) literally and physically feel your meaning is infinitely more powerful than argument."[46]

In her book *Influence is Your Superpower*, Yale researcher Zoe Chance shares an example of this principle courtesy of eccentric Brazilian billionaire Chiquinho Scarpa.

When Scarpa announced he had been inspired by the pharaohs to bury his $500,000 Bentley in his back garden, the response was one of shock, confusion, and criticism. Chance recounts, "The day of the burial was a media circus, buzzing with journalists, camera crews, and helicopters overhead. As the Bentley was being lowered into its grave, Scarpa suddenly called the proceedings to a halt and invited the crowd inside his mansion, where he made a prepared statement."

Acknowledging how absurd and wasteful it was to bury such a beautiful and expensive vehicle, Scarpa pointed out that we bury something infinitely more valuable every day of the week: our organs. He went on to plead with Brazilians to consider registering to donate their organs and the call to action was both swift and effective. Within a month, organ donations had increased by 32 percent.[47]

Stepping into "enemy territory"

When it comes to getting a visceral experience of the other side of an issue, there is nothing quite as powerful as stepping into "enemy territory." This was certainly the experience of Democratic voter Karlyn Borysenko in the lead up to the 2020 U.S. federal election.

The election campaign had been bitter and polarized with Trump supporters united in their fear and vitriol towards Joe Biden and his "socialist agenda."

By the same token, liberal voters were incensed by the blatant mistruths and character flaws evident in President Trump. In workplaces, social settings, and families, reasoned discussion or exchange between opposing sides seemed near-impossible.

Against this backdrop, Borysenko penned an article titled "The Rally that Changed My Mind." The article's opening sentence left no doubt as to where the author's political affiliation lay: "I wouldn't be caught dead at a Donald Trump rally," Karlyn Borysenko declared. And yet in February 2020, this is precisely where she found herself—surrounded by 11,000 passionate supporters at a Republican Party function.

How did this happen? "Well, it all started with…knitting," Karlyn says. After watching many months of daily insults, name-calling, and attacks directed at Trump supporters in online knitting forums, she'd grown curious: "Could those Trump supporters, some of whom were literally my neighbors, really be as irredeemable as they said? I assumed the answer was yes, but I had to find out."

So, when she read news of a Trump rally in her home state of New Hampshire, she went along out of curiosity more than anything else. "My friends urged me not to go. They feared for my safety," Karlyn recalled. One friend even offered to give her a can of pepper spray to take along.

Arriving four hours before the rally was scheduled to start, Karlyn joined a line outside the arena that was already a mile long and opted to keep to herself. She was anxious being around this crowd of people who were not "like her" and feared it may get uncomfortable if she revealed the fact that she was a fan of Bernie Sanders.

"But then, as people are wont to do when stuck in a long line, we started to chat—first pleasantries, and then to more serious topics. And here's what I discovered: These people were soooo nice! No one harassed me. No one intimidated me. No one threatened me." Even Karlyn's admission that she was a Democrat was no big deal. "Their response was invariably a smile and 'welcome.'"

Beyond their warm demeanor and welcome, Karlyn was amazed at how diverse the Trump supporters were. "These were decent, hardworking people from every walk of life: electricians, lawyers, schoolteachers, small business owners, veterans. I might question some of the policies they supported— they were only too happy to debate me—but I couldn't question their good intentions or decency. These people were not stupid, not brainwashed, and, as far as I could tell, not racist, sexist, or phobic-anything."

Afterwards, Karlyn reflected on the experience, saying "So, did going to a Trump rally change me? Well, my values are the same, but my perspective is different. I'll even say the experience made me a better person. I learned that the people who come to these rallies aren't there because they hate anybody. The rally also reminded me that we are all people. Yes, we have fierce disagreements on how to solve our problems. But those who differ with us are not evil. Thinking that they are—that's the problem. That's what's tearing us apart. I refuse to add to the divisiveness any longer. I refuse to hate people I don't know simply because I don't like the way they vote."[48]

While attending a Republican rally may not have persuaded Karlyn Borysenko to vote differently, it certainly changed her mind in other ways. And real-life experiences have a unique capacity to do this. Karlyn could have read about the traits of everyday Trump supporters or even watched a documentary, but it was meeting them and experiencing them as three-dimensional people that made the difference.

Encounters that enlarge our view

Former National Public Radio CEO Ken Stern had a very similar set of experiences, which he recounted in his book *Republican Like Me: How I Left the Liberal Bubble and Learned to Love the Right*. A few years ago, Stern set out to better understand "conservative America."

Over the course of a number of months, he deliberately placed himself in unfamiliar environments with unfamiliar people. He "went to evangelical churches, shot a hog in Texas, stood in pit row at a NASCAR race, and hung out at Tea Party meetings."

Reflecting on his experiences and encounters, Stern said that these face-to-face interactions showed that "Americans aren't as divided as you think." Even when interacting with people whose views and values were wildly different from his own, Stern was "almost always able to find more points of agreement and commonality than I thought was possible."

The overarching theme of Stern's book is that common ground is possible to find—even in the midst of political division—when we meaningfully engage in-person rather than online. As a testament to the persuasive impact of this experience, Stern opted to denounce his Democratic affiliation at the conclusion of his road trip and became an independent voter.[49]

In reading Stern's account of these perspective-shifting encounters, I am reminded of the words of Spanish philosopher and writer Miguel de Unamuno: "Fascism is cured by reading, and racism is cured by traveling." When we have a visceral experience, our views invariably change.

In a legendary example of the power of using visceral experience to make a point, consider Nikita Khrushchev's response to a heckler during a speech in 1956 when he publicly denounced Stalin's many crimes. "You were a colleague of Stalin's," the heckler shouted, "why didn't you stop him then?"

As an icy silence descended, Khrushchev scanned the audience trying to work out who the heckler was. "Who said that?" he snarled. No one moved a muscle, much less raised their hand. It was as if all the oxygen had been sucked out of the room.

After a few moments, Khrushchev regained his composure and said in a calm voice, "Now you know why I didn't stop him."

It was a masterstroke of persuasion. Rather than trying to justify his perceived complicity or explain the constant terror anyone in Stalin's orbit lived with due to his paranoia and murderous rage, Khrushchev forced the audience to experience those same emotions. When this point was made, no further argument was necessary.[50]

Simulations that help us see

Of all the strategies for using experience to foster empathy, the power of simulation is often overlooked and underrated.

I vividly remember a simulated experience that forever changed my perspective on the plight of refugees. A number of years ago, my family and I spent a few weeks volunteering at an aid agency in Hong Kong called Crossroads. While Crossroads's core work is the shipment of essential aid and materials to impoverished people around the globe, they also have a commitment to education and community engagement.

One of the initiatives they had recently launched was a refugee simulation in which participants would get a sense of what it was like to face the impossibly dreadful decisions those fleeing war and strife around the world are confronted with every day.

I knew full well how the simulation was going to function before it began—part of the work we'd done as volunteers was to install the electrical wiring and paint the scene panels for the various rooms that participants would go through.

But on the evening of the first live simulation, nothing could have prepared my family and me for what we were about to experience. We were marshaled into huddled groups, assigned names, stories, and identities before the room dramatically went black and the sound of gunshots rang out. A few seconds later, the doors burst open and "armed" soldiers entered the room with helmet torches and shouts in foreign languages.

Families and loved ones were separated. Bribes were offered. Our documentation and passports—along with my wristwatch—were confiscated, food was taken from us, and some attendees were informed that they could perform sexual acts for the guards in return for special treatment.

Naturally, none of this was real and the guards were the very Crossroads employees we'd been working alongside all week. But that hardly mattered. Within a few moments, we were all transported into the world of a confused, terrified, and victimized refugee with few options and even less power. After forty-five minutes (which felt more like four to five hours), the lights were switched on, the soldiers removed their headgear and their plastic weapons, and we all gathered for a debrief.

A sense of relief and terror lingered in the group even as cups of tea and supper were handed out by the very "guards" who had been shouting at us moments before. It probably took twenty minutes before any sense of normality returned to the group as we reflected on the experience we'd just had.

Many years later, that evening in Hong Kong stays with me as one of the most formative influences on my view of the issue of refugees and asylum seekers. Why? Because, even in some minuscule way, I could deeply empathize with what their felt experience must be.

Technology-enabled empathy

While large-format simulations like this can be a powerful way of creating an impactful experience, immersive technologies such as virtual reality (VR) offer more cost-effective ways to achieve the same result at scale.

The beauty of immersive VR is that it can make unfamiliar experiences feel very real. Anyone who has spent much time using virtual reality will know how quickly our minds get tricked into thinking that what we're seeing or experiencing is actually happening. Our bodies and emotions respond as if it were indeed real. Our pulse races, our palms get sweaty, our limbic system engages. Put simply, VR is a powerful primer for empathy.

The former UN Secretary-General Ban Ki-moon offered a compelling example of VR's capacity to raise public awareness about global issues. In 2016, Ban Ki-moon invited a VR crew to travel with him to a series of countries that had been severely impacted by warfare or natural disasters. His goal was to offer viewers a glimpse into the life and experiences of some of the most disadvantaged people on the planet.

After the project's launch, Ban shared in a *Time* magazine interview that he believed VR had a unique power to "make people perceive and feel one another's reality and, in so doing, can help create empathy and compassion in a world that needs it more than ever."[51]

In another example of the power of this technology, a team of journalists at the BBC joined forces a few years ago with a group of documentary producers and ex-prisoners to create a VR depiction of what solitary confinement in prison really feels like. The goal was to help everyday people experience something they otherwise never would and, in doing so, raise support to end the practice.[52]

The machine to be another

While VR is a powerful way to raise awareness of global and societal issues, it is just as effective at an interpersonal level. Performance artist Philippe Bertrand offers a potent example of this with a VR experience he developed called *The Machine to Be Another*. This initiative is designed to help people see the world through eyes very different than their own—be they the eyes of a child, a close friend, or someone with a disability.

In his own words, Bertrand says that while VR technology is disorienting, "afterwards, you now know someone in an intimate way and that helps you connect."

In a unique application of this approach, one of the most noteworthy entries in the 2016 Tribeca Film Festival was an immersive experience called *Notes on Blindness*. Unlike most VR applications, this project made no use of visuals but instead relied on 3D sound to give the audience a deep understanding of what it feels like to be blind.[53]

Jeremy Bailenson of Stanford University's Virtual Human Interaction Lab says these sorts of technologies have never been more important. "We are entering an era that is unprecedented in human history, where you can transform the self and experience anything the animator can fathom. The research shows it can have a deep effect on behavior."

Bailenson's own work has been to use virtual reality to foster what he describes as "Empathy at Scale." His research has demonstrated that using VR to see the world through the eyes of a color-blind person, for instance, will make someone twice as likely to help him or her.[54]

Subsequent research points to promising signs that VR does offer solutions that are unique and powerful. One Stanford University study involved people being exposed to what are known as "virtual shoes" experiments where they experience the realities of prejudice and disadvantage of individuals based on age, race, disability, or economic status. After the virtual immersion, subjects are tested for changes in levels of empathy and bias and the results are extraordinarily promising. With the help of neuroscientists, the Stanford team has been able to demonstrate a dynamic they've called "self-other merging," which indicates that VR can cause physical changes to the brain that reduce bias and prejudice.[55]

Regardless of whether an experience is virtual or not, what matters is that it's visceral. When we are forced to see the world from the perspective of another, something powerful happens to our own preconceptions.

■ ■ ■

In the words of famed blogger Tim Urban, "Arrogance is ignorance plus conviction."[56] In considering the nature of ignorance in Urban's equation, this is about more than simply a lack of understanding. Instead, ignorance is often a function of distance or detachment.

The further removed we are from an issue, idea, or individual, the simpler our judgments tend to be. Pastor and author Andy Stanley suggests that when this happens, getting up close and personal is the best way forward. "When we get close, when we are confronted with the complexity disguised by the distance...we are forced to consider someone's current reality and context. In those moments, our well-rehearsed, simplistic, politically informed solutions become mostly irrelevant."[57]

This tends to result in moments of empathy and clarity that translate into phrases like:

Oh! I've always assumed...

Oh! I thought people like that were...

Oh! I never took into account...

Oh! I didn't know...[58]

Carl Sagan wisely observed that "At too great a distance, we can mistake ignorance for perspective." In seeking to persuade others, then, we'd do well to leverage the power of meaningful experiences in order to build empathy and inform perceptions.

PERSUASION TOOL #15 PRO TIPS

1. Ideas become far more compelling when they are demonstrated as opposed to when they are debated. The fastest and most effective way to make any point is to give people a visceral experience that transcends the theoretical.

2. When deep prejudice is involved, try engineering opportunities for individuals to get up close and personal with those they might otherwise struggle to identify or agree with. Some of the most powerful learning happens in "enemy territory."

3. Simulations have a unique ability to help people experience what you might be trying to explain. While it can take some creativity, time, and resources, never underestimate the power of creating purposeful experiences. Remember, the truth is generally seen rather than heard.

4. Consider embracing the emerging possibilities of virtual reality to help people, literally, see the world from another person's perspective. These amazing new technology tools enable deep empathy at scale.

5. Never forget that arrogance is ignorance plus conviction. The most mind-stuck people are often unaware that their perceptions and judgments are more incomplete than they are inaccurate views of reality. The best antidote for ignorance is intimacy so try facilitating meaningful interpersonal interactions that will broaden an individual's frame of reference.

CLOSING REFLECTIONS
ON EMPATHY

In 375 BC, Plato summed it up best in his seminal work *Republic*: "Opinion is really the lowest form of human knowledge. It requires no accountability, no understanding. The highest form of knowledge is empathy, for it requires us to suspend our egos and live in another's world."

In an age dominated by dogma, ideology, and opinion, the sort of empathy Plato refers to is needed more than ever. It is our ability to empathize that makes us truly human. As such, there is tremendous persuasive power in tapping into this capacity for identifying with, relating to, and feeling for others.

Whether by humanizing and personalizing ideas or issues, offering an alternative perspective, or crafting a meaningful experience, the avenues for fostering empathy are many and varied. What matters most is that we don't overlook the importance of engaging people's hearts in order to change their minds.

EPILOGUE
LEAVING OUR TRENCHES BEHIND

The Christmas of 1914 is not one that the world remembers fondly. With the "war to end all wars" having broken out with all the force of the twentieth-century's deadliest new technology, this Christmas fell within one of the world's darkest winters. Amidst all the gut-wrenching tales of misery and horror that emerged from World War I, however, there is one heartwarming story of humanity that transpired that festive season.

Having spent four months bogged down in the mud and muck of Flanders, German and Allied troops had scarcely moved positions in months. Although the trenches were at some points only a few hundred meters apart, these were troops that believed they had little in common with their enemy and had deeply ingrained hatred for each other.

British and French media outlets had stoked a righteous disdain for their opponents by using propaganda that perpetuated myths of barbaric Germans melting down innocent people to manufacture soap. For their part, Germans were also well-schooled in hatred having been taught as children to recite Ernst Lissauer's "Hymn of Hate:"

You we will hate with a lasting hate, We will never forbear our hate, Hate by water and hate by land, Hate of the head and hate of the hand, Hate of the hammer and hate of the crown, Hate of seventy millions choking down. We love as one, we hate as one, We have one foe and one alone—ENGLAND!

Against this backdrop of deep-seated enmity, something truly extraordinary occurred.

It started with singing.

As one British soldier recalled, "The Germans would sing one of their carols and then we would sing one of ours, until when we started up 'O Come, All Ye Faithful.' The Germans immediately joined in singing the same hymn to the Latin words Adeste Fideles. And I thought, well, this is really a most extraordinary thing: two nations both singing the same carol in the middle of a war."[1]

As each side took turns singing familiar festive tunes in their own language, each "performance" was met with applause, cheering, and even playful jeering. After a number of musical exchanges, an even more astonishing thing happened: soldiers began emerging from their trenches. I try to imagine how terrified the first soldier who did this must have felt. After all, just an hour earlier, the lighting of a match was enough to invite sniper fire from the enemy.

The soldiers who had clambered out of their trenches calmly approached each other in no-man's land. One of the Germans called out in English "I am a lieutenant! Gentlemen, my life is in your hands, for I am out of my trench and walking toward you. Will one of your officers meet me halfway? You don't shoot, we don't shoot."

Despite their learned suspicion, enemy soldiers approached each other and began to interact. They ate, drank, and cooked together. They played a game of soccer, they exchanged photos, and even helped each other bury the fallen.

While this moment was indeed remarkable, what's extraordinary is that it was far from an isolated event. Tens of thousands of men along two-thirds of the battlefront reported the same experience. The recorded diary entries of soldiers from both sides reflected just how surreal the experience was with many describing it as something of a "waking dream."

While the Christmas Truce is often viewed as a seemingly spontaneous event, Daniel Coyle in *The Culture Code* examined how it actually began many weeks earlier with "a steady flow of interactions that created bonds of safety, identity, and trust." Each side had come to an informal agreement to withhold fire when troops ventured out to collect dry straw for bedding. These cease-fires eventually extended to include an unspoken rule to not fire upon latrines or target supply lines. Both sides were willing to make allowances to allow the other to enjoy some semblance of peace and dignity even in the midst of bitter fighting. There were also elements of playfulness in the exchanges. One British soldier described his "pet sniper" on the German side who would fire off a "good night kiss" every night promptly at 9:15 p.m. and then not fire again until morning.

In the midst of a war that depended on the demonization and dehumanization of the enemy, humanity worked its way in and emerged in moments of vulnerability and connection. Daniel Coyle summed up the Christmas Truce and the events that led up to it as a series of messages between warring sides that said: "We are the same. We are safe. I'll go if you will. And so, they did."[2]

In our mindstuck era, which seems increasingly characterized by ideological entrenchment and animosity, the need to find ways to come together is more pressing than ever. As we, in our various tribes and debates, have stubbornly dug into our trenches and vilified our opponents, the call comes to venture courageously into no-man's land and humbly meet our opponents halfway.

While we've been conditioned to see our opponents as enemies that need to be subdued, healthy persuasion always rests on sincere dialogue. For this to take place, we need to re-learn the skills of seeing others and their ideas as complex, nuanced and three-dimensional.

Although we like to believe ourselves to be enlightened, rational and open-minded, and our opponents to be stubborn and stuck in their ways, the reality is that progress is always a two-way affair. Taking a step towards meaningful influence and healthy persuasion means taking a step into the dangerous territory beyond our trenches, risking vulnerability, and forfeiting our egos for the sake of engaging our counterparts.

As we continue to navigate an age of culture wars and conspiracies, tribal ideology and identity politics, division and debate, it is worth reflecting on the story of the soldiers who sang through an especially dark Christmas night in 1914. Enemy became ally and foe became friend as each side recognized themselves in the other. And we would do well to remember that the action which really moved the enemy that night came with one soldier who was bold enough to walk unarmed out onto common ground, speak the language of his opponent and humbly ask, "Will one of you meet me halfway?"

What a difference it would make if we were all willing to do the same.

ENDNOTES

Introduction

1   Caldwell, F. 2021, 'Scare campaign over recycled water could be worse than 'Poowoomba': Turnbull', *The Sydney Morning Herald*, 24 August.

2   2019, *All Options on the Table*, Water Services Association of Australia, p 4.

3   2019, *All Options on the Table*, Water Services Association of Australia, p 4.

4   2017, Editorial Board, 'San Diego will drink water recycled from sewage. Cheers.' *The San Diego Union-Tribune,* 11 May.

5   Ross, H. 2008, 'Proven Strategies for Addressing Unconscious Bias in the Workplace,' *CDO Insights,* August.

6   Thaler, R. and Sunstein, C. 2009, *Nudge*, Penguin, New York, pp. 22, 23.

7   Stephens, M. 2021, *The End of Thinking*, Acorn Press, Sydney, p. 11.

8   Berger, J. 2020, *The Catalyst*, Simon and Schuster, London, pp. 5, 6.

9   Pink, D. 2012, *To Sell is Human*, Riverhead Books, New York, pp. 21, 22.

10 Berger, J. 2020, *The Catalyst*, Simon and Schuster, London, pp. 5, 6.

11 Williams, H. 2006, Days that Changed the World, Quercus Publishing, London, p. 163.

12 Burg, B. 2011, The Art of Persuasion, Sound Wisdom Books, Shippensburg, p. 163.

13 Shapiro, B. 2019, *The Right Side of History*, Broadside Books, New York, pp. 108-109.

14 Williams, H. 2006, *Days that Changed the World*, Quercus Publishing, London, p. 78.

15 Heath, C. and Heath, D. 2010, *Switch*, Broadway Books, New York, pp. 112-113.

16 Grant, A. 2021, *Think Again*, WH Allen, London, p. 143.

17 Denning, S. 2005, *The Leader's Guide to Storytelling*, Jossey-Bass, San Francisco, p. 47.

Part I

1   Berger, J. 2020, *The Catalyst*, Simon and Schuster, London, p. 221.

Chapter 1

1   Heath, C. and Heath, D. 2010, *Switch*, Broadway Books, New York, pp. 6-7.

2   Burow, P. et al, *Behavioural Economics for Business*, Peter Burow, Australia, p. 14.

3   Rom 8:6, *The Holy Bible - American Standard Version*, Star Bible Publishers, Hurst, Texas.

4   Burow, P. et al, *Behavioural Economics for Business*, Peter Burow, Australia, p. 2.

5   Burow, P. et al, *Behavioural Economics for Business*, Peter Burow, Australia, pp. 29-30.

6   Kahneman, D. 2011, *Thinking, Fast and Slow*, FSG, New York, pp. 20-21.

7   Chance, Z. 2022, *Influence Is Your Superpower*, Penguin Random House, London, p. 24.

8   Dooley, R. 2012, *Brainfluence*, Wiley, New Jersey, p. 1.

9   Thaler, R. and Sunstein, C. 2009, *Nudge*, Penguin, New York, pp.19-22.

10   Zak, H. 2020, 'Adults Make More Than 35,000 Decisions Per Day,' *Inc Australia*, 22 January.

11   Kahneman, D. 2011, *Thinking, Fast and Slow*, FSG, New York, pp. 20-21.

12   Kahneman, D. 2011, *Thinking, Fast and Slow*, FSG, New York, p. 105.

13   Weinschenk, S. 2013, *How to Get People to Do Stuff*, Pearson Education, London, p. 126.

14   Milkman, K. 2021, *How to Change*, Penguin, New York, p. 119.

15   Stephens, M. 2021, *The End of Thinking*, Acorn Press, Sydney, p. 12.

16   Thaler, R. and Sunstein, C. 2009, *Nudge*, Penguin, New York, pp. 19-22.

17   Taleb, N. 2010, *The Black Swan*, Random House, New York, p. 66.

18   Taleb, N. 2010, *The Black Swan*, Random House, New York, pp. 81-82.

19   Kahneman, D. 2011, *Thinking, Fast and Slow*, FSG, New York, p. 105.

20   Ellerton, P. 2014 'What you think is right may actually be wrong – here's why', *The Sydney Morning Herald*, 16 January.

21   Weinschenk, S. 2013, *How to Get People to Do Stuff*, Pearson Education, London, p. 126.

22   Cialdini, R. 2016, *Pre-Suasion*, Random House, London, p. 198.

23   Gladwell, M. 2005, *Blink*, Penguin, London, pp. 13-14.

24   2014, 'Bill Nye to climate change deniers: you can't ignore facts forever,' *Big Think*, 7 August.

25   Harman, G. 2014, 'Your brain on climate change', *The Guardian*, 11 November.

26   Mannix, L. 2021, 'Worried about AstraZeneca? Me too. The way we think about risk might be the problem,' *The Sydney Morning Herald*, 20 July.

27   Dvorsky, G. 2013, 'The 12 cognitive biases that prevent you from being rational,' *io9*, 1 September.

28   Kahneman, D. 2011, *Thinking, Fast and Slow*, FSG, New York, pp. 159-160.

29   R.L. Isaacson. 2001, *International Encyclopedia of the Social & Behavioral Sciences*, Pergamon, Oxford.

30   2022, 'The Limbic System', *Queensland Brain Institute*,

31   Burton, R. 2008, *On Being Certain*, St Martin's Press, New York, p. 158.

32   Hamilton, D. 2015, 'Calming your brain during conflict', *Harvard Business Review*, 22 December.

33   Queenan, J. 2018, 'How your brain is keeping you from changing your mind.' *The Rotarian*, 16 May.

34   Offord, C. 2020, 'How Social Isolation Affects the Brain', *The Scientist*, 13 July.

35   Kahneman, D. 2011, Thinking, Fast and Slow, FSG, New York, pp. 43-44.

36   Goldstein, N. et al. 2008, *Yes! 50 Scientifically Proven Ways to be Persuasive*, Simon and Schuster, New York, pp. 197-199.

37   Dean, J. 2010, 'Caffeine makes us easier to persuade,' *PsyBlog*, November.

Chapter 2

1   Burton, R. 2008, *On Being Certain*, St Martin's Press, New York, p. xiii.

2   Fitzsimons, T. 2020, 'Man who died of coronavirus wins election for North Dakota state legislature,' *NBC News*, 5 November.

3   Berger, J. 2020, *The Catalyst*, Simon and Schuster, London, pp. 189-191.

4   Ramadan, A. et al. 2016, *Play Bigger*, HarperCollins, New York, pp. 31-32.

5   Stephens, M. 2021, *The End of Thinking*, Acorn Press, Sydney, p. 22.

6   Dvorsky, G. 2013, 'The 12 cognitive biases that prevent you from being rational,' *io9*, 1 September.

7   Dvorsky, G. 2013, 'The 12 cognitive biases that prevent you from being rational,' *io9*, 1 September.

8   Durkin, P. 2023, '76pc of Aussies refuse to help someone with opposing views', *The Australian Financial Review*, 8 February.

9   Buliga, E. 2020, '"How do you like them now?" Expected reactions upon discovering that a friend is a political out-group member', *Journal of Social and Personal Relationships*, 14 July.

10   Pinker, S. 2021, *Rationality*, Allen Lane, London, pp. 293-294.

11   Pinker, S. 2021, *Rationality*, Allen Lane, London, p. 295.

12   Kolbert, E. 2017, 'Why facts don't change our minds', *The New Yorker*, 27 February.

13   Heinrichs, J. 2013, *Thank You for Arguing*, Three Rivers Press, New York, pp. 318-326.

14   Graves, C. 2015, 'Why debunking myths about vaccines hasn't convinced dubious parents,' 20 February.

15   Dickson, J. 2011, 'Art of persuasion not so simple,' *The Sydney Morning Herald*, 9 July.

16   Ecker, U. 2018, 'Political Attitudes and the Processing of Misinformation Corrections,' *Political Psychology Wiley Online Library*, 1 October.

17   Berger, J. 2020, *The Catalyst*, Simon and Schuster, London, pp. 91-93.

18   Kruger, A. 2022, 'A climate for mis- and disinformation', *First Draft News*, 25 July.

19   Lukianoff, G. and Haidt, J. 2018, *The Coddling of the American Mind*, Penguin Random House, New York, pp. 58-59.

20   Kolbert, E. 2017, 'Why facts don't change our minds', *The New Yorker*, 27 February.

21   Urban, T. 2023, *What's Our Problem? A Self-Help Book for Societies*, Wait But Why, Chapter 4.

22   Urban, T. 2023, *What's Our Problem? A Self-Help Book for Societies*, Wait But Why, Chapter 7.

23   Bail, C. 2021, Breaking the Social Media Prism, Princeton University Press, New Jersey, pp. 49.

24　Gregory D. and Flanagan, K. 2015, *Selfish, Scared & Stupid*, Wiley, Melbourne, p. 125.

25　Dooley, R. 2012, *Brainfluence*, Wiley, New Jersey, p. 65-67.

26　De Bono, E. 1991, *I Am Right You Are Wrong*, Penguin Books, London, pp. 156-157.

27　Urban, T. 2019, 'The story of us', *Wait, but Why?*, 26 August.

28　Urban, T. 2019, 'The story of us', *Wait, but Why?*, 26 August.

29　Moore, N. 2015, 'Silence isn't golden when it comes to free speech,' *ABC News*, 7 May.

30　Graham, P. 2009, 'Keep your identity small', *Paul Graham Blog*, February.

31　Urban, T. 2023, *What's Our Problem? A Self-Help Book for Societies*, Wait But Why, Chapter 7.

32　Grant, A. 2021, *Think Again*, WH Allen, London, p. 62.

33　Pariser, E. 2011, *The Filter Bubble*, Penguin, London, p. 77.

34　De Bono, E. 1991, *I Am Right You Are Wrong*, Penguin Books, London, pp. 17-18.

35　O'Keeffe, A. 2011, *Hardwired Humans*, Roundtable Press, Sydney, p. 60.

36　Gregory D. and Flanagan, K. 2015, *Selfish, Scared & Stupid*, Wiley, Melbourne, p. 40.

37　De Bono, E. 1991, *I Am Right You Are Wrong*, Penguin Books, London, p. 181.

38　De Bono, E. 1991, *I Am Right You Are Wrong*, Penguin Books, London, p. 215.

39　Grant, A. 2021, *Think Again*, WH Allen, London, p. 25.

40　Lakhani, D. 2005, *Persuasion: The Art of Getting What You Want*, Wiley, New Jersey, p. 83.

41　McRaney, D. 2012, *You Are Not So Smart*, Gotham Books, New York, pp. 168-169.

42　McRaney, D. 2012, *You Are Not So Smart*, Gotham Books, New York, p. 30.

43　McRaney, D. 2012, *You Are Not So Smart*, Gotham Books, New York, p. 30.

44　Wyman, B. 2023, 'Hoo boy! Fox News trumpeting conspiracies is worse than we thought,' *The Sydney Morning Herald,* 3 March.

45　Weinberg, G. and McCann, L. 2019, *Super Thinking*, Penguin, London, pp. 27-28.

46　Grant, A. 2021, *Think Again*, WH Allen, London, p. 59.

47　Pierre, J. 2019, 'Behind the curve: the science fiction of flat earthers,' *Psychology Today,* 26 February.

48　Nyhan, B. 2014, 'Effective messages in vaccine promotion', *Pediatrics,* 3 March.

49　Nyhan B. et al. 2014, 'Does correcting myths about the flu vaccine work,' *Elsevier*, 8 December.

50　Berger, J. 2020, *The Catalyst*, Simon and Schuster, London, p. 91-94.

51　Wilson, T. 2011, *Redirect*, Back Bay Books, New York, p. 53.

52　O'Keeffe, A. 2011, *Hardwired Humans*, Roundtable Press, Sydney, p. 173.

53　Grant, A. 2021, *Think Again*, WH Allen, London, p. 4.

54　Jones, M. 2020, *Beliefonomics,* Filtered Media, Sydney, pp. 95-101.

55　Kolbert, E. 2017, 'Why facts don't change our minds', *The New Yorker*, 27 February.

56　Burton, R. 2008, *On Being Certain*, St Martin's Press, New York, p. 135.

57　Pierre, J. 2016, 'Does the internet promote delusional thinking?' *Psychology Today*, 25 January.

58　Grant, A. 2021, *Think Again*, WH Allen, London, pp. 67-68.

59 Pierre, J. 2016, 'Does the internet promote delusional thinking?' *Psychology Today*, 25 January.

60 Streitfeld, D. 2017. '"The internet is broken,' says Twitter co-founder Evan Williams,' *The Sydney Morning Herald*, 22 May.

61 Drummond, C. 2017, 'Individuals with greater science literacy and education have more polarized beliefs on controversial science topics,' *PNAS*, 21 August.

62 McRaney, D. 2014, *You Are Not So Smart* Podcast: Episode 016, 'Interview with Steven Novella,' 16 January.

63 Aubrey, S. 2020, 'Playing with fire: The curious marriage of QAnon and wellness', *The Sydney Morning Herald,* 27 September.

64 McRaney, D. 2014, *You Are Not So Smart* Podcast: Episode 016, 'Interview with Steven Novella,' 16 January.

65 Kolbert, E. 2017, 'Why facts don't change our minds', *The New Yorker*, 27 February.

66 Funnell, A. 2021, 'Are some of us destined to be dumb and is there anything we can do about it?' *ABC News,* 23 December.

67 Britannica, The Editors of Encyclopaedia. "a priori knowledge". Encyclopedia Britannica, 3 Dec. 2020, https://www.britannica.com/topic/a-priori-knowledge. Accessed 6 October 2021.

68 Burton, R. 2008, *On Being Certain*, St Martin's Press, New York, p. 95.

69 Epstein, Seymour (30 November 2010). "Demystifying Intuition: What It Is, What It Does, and How It Does It". Psychological Inquiry. 21 (4): 295–312. doi:10.1080/1047 840X.2010.523875. S2CID 145683932.

70 Burton, R. 2008, *On Being Certain*, St Martin's Press, New York, p. 89.

71 Elejalde-Ruiz, A. 2012, 'Going with your gut', *Chicago Tribune,* 13 June.

72 O'Keeffe, A. 2011, *Hardwired Humans*, Roundtable Press, Sydney, pp. 61-62.

73 O'Keeffe, A. 2011, *Hardwired Humans*, Roundtable Press, Sydney, pp. 72-73.

74 Burton, R. 2008, *On Being Certain*, St Martin's Press, New York, p. xiv.

75 Burton, R. 2008, *On Being Certain*, St Martin's Press, New York, p. 138.

76 Goff, B. 2012, *Love Does*, Thomas Nelson, Nashville, Tennessee, p. 138.

77 Lawson, Todd (23 September 2005). Reason and Inspiration in Islam: Theology, Philosophy and Mysticism in Muslim Thought. London: I.B touris co ltd. pp. 210–225. ISBN 1-85043-470-0. Retrieved 26 December 2014.

78 Burton, R. 2008, *On Being Certain*, St Martin's Press, New York, p. 67.

79 Burton, R. 2008, *On Being Certain*, St Martin's Press, New York, p. 67.

80 Lakoff, G. 1999, 'Philosophy in the flesh - a conversation with George Lakoff,' *Edge*, 8 March.

81 Burton, R. 2008, *On Being Certain*, St Martin's Press, New York, p. 139.

82 Verny, T. 2021, *The Embodied Mind*, Pegasus Books, New York, p. 117.

83 Verny, T. 2021, *The Embodied Mind*, Pegasus Books, New York, p. 118.

84 Verny, T. 2021, *The Embodied Mind*, Pegasus Books, New York, p. 120.

85 Underwood, E. 2018, 'Your gut is directly connected to your brain, by a newly discovered neuron circuit', *Science Magazine,* 20 September.

86 Schemann, M. et al. 2019, 'To learn, to remember, to forget - how smart is the gut?', Acta Physiol (Oxf). 2020 Jan; 228(1): e13296.

87 Burton, R. 2008, *On Being Certain*, St Martin's Press, New York, pp.148-149.

88 Pierre, J. 2016, 'The death of facts: the emperor's new epistemology,' *Psychology Today*, 4 December.

89 Pierre, J. 2016, 'The death of facts: the emperor's new epistemology,' *Psychology Today*, 4 December.

Part II

1   Heinrichs, J. 2013, *Thank You for Arguing*, Three Rivers Press, New York, pp. 39-40.

2   Mortensen, K. 2004, *Maximum Influence,* HarperCollins Australia, p. 17.

3   Dickson, J. 2011, 'Art of persuasion not so simple,' *The Sydney Morning Herald,* 9 July.

4   Garvey, J. 2016, *The Persuaders*, Icon Books, London, pp. 227-228.

5   Jones, M. 2020, *Beliefonomics,* Filtered Media, Sydney, pp. 95-101.

6   Ross, H. 2008, 'Proven Strategies for Addressing Unconscious Bias in the Workplace,' *CDO Insights,* August.

7   Cialdini, R. 1984, *Influence*, William Morrow and Company, New York, pp. 222-223.

8   Stulp, G. et al. 2015, 'Human Height Is Positively Related to Interpersonal Dominance in Dyadic Interactions,' *PLOS One,* 26 February.

9   Heinrichs, J. 2013, *Thank You for Arguing*, Three Rivers Press, New York, pp. 47-49.

10 Pierre, J. 2015, 'The psychology of guns,' *Psychology Today*, 4 October.

11 Ferrier, A. 2014, *The Advertising Effect*, Oxford University Press, South Melbourne, pp. 83-84.

12 Queenan, J. 2018, 'How your brain is keeping you from changing your mind.' *The Rotarian*, 16 May.

13 O'Keeffe, A. 2011, *Hardwired Humans*, Roundtable Press, Sydney, p. 54.

14 Dean, J. 2010, 'The battle between thoughts and emotions,' *PsyBlog*, November.

15 Heath, C. and Heath, D. 2010, *Switch*, Broadway Books, New York, p. 105.

16 Ferrier, A. 2014, *The Advertising Effect*, Oxford University Press, South Melbourne, pp. 83-84.

17 Kahneman, D. 2011, *Thinking, Fast and Slow*, FSG, New York, p. 302.

18 Heath, C. and Heath, D. 2010, *Switch*, Broadway Books, New York, pp. 121-123.

19 Grant, A. 2021, *Think Again,* WH Allen, London, pp. 178-181.

20 Grant, A. 2021, *Think Again,* WH Allen, London, pp. 178-181.

21 Foley, D. 2014, 'What Are Room Resonances & How Should You Locate Them?', *www. acousticfields.com*, 28 May.

22 Bhalla, J. 2016, 'What Trump can teach reason-loving smart folks,' *Big Think*, 9 October.

23 De Bono, E. 1991, *I Am Right You Are Wrong*, Penguin Books, London, p. 23.

24 De Bono, E. 1991, *I Am Right You Are Wrong*, Penguin Books, London, p. 23.

25 Weinberg, G. and McCann, L. 2019, *Super Thinking*, Penguin, London, pp. 25-26.

26 Gallo, C. 2019, 'The art of persuasion hasn't changed in 2,000 years,' *Harvard Business Review*, 15 July.

Chapter 3

1   2015, 'The logic question six-year-olds can answer, but leaves adults baffled,' *The Sydney Morning Herald*, 18 June.
2   Amlen, D. 2017, 'We do not see things as they are,' *The New York Times,* 4 August.
3   Bryson, B. 2019, *The Body: A Guide for Occupants*, Transworld Publishers, London, p. 56.
4   Grant, A. 2021, *Think Again,* WH Allen, London, pp. 128-129.
5   Mosher, D. 2020, 'Astronauts often describe a powerful 'overview effect' when gazing at Earth,' *Business Insider Australia*, 4 June.
6   Coulson, J. 2018, *10 Things Every Parent Needs to Know*, ABC Books, Sydney, p. 76.
7   Desjardins, J. 2018, 'Here are 24 cognitive biases that are warping your perception of reality,' *World Economic Forum,* 6 December.
8   Cialdini, R. 1984, *Influence*, William Morrow and Company, New York, p. 64.
9   Blain, L. 2014, 'Motorcycle lane splitting: Better for riders, better for drivers, and safer than sitting in traffic,' *New Atlas*, 27 October.
10 Kahneman, D. 2011, *Thinking, Fast and Slow*, FSG, New York, p. 88.
11 Kahneman, D. 2011, *Thinking, Fast and Slow*, FSG, New York, pp. 330-331.
12 Collister, P. 2017, *How to Use Innovation and Creativity in the Workplace*, Pan Macmillan, London, pp. 146-147.
13 Cook, J. and Lewandowsky, S. 2011, The Debunking Handbook. St. Lucia, Australia: University of Queensland, p 5.
14 Stephens, M. 2021, *The End of Thinking*, Acorn Press, Sydney, pp. 13-14.
15 Kahneman, D. 2011, *Thinking, Fast and Slow*, FSG, New York, p. 363.
16 Weinberg, G. and McCann, L. 2019, *Super Thinking*, Penguin, London, pp. 13-14.
17 Nordgren, L. 2017, 'Four tips to persuade others your idea is a winner,' *Kellogg Northwestern*, 3 February.
18 Ariely, D. 2008, *Predictably Irrational*, HarperCollins, New York, pp. 218-219.
19 Brafman, O. and Brafman, R. 2008, *Sway*, Crown Business, New York, pp. 49-50.
20 Ariely, D. 2008, *Predictably Irrational*, HarperCollins, New York, pp. 218-219.
21 Ariely, D. 2008, *Predictably Irrational*, HarperCollins, New York, pp. 218-219.
22 Dooley, R. 2012, *Brainfluence*, Wiley, New Jersey, pp. 17-18.
23 Wilson, T. 2011, *Redirect*, Back Bay Books, New York, p. 7.
24 Kahneman, D. 2011, *Thinking, Fast and Slow*, FSG, New York, pp. 123-124.
25 Kahneman, D. 2011, *Thinking, Fast and Slow*, FSG, New York, pp. 124-125.
26 Kolenda, N. 2013, *Methods of Persuasion*, Kolenda Entertainment, Grand Rapids, p. 22, 23.
27 Kolenda, N. 2013, *Methods of Persuasion*, Kolenda Entertainment, Grand Rapids, p. 27.
28 Cialdini, R. 2016, *Pre-Suasion*, Random House, London, 151

29   Cialdini, R. 2016, *Pre-Suasion*, Random House, London, p. 5.

30   Thaler, R. and Sunstein, C. 2009, *Nudge*, Penguin, New York, p. 24.

31   Kahneman, D. 2011, *Thinking, Fast and Slow*, FSG, New York, p. 135.

32   Kolenda, N. 2013, *Methods of Persuasion*, Kolenda Entertainment, Grand Rapids, p. 46.

33   Weinschenk, S. 2013, *How to Get People to Do Stuff,* Pearson Education, London, pp. 132-133.

34   Goldstein, N. et al. 2017, *Yes! 60 Secrets from the Science of Persuasion*, Profile Book, London, pp. 49-51.

35   Weinschenk, S. 2013, *How to Get People to Do Stuff,* Pearson Education, London, pp. 19-20.

36   Cialdini, R. 1984, *Influence*, William Morrow and Company, New York, p. 68.

37   Kahneman, D. 2011, *Thinking, Fast and Slow*, FSG, New York, pp. 131-132.

38   Burow, P. et al, *Behavioural Economics for Business*, Peter Burow, Australia, p. 27.

39   Goldstein, N. et al. 2008, *Yes! 50 Scientifically Proven Ways to be Persuasive*, Simon and Schuster, New York, p. 69-70.

40   Chance, Z. 2022, *Influence Is Your Superpower*, Penguin Random House, London, p. 130.

41   Eyal, N. 2014, *Hooked*, Penguin, New York, p. 88.

42   Hogan, K. 2013, *Invisible Influence*, Wiley, New Jersey, pp. 139-140.

43   Garvey, J. 2016, *The Persuaders*, Icon Books, London, p. 232.

44   Tormala, Z. and Rucker, D. 2015, 'How certainty transforms persuasion,' *Harvard Business Review*, September.

45   Kruger, A. 2022, 'A climate for mis- and disinformation', *First Draft News*, 25 July.

46   Tormala, Z. and Rucker, D. 2015, 'How certainty transforms persuasion,' *Harvard Business Review*, September.

47   Roozenbeek, J. and Van der Linden, S. 2019, 'Fake news game confers psychological resistance against online misinformation,' *Humanities and Social Sciences Communications*, 25 June.

48   Van der Linden, S. et al. 2020, 'Inoculating against fake news about COVID-19,' *Frontiers in Psychology*, 23 October.

49   Cook, J. 2017, 'Inoculation theory - using misinformation to fight misinformation,' *The Conversation*, 15 May.

50   Miller, G. 2021, 'The enduring allure of conspiracy theories,' *Nieman Journalism Lab*, 19 January.

51   Dean, J. 2013, '9 Ways the mind resists persuasion and how to sustain or overcome them,' PsyBlog, May.

52   Van der Linden, S. et al. 2020, 'Inoculating against fake news about COVID-19,' *Frontiers in Psychology*, 23 October.

53   Grant, A. 2021, *Think Again,* WH Allen, London, pp. 163-166.

54   Grant, A. 2021, *Think Again,* WH Allen, London, pp. 163-166.

55   Grant, A. 2021, *Think Again,* WH Allen, London, pp. 163-166.

56   Kolenda, N. 2013, *Methods of Persuasion*, Kolenda Entertainment, Grand Rapids, pp. 28-29.

57   2020, 'Trust misplaced: A report on the future of trust in media,' *Ipsos Views,* October.

58 Hameiri, B. et al. 2014, 'Paradoxical thinking as a new avenue of intervention to promote peace,' *PNAS*, 18 June.

59 Lakhani, D. 2005, *Persuasion: The Art of Getting What You Want*, Wiley, New Jersey, pp. 230-231.

60 Gregory D. and Flanagan, K. 2015, *Selfish, Scared & Stupid*, Wiley, Melbourne, p. 173.

61 Weinschenk, S. 2013, *How to Get People to Do Stuff*, Pearson Education, London, p. 4.

62 Cialdini, R. 2016, *Pre-Suasion*, Random House, London, pp. 168-169.

63 Cialdini, R. 2016, *Pre-Suasion*, Random House, London, pp. 168-169.

64 Thaler, R. and Sunstein, C. 2009, *Nudge*, Penguin, New York, p. 71.

65 Cialdini, R. 2016, *Pre-Suasion*, Random House, London, pp. 168-169.

66 Goldstein, N. et al. 2008, *Yes! 50 Scientifically Proven Ways to be Persuasive*, Simon and Schuster, New York, pp. 73-74.

67 Cialdini, R. 2016, *Pre-Suasion*, Random House, London, pp. 168-169.

68 Goldstein, N. et al. 2008, *Yes! 50 Scientifically Proven Ways to be Persuasive*, Simon and Schuster, New York, pp. 73-74.

69 Milkman, K. 2021, *How to Change*, Penguin, New York, pp. 76-79.

70 Goldstein, N. et al. 2008, *Yes! 50 Scientifically Proven Ways to be Persuasive*, Simon and Schuster, New York, pp 80-82.

71 Grant, A. 2022, 'You can't say that: How to argue better,' *The Guardian*, 30 July.

72 Grant, A. 2021, *Think Again*, WH Allen, London, p.252-255.

73 Hutson, M. 2020, 'Why you don't really know what you know,' *MIT Technology Review*, 21 October.

74 Kolbert, E. 2017, 'Why facts don't change our minds', *The New Yorker*, 27 February.

75 Singal, J. 2014, 'How to win your next political argument,' *The Cut*, 14 May.

76 Luntz, F. 2007, *Words That Work*, Hachette, New York, pp. 107-108.

77 Berger, J. 2020, *The Catalyst*, Simon and Schuster, London, pp. 6-11.

78 Gregory D. and Flanagan, K. 2015, *Selfish, Scared & Stupid*, Wiley, Melbourne, p. 61.

79 Garber, M. 2019, 'The myth of the 'Underage Woman,'' *The Atlantic*, 15 August.

80 Jolles, R. 2013, *How to Change Minds*, Berrett-Koehler, Oakland, p. 62.

81 Thaler, R. and Sunstein, C. 2009, *Nudge*, Penguin, New York, pp. 36-37.

82 Grant, A. 2021, *Think Again*, WH Allen, London, pp. 173-174.

83 Garvey, J. 2016, *The Persuaders*, Icon Books, London, p. 116-117.

84 Hogan, N. and Speakman, J. 2006, *Covert Persuasion*, Wiley, New Jersey, pp. 79-84.

85 Hogan, K. 2013, *Invisible Influence*, Wiley, New Jersey, pp. 105-106.

86 Weinberg, G. and McCann, L. 2019, *Super Thinking*, Penguin, London, pp. 13-14.

87 Kolenda, N. 2013, *Methods of Persuasion*, Kolenda Entertainment, Grand Rapids, p. 14.

88 McRaney, D. 2012, *You Are Not So Smart*, Gotham Books, New York, pp. 10-11.

89 De Bono, E. 1991, *I Am Right You Are Wrong*, Penguin Books, London, p. 156.

90 Goldstein, N. et al. 2008, *Yes! 50 Scientifically Proven Ways to be Persuasive*, Simon and Schuster, New York, pp. 164-165.

91 Kahneman, D. 2011, *Thinking, Fast and Slow*, FSG, New York, pp. 62-63.

92 Kawasaki, G. 2011, *Enchantment*, Penguin, New York, pp. 21-22

93   Roeder, M. 2011, *The Big Mo*, Virgin Books, London, p. 86.

94   Heinrichs, J. 2013, *Thank You for Arguing*, Three Rivers Press, New York, p. 87.

95   Bowden, M. 2013, *How to Present*, Wiley, Melbourne, p. 207.

96   Mortensen, K. 2004, *Maximum Influence*, HarperCollins Australia, p. 61.

97   Mortensen, K. 2004, *Maximum Influence*, HarperCollins Australia, p. 61.

98   Cialdini, R. 2016, *Pre-Suasion*, Random House, London, p. 102.

99   Kozicki, S. 1993, *The Creative Negotiator*, Gower Publishing, St Ives, p. 173.

Chapter 4

1   Coyle, D. 2018, *The Culture Code*, Bantam Books, New York, pp. 22-23.

2   Heinrichs, J. 2013, *Thank You for Arguing*, Three Rivers Press, New York, p. 284.

3   Bernstein, E. 2020, 'Worried about a difficult conversation? Here's advice from a hostage negotiator,' *The Wall Street Journal*, 14 June.

4   Ward, A. 2020, 'Joe Biden in victory speech: Let this grim era of demonization in America begin to end,' *Vox*, 7 November.

5   Stanley, A. 2022, *Not in It to Win It*, Zondervan, Grand Rapids, Michigan, p. 3.

6   Garvey, J. 2016, *The Persuaders*, Icon Books, London, pp. 217-225.

7   Garvey, J. 2016, *The Persuaders*, Icon Books, London, pp. 217-225.

8   Heinrichs, J. 2013, *Thank You for Arguing*, Three Rivers Press, New York, p. 19.

9   De Bono, E. 1991, *I Am Right You Are Wrong*, Penguin Books, London, pp. 4-7.

10   De Bono, E. 1991, *I Am Right You Are Wrong*, Penguin Books, London, pp. 4-7.

11   Garvey, J. 2016, *The Persuaders*, Icon Books, London, pp. 241-243.

12   Pink, D. 2012, *To Sell is Human*, Riverhead Books, New York, p. 205-206.

13   Stephens, M. 2020, 'Ever wondered how someone could possibly believe their own words?' *The Canberra Times*, 23 May.

14   Grant, A. 2021, *Think Again*, WH Allen, London, p. 114.

15   McRaney, D. 2012, *You Are Not So Smart*, Gotham Books, New York, pp. 103-104.

16   Graham, P. 2008, 'How to disagree,' *Paul Graham Blog*, March.

17   Lakoff, J. and Johnson, M. 2003, *Metaphors We Live By*, University of Chicago Press, Chicago.

18   Lakoff, J. and Johnson, M. 2003, *Metaphors We Live By*, University of Chicago Press, Chicago.

19   Grant, A. 2021, *Think Again*, WH Allen, London, pp. 104-106.

20   Grant, A. 2021, *Think Again*, WH Allen, London, p 107.

21   Grant, A. 2021, *Think Again*, WH Allen, London, pp. 104-106.

22   Grant, A. 2021, *Think Again*, WH Allen, London, pp. 112-113.

23   Pink, D. 2012, *To Sell is Human*, Riverhead Books, New York, p. 198.

24   Grant, A. 2021, *Think Again*, WH Allen, London, p. 97.

25   Grant, A. 2021, *Think Again*, WH Allen, London, pp. 252-255.

26   Graham, P. 2009, 'Keep your identity small', *Paul Graham Blog*, February.

27   Pink, D. 2012, *To Sell is Human*, Riverhead Books, New York, p. 198.

28   Spence, G. 1995, *How to Argue and Win Every Time*, St Martin's Press, New York, p. 22-25.

29   Snow, S. 2017, 'Why Major Institutions Lost Public Trust, And How They Can Get It Back Again', *The Content Strategist*, 15 December.

30   Coyle, D. 2018, *The Culture Code*, Bantam Books, New York, pp. 76-77.

31   Cialdini, R. 2016, *Pre-Suasion*, Random House, London, pp. 165-166.

32   Heinrichs, J. 2013, *Thank You for Arguing*, Three Rivers Press, New York, pp. 77-78.

33   Heinrichs, J. 2013, Thank You for Arguing, Three Rivers Press, New York, pp. 77-78.

34   Cialdini, R. 2016, *Pre-Suasion*, Random House, London, pp. 165-166.

35   Grant, A. 2021, *Think Again*, WH Allen, London, pp. 117-119.

36   Kolenda, N. 2013, *Methods of Persuasion*, Kolenda Entertainment, Grand Rapids, p. 145.

37   Goldstein, N. et al. 2008, *Yes! 50 Scientifically Proven Ways to be Persuasive*, Simon and Schuster, New York, pp. 112-114.

38   Bail, C. 2021, Breaking the Social Media Prism, Princeton University Press, New Jersey, pp. 112.

39   Goldstein, N. et al. 2008, *Yes! 50 Scientifically Proven Ways to be Persuasive*, Simon and Schuster, New York, p. 115.

40   Dean, J. 2010, 'Balanced arguments are more persuasive,' *PsyBlog*, November.

41   Cialdini, R. 2016, *Pre-Suasion*, Random House, London, pp. 165-166.

42   Grant, A. 2021, *Think Again*, WH Allen, London, pp 173-174.

43   Cialdini, R. 2016, *Pre-Suasion*, Random House, London, pp. 165-166.

44   Goldstein, N. et al. 2008, *Yes! 50 Scientifically Proven Ways to be Persuasive*, Simon and Schuster, New York, pp. 112-114.

45   Goldstein, N. et al. 2008, *Yes! 50 Scientifically Proven Ways to be Persuasive*, Simon and Schuster, New York, pp. 112-114.

46   Cialdini, R. 2016, *Pre-Suasion*, Random House, London, pp. 201-202.

47   Harris, J. 2019, *The Soulful Art of Persuasion*, Penguin Random House, New York, p. 199.

48   Selinger-Morris, S. 2021, 'One of the greatest predictors of divorce: How to argue better,' *The Sydney Morning Herald*, 16 July.

49   Selinger-Morris, S. 2021, 'One of the greatest predictors of divorce: How to argue better,' *The Sydney Morning Herald*, 16 July.

50   Lakhani, D. 2005, *Persuasion: The Art of Getting What You Want*, Wiley, New Jersey, pp. 88-89.

51   Heinrichs, J. 2013, *Thank You for Arguing*, Three Rivers Press, New York, pp. 107-108.

52   Grant, A. 2021, *Think Again*, WH Allen, London, pp. 128-129.

53   Chance, Z. 2022, *Influence Is Your Superpower*, Penguin Random House, London, p. 143.

54   Bail, C. 2021, Breaking the Social Media Prism, Princeton University Press, New Jersey, pp. 73.

55   Stanley, A. 2022, *Not in It to Win It*, Zondervan, Grand Rapids, Michigan, p. 19.

56   Chance, Z. 2022, *Influence Is Your Superpower*, Penguin Random House, London, p. 143.

57   Gregory D. and Flanagan, K. 2015, *Selfish, Scared & Stupid*, Wiley, Melbourne, pp. 114-115.

58 Lakhani, D. 2005, *Persuasion: The Art of Getting What You Want*, Wiley, New Jersey, p. 95.

59 Lukianoff, G. and Haidt, J. 2018, *The Coddling of the American Mind*, Penguin Random House, New York, p. 60.

60 Weinschenk, S. 2013, *How to Get People to Do Stuff*, Pearson Education, London, pp. 25-26.

61 Cialdini, R. 2016, *Pre-Suasion*, Random House, London, pp. 194-195.

62 Thaler, R. and Sunstein, C. 2009, *Nudge*, Penguin, New York, p. 54.

63 Weinschenk, S. 2013, *How to Get People to Do Stuff*, Pearson Education, London, p. 22.

64 Pink, D. 2012, *To Sell is Human*, Riverhead Books, New York, pp. 76-77.

65 Cialdini, R. 2016, *Pre-Suasion*, Random House, London, pp. 110-111.

66 Weinschenk, S. 2013, *How to Get People to Do Stuff*, Pearson Education, London, p. 10.

67 Weinschenk, S. 2013, *How to Get People to Do Stuff*, Pearson Education, London, p. 10.

68 Cialdini, R. 2016, *Pre-Suasion*, Random House, London, pp. 110-111.

69 Cialdini, R. 2016, *Pre-Suasion*, Random House, London, pp. 110-111.

70 Cialdini, R. 2016, *Pre-Suasion*, Random House, London, pp. 110-111.

71 Weinschenk, S. 2013, *How to Get People to Do Stuff*, Pearson Education, London, p. 10.

72 Kolenda, N. 2013, *Methods of Persuasion*, Kolenda Entertainment, Grand Rapids, pp. 94-95.

73 Cialdini, R. 2016, *Pre-Suasion*, Random House, London, pp. 110-111.

74 Hogan, N. and Speakman, J. 2006, *Covert Persuasion*, Wiley, New Jersey, p. 69.

75 Botsman, R. 2018, *Who Can You Trust?*, Penguin Business, London, p. 1.

Chapter 5

1 Cialdini, R. 2016, *Pre-Suasion*, Random House, London, p. 72.

2 Dooley, R. 2012, *Brainfluence*, Wiley, New Jersey, pp. 127-128.

3 Cialdini, R. 2016, *Pre-Suasion*, Random House, London, p. 159.

4 Cialdini, R. 2016, *Pre-Suasion*, Random House, London, p. 159.

5 Greene, R. 1998, *The 48 Laws of Power*, Penguin, New York, p. 71.

6 Psalm 25:15, *The Holy Bible – The Passion Translation*, Broadstreet Publishing, Minnesota.

7 Maley, J. 2022, 'He's worked with Greta and Malala, and now Ed Coper has some bad news to share,' *The Sydney Morning Herald*, 10 March.

8 Levinovitz, A. 2017, 'Trump supporters refuse to believe their own eyes,' *Slate*, 27 January.

9 Kolenda, N. 2013, *Methods of Persuasion*, Kolenda Entertainment, Grand Rapids, pp. 64-66.

10 Burton, R. 2008, *On Being Certain*, St Martin's Press, New York, pp. 12-13.

11 Kolenda, N. 2013, *Methods of Persuasion*, Kolenda Entertainment, Grand Rapids, pp. 64-66.

12 Burton, R. 2008, *On Being Certain*, St Martin's Press, New York, pp. 12-13.

13 Miller, G. 2021, 'The enduring allure of conspiracy theories,' *Nieman Journalism Lab*, 19 January.

14 Yosufzai, R. 2021, 'QAnon followers realise their baseless conspiracy was 'all a lie' as President Joe Biden takes office,' *SBS News*, 21 January.

15 Bryant, N. 2022, 'Trump for 2024? It's all about justice,' *The Sydney Morning Herald*, 25 October.

16 Cialdini, R. 1984, *Influence*, William Morrow and Company, New York, pp. 57-58.

17 Ramadan, A. et al. 2016, *Play Bigger*, HarperCollins, New York, p. 31.

18 Brafman, O. and Brafman, R. 2008, *Sway*, Crown Business, New York, pp. 38-39

19 Stephens, M. 2021, *The End of Thinking*, Acorn Press, Sydney, p. 43.

20 O'Keeffe, A. 2011, *Hardwired Humans*, Roundtable Press, Sydney, pp. 92-93.

21 Pinker, S. 2021, *Rationality*, Allen Lane, London, pp. 289-290.

22 Thaler, R. 2015, *Misbehaving*, Penguin, New York, pp. 20-21.

23 Kahneman, D. 2011, *Thinking, Fast and Slow*, FSG, New York, p. 305

24 Acts 26: 28, *The Holy Bible – The Passion Translation*, Broadstreet Publishing, Minnesota.

25 Hogan, N. and Speakman, J. 2006, *Covert Persuasion*, Wiley, New Jersey, p. 90.

26 Oppong, T. 2019, 'Active listening lessons from FBI negotiators that will get you what you want,' *The Ladders*, 14 October.

27 Jolles, R. 2013, *How to Change Minds*, Berrett-Koehler, Oakland, p. 137.

28 Jakes, TD. 2021, 'Prayer and science led me to the vaccine,' *The Wall Street Journal*, 25 February.

29 Weinberg, G. and McCann, L. 2019, *Super Thinking*, Penguin, London, pp. 23-24.

30 Weinberg, G. and McCann, L. 2019, *Super Thinking*, Penguin, London, pp. 23-24.

31 Greene, R. 1998, *The 48 Laws of Power*, Penguin, New York, p. 398.

32 Greene, R. 1998, *The 48 Laws of Power*, Penguin, New York, p. 392.

33 Burg, B. 2011, *The Art of Persuasion*, Sound Wisdom Books, Shippensburg, pp. 164-165.

34 Dvorsky, G. 2013, 'The 12 cognitive biases that prevent you from being rational,' *io9*, 1 September.

35 Garvey, J. 2016, *The Persuaders*, Icon Books, London, pp. 88-89.

36 Berger, J. 2020, *The Catalyst*, Simon and Schuster, London, pp. 208-213.

37 Duhigg, C. 2014, *The Power of Habit*, Random House, New York, pp. 204-206.

38 Berger, J. 2020, *The Catalyst*, Simon and Schuster, London, pp. 208-213.

39 Duhigg, C. 2014, *The Power of Habit*, Random House, New York, pp. 204-206.

40 Berger, J. 2020, *The Catalyst*, Simon and Schuster, London, pp. 208-213.

41 Duhigg, C. 2014, *The Power of Habit*, Random House, New York, pp. 204-206.

42 Grant, A. 2021, 'Persuading the unpersuadable,' *Harvard Business Review*, March-April.

43 Hogan, N. and Speakman, J. 2006, *Covert Persuasion*, Wiley, New Jersey, pp. 107-108.

44 Keller, G. 2013, *The One Thing*, John Murray Publishers, London, p. 104.

45 Mortensen, K. 2004, *Maximum Influence,* HarperCollins Australia, p. 144.

46 Luntz, F. 2007, *Words That Work*, Hachette, New York, pp. 223-224.

47 Grant, A. 2021, *Think Again*, WH Allen, London, p. 18.

48 Burg, B. 2011, *The Art of Persuasion*, Sound Wisdom Books, Shippensburg, p. 184.

49 Hogan, N. and Speakman, J. 2006, *Covert Persuasion*, Wiley, New Jersey, pp. 174-176.

50 Weinschenk, S. 2013, *How to Get People to Do Stuff,* Pearson Education, London, p. 150.

51   Grant, A. 2021, *Think Again*, WH Allen, London, pp. 146-150.

52   Grenny, J. et al. 2013, *Influencer*, McGraw Hill, New York, pp. 86-88.

53   Grant, A. 2021, *Think Again*, WH Allen, London, pp. 146-150

54   Grant, A. 2021, *Think Again*, WH Allen, London, pp. 146-150

55   Grant, A. 2021, *Think Again*, WH Allen, London, pp. 146-150

56   Pink, D. 2012, *To Sell is Human*, Riverhead Books, New York, pp. 145-146.

57   Pink, D. 2012, *To Sell is Human*, Riverhead Books, New York, pp. 145-146.

58   Pantalon, M. 2011, *Instant Influence*, Hachette, New York, p. 85.

59   Pantalon, M. 2011, *Instant Influence*, Hachette, New York, pp. 90-91.

60   Pantalon, M. 2011, *Instant Influence*, Hachette, New York, pp. 154-155.

61   Jolles, R. 2013, *How to Change Minds*, Berrett-Koehler, Oakland, p. 45.

62   Pantalon, M. 2011, *Instant Influence*, Hachette, New York, p. 78.

63   Pantalon, M. 2011, *Instant Influence*, Hachette, New York, pp. 90-91.

64   Pantalon, M. 2011, *Instant Influence*, Hachette, New York, pp. 186-190.

65   Pantalon, M. 2011, *Instant Influence*, Hachette, New York, pp. 25-30.

66   Grant, A. 2021, *Think Again*, WH Allen, London, p. 156.

67   Stephens, M. 2021, *The End of Thinking*, Acorn Press, Sydney, pp. 61-62.

68   Herring, J. 2012, *How to Argue*, FT Press, New Jersey, p. 87.

69   Keller, G. 2013, *The One Thing*, John Murray Publishers, London, p.104.

70   Grenny, J. et al. 2013, *Influencer*, McGraw Hill, New York, p. 84.

71   Grenny, J. et al. 2013, *Influencer*, McGraw Hill, New York, p. 84.

72   Aly, W. 2021, 'Has solidarity succumbed to the rise of rage?' *The Sydney Morning Herald*, 24 September.

73   Aly, W. 2021, 'Has solidarity succumbed to the rise of rage?' *The Sydney Morning Herald*, 24 September.

74   Grenny, J. et al. 2013, *Influencer*, McGraw Hill, New York, pp. 86-88.

75   Weinschenk, S. 2013, *How to Get People to Do Stuff*, Pearson Education, London, pp. 103-104.

76   Chance, Z. 2022, *Influence Is Your Superpower*, Penguin Random House, London, p. 135.

77   Weinschenk, S. 2013, *How to Get People to Do Stuff*, Pearson Education, London, pp. 103-104.

78   Berger, J. 2020, *The Catalyst*, Simon and Schuster, London, pp. 30-32.

79   Berger, J. 2020, *The Catalyst*, Simon and Schuster, London, pp. 30-32.

80   Burg, B. 2011, *The Art of Persuasion*, Sound Wisdom Books, Shippensburg, p. 131.

81   Pantalon, M. 2011, *Instant Influence*, Hachette, New York, pp. 46-54.

82   Dean, J. 2013, 'The one (really easy) persuasion technique everyone should know,' *PsyBlog*, February.

83   Dean, J. 2010, '20 simple steps to the perfect persuasive message,' *PsyBlog*, 20 December.

84   Dean, J. 2010, 'The influence of positive framing,' *PsyBlog*, December.

85   O'Keefe, D. 2008, 'Do loss-framed persuasive messages engender greater message processing than do gain-framed messages? A meta-analytic review,' *Communication Studies Journal - Volume 59*, 11 March.

86 Glenister, S. 2019, 'Why we need to harness brain science to get environmental messages to stick,' *LinkedIn Article*, 9 April.

87 Glenister, S. 2019, 'Why we need to harness brain science to get environmental messages to stick,' *LinkedIn Article*, 9 April.

88 Ferrier, A. 2014, *The Advertising Effect*, Oxford University Press, South Melbourne, pp. 105-106.

89 Cialdini, R. 2016, *Pre-Suasion*, Random House, London, pp. 204-206.

90 Ferrier, A. 2014, *The Advertising Effect*, Oxford University Press, South Melbourne, pp. 37-38.

91 Luntz, F. 2007, *Words That Work*, Hachette, New York, p. xiv.

Chapter 6

1 Garvey, J. 2016, *The Persuaders*, Icon Books, London, pp. 40-41.

2 Garvey, J. 2016, *The Persuaders*, Icon Books, London, pp. 40-41.

3 2019, 'Social experiment: Information cascade,' *Cornell University*, 4 December.

4 Coyle, D. 2018, *The Culture Code*, Bantam Books, New York, pp. 23-26.

5 Coyle, D. 2018, *The Culture Code*, Bantam Books, New York, pp. 23-26.

6 Kolenda, N. 2013, *Methods of Persuasion*, Kolenda Entertainment, Grand Rapids, pp. 96-97.

7 Kolenda, N. 2013, *Methods of Persuasion*, Kolenda Entertainment, Grand Rapids, pp. 96-97

8 Garvey, J. 2016, *The Persuaders*, Icon Books, London, pp. 74-75.

9 Goldstein, N. et al. 2008, *Yes! 50 Scientifically Proven Ways to be Persuasive*, Simon and Schuster, New York, pp. 12-13.

10 Ferrier, A. 2014, *The Advertising Effect*, Oxford University Press, South Melbourne, p. 91-94.

11 Kolenda, N. 2013, *Methods of Persuasion*, Kolenda Entertainment, Grand Rapids, pp. 85-86.

12 Cialdini, R. 2016, *Pre-Suasion*, Random House, London, pp. 161-164.

13 Thaler, R. and Sunstein, C. 2009, *Nudge*, Penguin, New York, pp. 64-65.

14 Garvey, J. 2016, *The Persuaders*, Icon Books, London, p. 126.

15 Heath, C. and Heath, D. 2010, *Switch*, Broadway Books, New York, pp. 233-234.

16 Goldstein, N. et al. 2008, *Yes! 50 Scientifically Proven Ways to be Persuasive*, Simon and Schuster, New York, pp. 10-11.

17 Surowiecki, J. 2004, *The Wisdom of Crowds*, Anchor Books, New York, p. 43.

18 Thaler, R. and Sunstein, C. 2009, *Nudge*, Penguin, New York, p. 67.

19 Berger, P. 2019, 'How can New York get subway riders to pay up? Praise them,' *The Wall Street Journal*, 29 October.

20 Kolenda, N. 2013, *Methods of Persuasion*, Kolenda Entertainment, Grand Rapids, pp. 85, 86.

21 Goldstein, N. et al. 2008, *Yes! 50 Scientifically Proven Ways to be Persuasive*, Simon and Schuster, New York, pp. 26-29.

22 Goldstein, N. et al. 2008, *Yes! 50 Scientifically Proven Ways to be Persuasive*, Simon and Schuster, New York, pp. 9-10.

23 Kolenda, N. 2013, *Methods of Persuasion*, Kolenda Entertainment, Grand Rapids, p. 184.

24 Ferrier, A. 2014, *The Advertising Effect*, Oxford University Press, South Melbourne, p. 91-94.

25 Thaler, R. and Sunstein, C. 2009, *Nudge*, Penguin, New York, p. 59.

26 Ferrier, A. 2014, *The Advertising Effect*, Oxford University Press, South Melbourne, pp. 91-94.

27 Thaler, R. and Sunstein, C. 2009, *Nudge*, Penguin, New York, p. 56.

28 Thaler, R. and Sunstein, C. 2009, *Nudge*, Penguin, New York, p. 56.

29 Ferrier, A. 2014, *The Advertising Effect*, Oxford University Press, South Melbourne, p. 91-94.

30 Roeder, M. 2011, *The Big Mo*, Virgin Books, London, p. 156.

31 Brafman, O. and Brafman, R. 2008, *Sway*, Crown Business, New York, pp. 153-155.

32 Dean, J. 2010, '20 simple steps to the perfect persuasive message,' *PsyBlog*, 20 December.

33 Ferrier, A. 2014, *The Advertising Effect*, Oxford University Press, South Melbourne, p 93.

34 Urban, T. 2023, *What's Our Problem? A Self-Help Book for Societies*, Wait But Why, Chapter 1.

35 Burow, P. et al, *Behavioural Economics for Business*, Peter Burow, Australia, pp. 11-12.

36 Roeder, M. 2011, *The Big Mo*, Virgin Books, London, pp. 81, 82.

37 Heinrichs, J. 2013, *Thank You for Arguing*, Three Rivers Press, New York, pp. 262-263, 269.

38 Heinrichs, J. 2013, *Thank You for Arguing*, Three Rivers Press, New York, pp. 262-263, 269.

39 Brafman, O. and Brafman, R. 2008, *Sway*, Crown Business, New York, pp. 132-144.

40 Brafman, O. and Brafman, R. 2008, *Sway*, Crown Business, New York, pp. 132-144.

41 Brafman, O. and Brafman, R. 2008, *Sway*, Crown Business, New York, pp. 132-144.

42 Pink, D. 2009, *Drive*, Riverhead Books, New York, pp. 50-51.

43 Weinberg, G. and McCann, L. 2019, *Super Thinking*, Penguin, London, pp. 222-223.

44 Weinberg, G. and McCann, L. 2019, *Super Thinking*, Penguin, London, pp. 222-223.

45 Pink, D. 2009, *Drive*, Riverhead Books, New York, pp. 45-47.

46 Heinrichs, J. 2013, *Thank You for Arguing*, Three Rivers Press, New York, pp. 243-245.

47 Ernest-Jones, M. et al. 2010, 'Effects of eye images on everyday cooperative behavior: a field experiment,' *School of Psychology – Newcastle University*, 23 October.

48 Ernest-Jones, M. et al. 2010, 'Effects of eye images on everyday cooperative behavior: a field experiment,' *School of Psychology – Newcastle University*, 23 October.

49 Cialdini, R. 2016, *Pre-Suasion*, Random House, London, pp. 197-198.

50 Cialdini, R. 2016, *Pre-Suasion*, Random House, London, pp. 198-199.

51 Weinschenk, S. 2013, *How to Get People to Do Stuff*, Pearson Education, London, p. 188.

52 Cialdini, R. 1984, *Influence*, William Morrow and Company, New York, p. 18.

53   Mortensen, K. 2004, *Maximum Influence,* HarperCollins Australia, p. 45.

54   Mortensen, K. 2004, *Maximum Influence,* HarperCollins Australia, p. 44.

55   Cialdini, R. 2016, *Pre-Suasion*, Random House, London, pp. 153-154.

56   Cialdini, R. 2016, *Pre-Suasion*, Random House, London, pp. 153-154.

57   Goldstein, N. et al. 2008, *Yes! 50 Scientifically Proven Ways to be Persuasive*, Simon and Schuster, New York, pp. 53-55.

58   Goldstein, N. et al. 2008, *Yes! 50 Scientifically Proven Ways to be Persuasive*, Simon and Schuster, New York, pp. 60-62.

59   Mortensen, K. 2004, *Maximum Influence,* HarperCollins Australia, p. 53.

60   Dooley, R. 2012, *Brainfluence*, Wiley, New Jersey, p. 110.

61   Dooley, R. 2012, *Brainfluence*, Wiley, New Jersey, p. 110.

62   Weinschenk, S. 2013, *How to Get People to Do Stuff,* Pearson Education, London, p. 28.

63   Ferrier, A. 2014, *The Advertising Effect*, Oxford University Press, South Melbourne, p. 39.

64   Goldstein, N. et al. 2017, *Yes! 60 Secrets from the Science of Persuasion*, Profile Book, London, pp. 69-70.

65   Ferrier, A. 2014, *The Advertising Effect*, Oxford University Press, South Melbourne, p. 39.

Chapter 7

1   Diniejko, A. 2020, 'Charles Dickens as social commentator and critic,' *The Victorian Web*, 4 December.

2   Shields, B. 2021, 'A Hollywood film and a cunning plan: how Britain got its vaccine rollout right,' *The Sydney Morning Herald,* 13 February.

3   Roeder, M. 2011, *The Big Mo*, Virgin Books, London.

4   Kawasaki, G. 2011, *Enchantment*, Penguin, New York, p. 1.

5   Burg, B. 2011, *The Art of Persuasion*, Sound Wisdom Books, Shippensburg, p. 142.

6   Harris, J. 2019, *The Soulful Art of Persuasion,* Penguin Random House, New York, pp. 168-169

7   Grant, A. 2021, *Think Again,* WH Allen, London, pp. 178-181.

8   Bail, C. 2018, 'Twitter's flawed solution to political polarization,' *The New York Times*, 8 September.

9   Urban, T. 2019, 'The story of us', *Wait, but Why?,* 26 August.

10   Grant, A. 2021, *Think Again,* WH Allen, London, p. 158.

11   Moore, N. 2015, 'Silence isn't golden when it comes to free speech,' *ABC News*, 7 May.

12   Luntz, F. 2007, *Words That Work*, Hachette, New York, p. xi.

13   Boertje, O. et al. 2015, 'Fashion: The 2 Euro T-shirt – A social experiment,' *Geographically Sane*, 3 November.

14   Gregory D. and Flanagan, K. 2015, *Selfish, Scared & Stupid*, Wiley, Melbourne, pp. 56-57.

15   Enzinna, W. 2018, 'Renouncing Hate: What happens when a white nationalist repents,' *The New York Times*, 10 September.

16   Heath, C. and Heath, D. 2007, *Made to Stick*, Random House, New York, p. 165.

17   Taleb, N. 2010, *The Black Swan*, Random House, New York, p. 80.

18 Dooley, R. 2012, *Brainfluence*, Wiley, New Jersey, p. 149.

19 Heath, C. and Heath, D. 2007, *Made to Stick*, Random House, New York, pp. 165-167.

20 Graves, C. 2015, 'Why debunking myths about vaccines hasn't convinced dubious parents,' 20 February.

21 Irvine, J. 2015, 'How climate change could ruin your sex life,' *The Sydney Morning Herald*, 5 November.

22 Srinivasan, A. 2020, 'What have we done to the whale?' *The New Yorker*, 17 August.

23 2021, 'This radio station plays songs made by trees as they grow,' *Fast Company*, 3 August.

24 Pink, D. 2012, *To Sell is Human*, Riverhead Books, New York, pp. 133-134.

25 2014, 'Share the road,' *NZ Transport Agency*, 11 February.

26 Grant, A. 2021, *Think Again*, WH Allen, London, p. 139.

27 Mortensen, K. 2004, *Maximum Influence*, HarperCollins Australia, p. 65.

28 Hornik, J. 1991, 'Shoppingtime and purchasing behavior as a result of in-store tactile stimulation,' *Perceptual and Motor Skills*.

29 Hornik, J. 1991, 'Shoppingtime and purchasing behavior as a result of in-store tactile stimulation,' *Perceptual and Motor Skills*.

30 Carroll, P & Mui, C. 2008, *Billion Dollar Lessons*, Penguin, New York, p. 232

31 Hogan, K. 2013, *Invisible Influence*, Wiley, New Jersey, p. 138.

32 Patterson, K. 2002, *Crucial Conversations*, McGraw Hill, New York, pp. 106-114.

33 Patterson, K. 2002, *Crucial Conversations*, McGraw Hill, New York, pp. 106-114.

34 Herring, J. 2012, *How to Argue*, FT Press, New Jersey, p. 18.

35 Chance, Z. 2022, *Influence Is Your Superpower*, Penguin Random House, London, p. 152.

36 Ferrier, A. 2014, *The Advertising Effect*, Oxford University Press, South Melbourne, p. 111.

37 Weinberg, G. and McCann, L. 2019, *Super Thinking*, Penguin, London, p. 19.

38 Weinberg, G. and McCann, L. 2019, *Super Thinking*, Penguin, London, pp. 19-20

39 Weinberg, G. and McCann, L. 2019, *Super Thinking*, Penguin, London, pp. 20-21.

40 Desjardins, J. 2018, 'Here are 24 cognitive biases that are warping your perception of reality,' *World Economic Forum*, 6 December.

41 Desjardins, J. 2018, 'Here are 24 cognitive biases that are warping your perception of reality,' *World Economic Forum*, 6 December.

42 Weinberg, G. and McCann, L. 2019, *Super Thinking*, Penguin, London, p. 30.

43 Pink, D. 2012, *To Sell is Human*, Riverhead Books, New York, pp. 73-74.

44 Gardner, D. 2009, 'There's no reason only poor people should get malaria,' *Daily Mail Australia*, 6 February.

45 Queenan, J. 2018, 'How your brain is keeping you from changing your mind.' *The Rotarian*, 16 May.

46 Cialdini, R. 2016, *Pre-Suasion*, Random House, London, p. 73.

47 Chance, Z. 2022, *Influence Is Your Superpower*, Penguin Random House, London, pp. 94-95.

48 Borysenko, K. 2020, 'Transcript: The rally that changed my mind,' *PragerU*,

49 Pierre, J. 2018, 'Why has America become so divided?' *Psychology Today*, 5 September.

50   Cialdini, R. 2016, *Pre-Suasion*, Random House, London, p. 73.

51   Rogers, S. 2017 'How could virtual reality change politics?' *LBB Online*, 4 April.

52   Rogers, S. 2017 'How could virtual reality change politics?' *LBB Online*, 4 April.

53   Byrne, W. and Knauss, D. 2017, 'VR builds empathy - it can build more inclusive business too,' *Fast Company*, 30 January.

54   Alsever, J. 2015, 'Is virtual reality the ultimate empathy machine?' *Wired*, November.

55   Byrne, W. and Knauss, D. 2017, 'VR builds empathy - it can build more inclusive business too,' *Fast Company*, 30 January.

56   Grant, A. 2021, *Think Again*, WH Allen, London, p. 45.

57   Stanley, A. 2022, *Not in It to Win It*, Zondervan, Grand Rapids, Michigan, pp. 213-214.

58   Stanley, A. 2022, *Not in It to Win It*, Zondervan, Grand Rapids, Michigan, pp. 213-214.

Epilogue

1   Harris, J. 2019, *The Soulful Art of Persuasion*, Penguin Random House, New York, pp. 203-204.

2   Coyle, D. 2018, *The Culture Code*, Bantam Books, New York, pp. 27-36.

ACKNOWLEDGMENTS

As my wife will readily attest, there is something very fitting about me writing a book on stubbornness—you could almost describe me as Exhibit A. Whether it's a temperament or learned trait, my thinking is often characterized by a sense of certainty that can get in the way of open-mindedness. Something about the process of writing this book has been a wonderful reminder to always maintain a posture of curiosity.

And so, my first thanks must go to the many individuals who have helped shape the ideas and research in this book that has, in turn, shaped me personally. There are far too many individuals to list and some of the most influential figures along the way have been casual acquaintances, people I've sat next to on planes, or audience members I have had the privilege to learn from in conversations during conference lunch breaks.

But there are some people I simply must acknowledge for their influence on this book and the process of it coming together. A special thanks to Dan Gregory, Kieran Flanagan, Berni Dymet, Phil Slade, Josh Linkner, and Professor Mark Hutchison. Sincere appreciation too to Naren, Myles, and the crew at Amplified Publishing Group for believing in this book and helping it come to life.

Thanks also to the many people that have been a personal support and encouragement along the way. Thanks to my mum, Anne, along with Ross and Nessie, Toby and Kirryn, Adrian and Claire, Dave and Amber, Gus and Jo, Sam and Kristyn, Luke and Liz, and Richard and Cathie. Thanks too to the team at Ode Management for all your support and encouragement—especially Leanne, Steve, Arnold, and Anita.

There have been a number of key individuals who have made an outsized contribution to the book you hold in your hands. From my initial editor Deborah

Agar, to Julie Masters and your expert guidance around topic positioning. An extra special shout-out to the amazing Amy Galliford. Your incisive and brilliant mind coupled with your flair for language and your steadfast belief in this project has made a bigger difference than you'll ever know.

While my propensity for obstinance can sometimes be a shortcoming, the process of writing this book has also shown how much of an asset it can also be. Given this project took nine years and required me devouring hundreds of books and thousands of academic articles, the cost has indeed been high. Naturally, this price has been one that I have not paid alone. My deepest and most affectionate thanks must go to my amazing wife, Hailey, and my son, Max, whose patience, support and encouragement were key enabling factors. I love you both beyond words.